The King's Gambit As White

3rd. edition

●

Robert Raingruber
Lou Maser

Thinkers' Press
Davenport, Iowa
1995

The King's Gambit As White

First Edition: November 1984
Second Edition: January 1986

First Printing, Third Edition:
April 1995

ISBN: 0-938650-47-5

Requests for permissions and republication rights should be addressed in writing to:

Thinkers' Press
Bob Long
P.O. Box 8
Davenport, Iowa 52805-0008 USA

CONTENTS

SYMBOLS

⩲	With slight advantage for White
⩱	With slight advantage for Black
±	With advantage for White
∓	With advantage for Black
+−	White has a won position
−+	Black has a won position
=	With a balanced position
=∞	With compensation for the material
∞	Unclear
#	Checkmate (mate)
△	With the idea (in some lines) of playing …
!	Good move
!!	Excellent move
!?	Interesting move
?!	Doubtful move
?	Bad move
??	Losing move
1–0	White won
0–1	Black won
½–½	Drawn
Ch	Championship
f7	The square *f7*
f7	Pawn moves to *f7*
P/f4	Pawn on *f4*
Nf7/Nh7	With the double threat of Nf7 and Nh7
[ ]	Indicates a specific Theory Reference
Footnote	Indicates an identically numbered problem at the end of its section

FOREWORD

A whole slew of OTB and postal King's Gambit games have been played and analyzed in the international chess arena since the advent of the Second Edition of *The King's Gambit As White*. Most prominent of the opening's recent practioners is GM Joe Gallagher. Quite a few of his and other games have followed lines espoused in our book. Reflecting this, we have taken care to incorporate all relevant new information in the Third Edition, including numerous apropos games—yielding over twice as many as in the Second Edition!

Not surprisingly, new questions in the Problems sections have been added. Also, investigation of two novel Lesser Declined Variations (ch. 16)—2... Qf6 and 2... Nc6 has been undertaken. And, in the King's Gambit Accepted, perhaps more original than critical is Master Kevin Burnett's 3... c5 (cf. the Lesser Accepted Variations of ch. 10) in which fertile ground for fresh ideas awaits praxis by today's stalwart gambiteers. At press-time 3... Qe7 has reared its "ugly" head as well, requiring a serious look.

In addition, a few notable corrections have been attended to. For instance, a complete rewrite of the Fischer Variation line from Diagram 4C-1 has occurred. The critical Berlin Defense of the Kieseritzky Variation (cf. Diagram 3F-4) too has been renovated, after having been put under a cloud for awhile. And, occasionally, poignant illustrative games are given to reflect current trends and testing, which diverge from the beaten path lines of the text. A good example of this, again from the Berlin Defense (from Diagram 3F-1), is seen after 6... d6 7 Nd3 Ne4 8 Bf4 Qe7 when 9 Be2 has been tried in place of the "prosaic" 9 Qe2.

No opening system can be expected to go under the microscope without some new light being shed thereupon. Certainly, this has been true of the King's Gambit in the past few years. In a way this validates the opening itself, to be sure, but more importantly it allows for increased understanding of this complex gambit. We believe that the ebb and flow of new ideas in the King's Gambit will continue to enhance the material in this roadmap book for a good many years.

Bob Raingruber
January 1995

1: INTRODUCTION

1	e4	e5
2	f4	

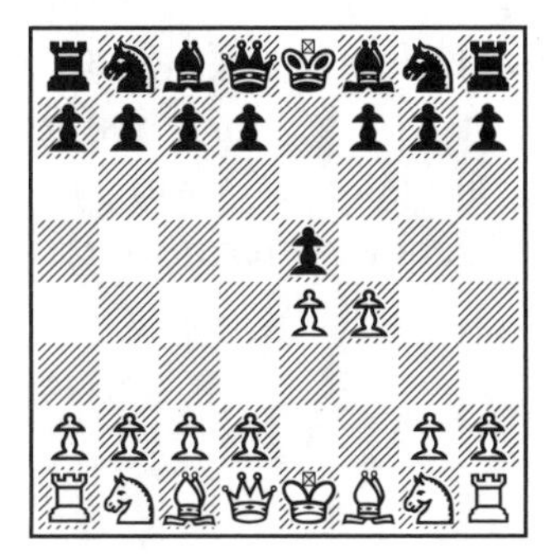

1-1

With his second move White initiates the King's Gambit by offering his P/f4 as bait. This pawn, superficially, appears free for the taking, but probing deeper one finds that the consequences abound in subtle complexities.

Nineteenth-century adherents commonly launched blitz attacks (on f7) against Black's king. Though a knockout frequently occurred, it was principally caused by a positional mishandling of the opening by their opponents. Today the first player usually enters the King's Gambit with a view to a favorable endgame. The list of moderns who have ventured this opening includes no less than: Spassky, Bronstein, Keres, Tal and Fischer(!). Since periodic attempts at refutation have not succeeded, the King's Gambit continues to crop up in Grandmaster praxis.

An openings repertoire is best determined by an individual's style. The King's Gambit will suit the aggressive player who favors hand-to-hand combat from the earliest moves. Moreover, the typically unbalanced pawn structures and piece configurations ensure a hard fight even in the endgame. Ironically, however, this opening often requires positional play of a very high order. Examples include the Fischer and Classical Declined variations.

The text is primarily oriented toward a system of concepts and plans in the King's Gambit, complete from only the White point of view. Although new lines do appear in this work, time-tested variations comprise the basis of the material.

Strongest play for both sides, in a given continuation, is presented in the main reference lines. Significant alternatives for White, which may appeal to players with different styles, are mentioned parenthetically (and sometimes as problems), but weaker lines by White, unless particularly instructive, are excluded altogether. Of course, inferior responses by Black require attention. Those of special interest are analyzed in the main body; the rest, are handled by notes and problems.

Every *numbered footnote* refers to an identically numbered problem at the end of its section. Thus "footnote 1" in Section 4B on p. 55 pinpoints the move (in this case Black's 7th) on which Problem 4B#1 (p. 61) begins. On the other hand, a *bracketed number* is used to cite one of the theory references listed in the bibliography. Answers to all problems can be located in the back and are coded by sections for convenience.

Summing up, it is hoped that the reader will gain considerable insight into the venerable (but not staid) King's Gambit. Strategically complex and tactically sound, it decries being treated mechanically, is not drawish, and begets middlegames rich in profound piece and pawn interplay. Though most lines require original ideas, perhaps familiarity will breed enthusiasm. As a study of the text should reveal, there is still life in this traveled opening. Indeed, novel continuations are even suggested here! But the bottom line is simply that the King's Gambit is fun to play. For this reason alone, it deserves strongly to be considered as a lifetime opening.

2: INTRODUCTORY REMARKS

The text is divided into two main parts based on whether or not Black takes White's proffered P/f4. In the King's Gambit Accepted (KGA), which is normally reached by **1 e4 e5 2 f4 ef4,** Black, in effect, challenges White to prove the opening. By continuing with 3 Nf3, White enters the King Knight's Gambit, the subject of the first part of this book. This flexible approach avoids the risky 3 Nc3 Qh4 4 Ke2 d5! yet still gives White time to determine on which square his king bishop will function best.

In all lines of the KGA White enjoys a central pawn majority. Thus d4 is a thematic thrust, establishing a duo on *d4* and *e4* (whenever feasible) to gain space and procure open lines for both White bishops. Germane as well is an understanding of when h4 is appropriate; whereas, for Black, a properly timed ...d6, ...d5, ...g5 or ...f5 is fundamental.

One of the most notable features of the KGA is the striking positional imbalance created by Black's doubled f-file pawns. Although Black obtains, at best, a 4–2 majority on the K-side, his pawns occupy only three files. Black, therefore, cannot achieve a front duo (such as a P/f5 and P/g5) in the middlegame without seriously weakening his K-side. By contrast, White can safely create a front duo with his 4–3 Q-side majority even if his king is castled there. Such a phalanx will give White central pressure and possibilities for developing a promotable passed pawn. Thus White can expect winning chances in many positions where Black remains a pawn ahead.

Briefly stated, while White seeks good squares for his pieces, Black will either strain to hold his extra pawn, or try to equalize by returning it at a propitious moment. In the latter regard, it is worth mentioning Reuben Fine's principle that given the presence of more than three pawns per side in a pieceless ending of equal material, the player with the greater number of center pawns has an advantage.

Black, of course, does not have to capture the P/f4. Though declining the gambit makes no attempt to refute it, Black, in several variations, can expect to attain level play. Among his replies, 2... d5, 2... Bc5, 2... d6, 2... Nf6, 2... Qh4 and 2... f5 all receive special mention in the second part of the text. (The 2... Nc6 line generally transposes to the 2... d6 variation.) Each of these choices is based on almost entirely different concepts. Center counterattack, rapid development, interference with castling intentions, and stubborn defense are variously undertaken. As one might expect, play in these lines proceeds along disparate paths.

ACKNOWLEDGMENTS

A particular thanks is extended to Grandmaster Nick DeFirmian for his careful corroboration of the problem solutions. Also, special mention goes to Trevor Hay for his creative work on the King's Gambit. Most of all, much gratitude goes out to Larry Christiansen for his monumental assistance in original analysis given in this work. Last but not least, a note of appreciation to Lyon's Restaurant of Modesto, CA, for their continued hospitality during the writing of the original manuscript.

Part I

THE KING'S GAMBIT ACCEPTED

The King's Knight Gambit

3: KIESERITZKY VARIATION (A)

One of the most critical variations of the King's Gambit is the Kieseritzky Variation:

1	**e4**	**e5**
2	**f4**	**ef4**
3	**Nf3**	**g5**
4	**h4**	**g4**[1]
5	**Ne5**	

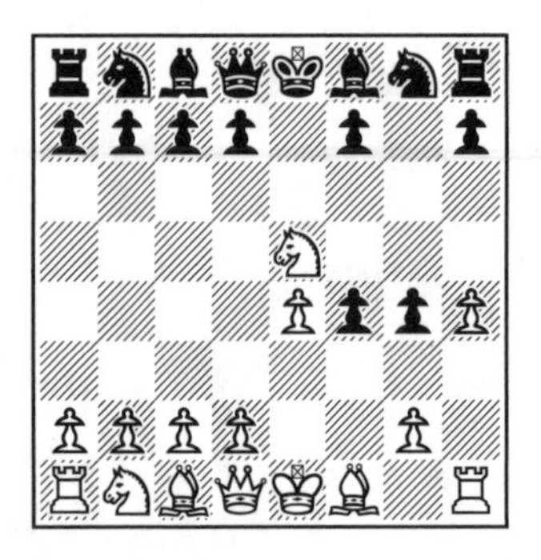

3A-1

The enterprising 3... g5 announces that Black intends to hold his extra pawn in the most direct fashion possible (cf. The Fischer Var. Chap. 4). White's reply, 4 h4, immediately challenges this plan and, unlike 4 Bc4, does not give Black time to construct a sturdy pawn chain by ...Bg7-h6. Instead, 4... g4 becomes necessary, whereupon White avoids the tempting but speculative Allgaier Gambit (5 Ng5) and finally initiates the Kieseritzky Variation with 5 Ne5.

As his P/g4 is now under fire, Black must resolve the question of its defense. A risky solution is 5... h5 (see Section 3B), but even the diverse counterattacks at Black's disposal often contain hidden resources for White.

For instance, after 5... Be7 (doubly attacking the P/h4) 6 Bc4! Bh4 7 Kf1(!), White is already better — despite being two pawns down! — because of the double-threat Nf7/Ng4 and his superior development. Black's advanced pawns are more vulnerable than venerable, and the B/h4 is sadly misplaced. Although White cannot castle, Black's f-file pawns act as a shield for White's king from subsequent attacks on that file. Ironically, after 7... Nh6[2] 8 Ng4 Ng4 9 Qg4 d5 (9... Bg5 10 Qh5

Qe7 11 d4) 10 Qf4 dc4 11 Rh4± [11] it is Black who must attend to the safety of his king!

The alternative **5... Qe7** is not so clearly desirable for Black either. Nevertheless, after **6 d4! Nf6**[3] (6... Bg7 7 Qg4) **7 Bc4,** White must tread carefully when the natural kicking maneuver **7... d6** (unproductive are 7... Nc6 8 Bf4 and 7... Ne4 8 Qg4!) is employed. Following **8 Bf7** (not 8 Nf7? Qe4 △ ...d5) **Kd8 9 Bf4** (playing in true gambit style to get a favorable trade-off of at least two pawns and an attack for a knight) **de5** (9... Nbd7 or 9... Bd7 can be met by 10 Bb3 with play similar to the main line) **10 de5 Bd7,** White maintains the pressure with **11 Bb3!**

Here White wisely preserves his light-squared bishop, while shielding the P/b2, since on 11 Bd5?! Nd5! 12 Bg5 Kc8 13 Be7 Ne7 △ ...Nbc6-Ne5 Black gets a lot of wood for his queen. Next **11... Qb4** (11... Ne4 12 Nd2 transposes) can lead to **12 Nd2 Ne4 13 c3 Nc3 14 Bg5 Be7** (14... Kc8? is refuted by 15 bc3 △ Bf6) **15 bc3 Qc3 16 Be7** [9] **Ke7 17 0–0±.**

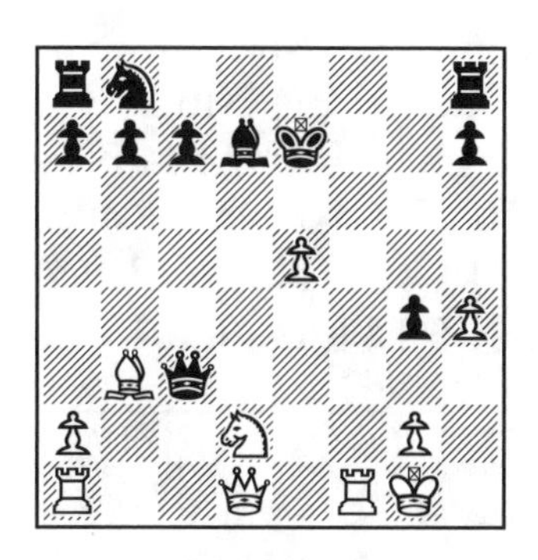

3A-2

White's attack looks irresistible; his P/e5 is taboo while *f7* is an especially weak target square which Black cannot easily defend. For example, 17... Rf8? 18 Rf8 Kf8 19 Qf1! Ke8 20 Qf7 is crushing, and 17... Qd4 18 Kh1 g3? (△ Qh4-Qh2 mate) is thwarted by a pretty "piece offering" involving 19 Qh5+–. Black should probably try 17... Qd4 18 Kh1 Be8 although 19 Rc1 △ Rc4, x-raying his P/g4, will prove hard to meet.

Returning to **5... Qe7 6 d4!,** Black's best try is **6... d6!** The most accurate response is **7 Ng4,** after which 7... Qe4 8 Qe2 Bf5 (for 8... Qe2 9 Be2 see Illustrative Game II, and 8... d5 9 Nf2 Qe2 10 Be2 Bd6 11 Nd3 Nc6 12 c3, or 8... f5 9 Nf2 Qe2 10 Be2 Nc6 11 c3 Bh6 12 Nd3 Nf6 13 Bf4 Bf4 14 Nf4 Ne4 15 Rh3! △ Nd2-Re3) 9 Bf4[4] (c3!?) is convenient for White, but even **7... f5 8 Nf2 Nf6** (8... fe4 9 Qh5 Kd8 10 Bf4 Nf6 11 Qe2 — cf. Diagram 3E-7) **9 Bf4 Ne4** (9... fe4 10 d5!) **10 Qh5 Kd8** (10... Qf7 11 Qf7 △ Ne4-Nc3-Bc4) **11 Be2 Nf6 12 Qf3 Nc6 13 c3**± [9]

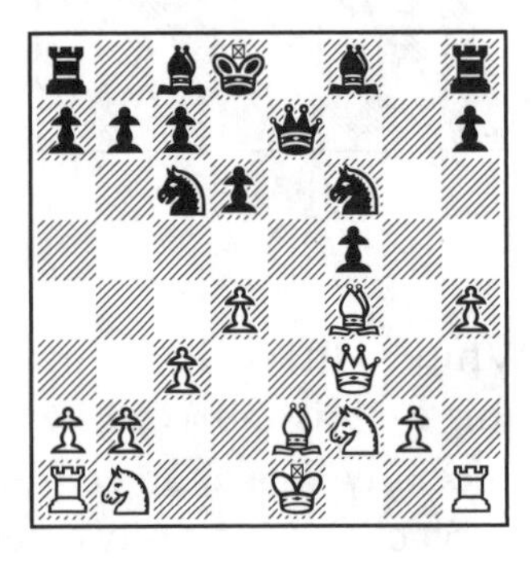

3A-3

fails to appreciably slow White's initiative.

White attains this good position without the usual pawn sacrifice. His rapidly developing pieces can easily exploit Black's exposed P/f5. Black, by contrast, cannot castle and must therefore lose more time while improving his king's location and developing his queen rook. Play might proceed 13... Bg7 (13... Be6 14 Nd2 Kd7?! 15 Bg5!) 14 0–0 h6 15 Nd2 △ Rae1-Bd3. On 13... h6 even 14 Nd2 △ 0–0–0-Rde1 comes into consideration.

Not well-known but intriguing is the provocative **5... Nc6** (from Diagram 3A-1) after which it is incumbent upon White to declare his intentions regarding his N/e5. After **6 d4! Ne5**[5] (doubly isolating White's center pawns) **7 de5 d6 8 Bf4,** Black has two good lines from which to choose: **8... Bg7** and 8... Qe7. The first of these seeks to dispute the a1-h8 diagonal dark squares, in particular *e5*. However, continuing with **9 Nc3 de5** (9... Be5 10 Be5 de5 11 Qd8 △ 0–0–0±) **10 Qd8 Kd8 11 0–0–0 Bd7** (11... Ke8 12 Bg3 c6 13 Bc4±) **12 Be3**⩲ [9]

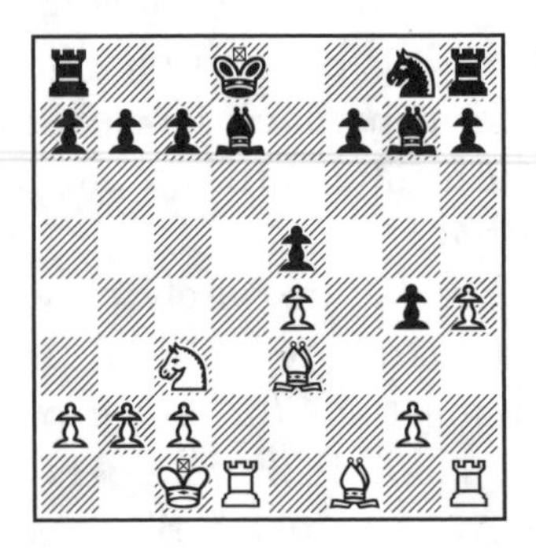

3A-4

White achieves castling with tempo, rapid and harmonious development with open lines for his bishops, and disruption of Black's castling notions.

Here White can already think about taking advantage of Black's weak pawns on *f7* and *g4*. Perhaps

White should keep Bc4-g3-Rhf1 in mind, and if ...Nf6?!, then Bg5, in conjunction with a rook on the f-file, will have a point. White may also effectively isolate the P/g4 by playing h5 with h6 in reserve. For example, a worthy plan is Nd5-Bg5-h5-Ne3-Be2-Ng4. Of course, Black's P/e5 could become a target as well, particularly in the event of ...f5.

If again (from Diagram 3A-1) **5... Nc6 6 d4! Ne5 7 de5 d6** (7... f3!? 8 Be3) **8 Bf4,** Black might select **8... Qe7,** attacking White's center (or 8... Bg7 9 Nc3 de5 — 9... Be5 10 Be5 de5 11 Qd8 — 10 Qd8 Kd8 11 0–0–0 Bd7 12 Be3±). Here **9 ed6** (or 9 Bb5 c6 10 ed6 Qe4 11 Qe2) **Qe4 10 Qe2 Qe2 11 Be2 Bd6 12 Bd6 cd6 13 Nc3=** [1]

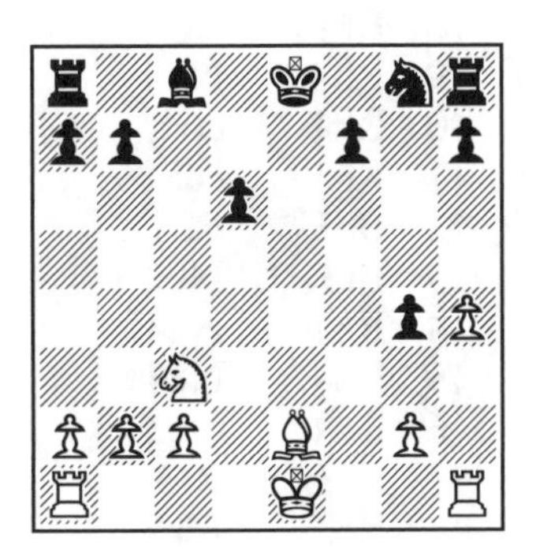

3A-5

gives White his usual edge in development for a pawn. White threatens to castle long with tempo (attacking the isolated P/d6) and *f4* may prove to be a strong outpost square for either of his rooks. One of White's principal strategies will be to focus pieces on the P/d6. Black's king will be subject to attack if it remains in the center to safeguard this pawn.

Furthermore, after 0–0–0-Bc4-(g3)-Rhf1 yet another weakness in Black's camp may be exposed—the square *f7*. Optionally, the plan h5-g3-0–0–0-Nd5-Rdf1-Rf4 would pile up attackers on the P/g4 while gaining time by menacing the P/d6 and contemplating Nc7. Thus, with the presence of bishops of the same color, Black's isolani and K-side pawn distortion offer White good winning chances.

ILLUSTRATIVE GAME I

Szewczak—Donato
1980 Golden Knights

1	e4	e5
2	f4	ef4
3	Nf3	g5
4	h4	g4
5	Ne5	Qe7
6	d4	f5
7	Bc4!	Nh6
8	Bf4	Qb4
9	Nc3	d6
10	a3	Qb6
11	Nd5	Qb2
12	Nc7	Kd8
13	Nb5	a6
14	Rb1	Qb1
15	Qb1	ab5
16	Bh6	de5
17	Bg5	Be7
18	Be7	Ke7
19	Qb4	1–0

ILLUSTRATIVE GAME II

David—Sherzer
Germany 1992

1	e4	e5
2	f4	ef4
3	Nf3	g5
4	h4	g4
5	Ne5	Qe7
6	d4!	d6
7	Ng4	Qe4
8	Qe2	Qe2
9	Be2	Nc6
10	c3	h5
11	Nf2	Bh6
12	0–0	Nge7
13	Na3	Nf5
14	Ne4	Nh4
15	Bf4	Bf4
16	Rf4	Ng6
17	Rf2	Nce7
18	Nb5	Kd8
19	Ng5 (Rf7)	Be6
20	Nf7	Bf7
21	Rf7	a6
22	Na3	Kd7
23	Raf1	Rag8
24	Nc4	h4
25	Bg4	Ke8
26	Ne3	Rf8
27	Rf8	Rf8
28	Nf5	Rg8
29	Ne7	Ke7
30	Bf5	Kf6
31	Kh2	Kg5
32	Be6	Re8
33	Rf5	Kh6
34	d5	Ne5
35	Kh3	Kg6
36	Rf4	Kg5
37	Rf5	Kg6
38	Rf4	Kg5
39	Rh4	Nd3
40	Rh7	c6
41	Kg3	cd5
42	Bd5	Re3
43	Bf3	Nb2
44	Rb7	Na4
45	Rb4	Nc3
46	Rd4	Ne2
47	Kf2	Rf3
48	Ke2	Ra3

½–½

PROBLEMS

1. Use Diagram 3A-6 to:

a) Determine whether **4... f6** is playable.
b) Find White's best response to **4... gh4 5 d4 Bh6.**

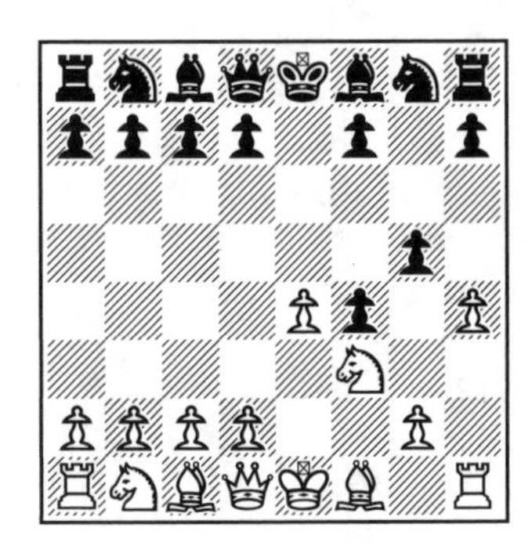

3A-6

c) Discover White's preferred procedure for handling **4... Be7 5 hg5 Bg5 6 d4 d6** (see Diagram 3A-7). Note that 6... Qe7 7 Nc3 △ g3 is good for White.

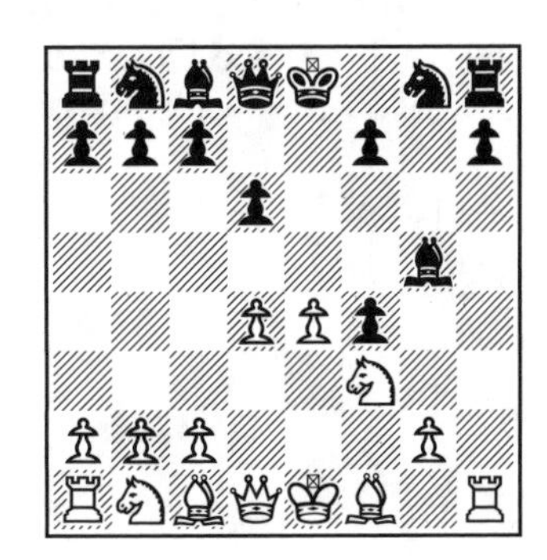

3A-7

2. Instead, Black can return a pawn to gain time for development by **7... d5 8 Bd5 Nh6 9 d4 Bg5** (9... Qg5 10 Qd2 Bg3 11 Nc3±) **10 Nc3! c6 11 Bb3** (see Diagram 3A-8). White's advantage resides in the contortions Black must undergo to maintain the pawns on **f4** and **g4.** Analyze:

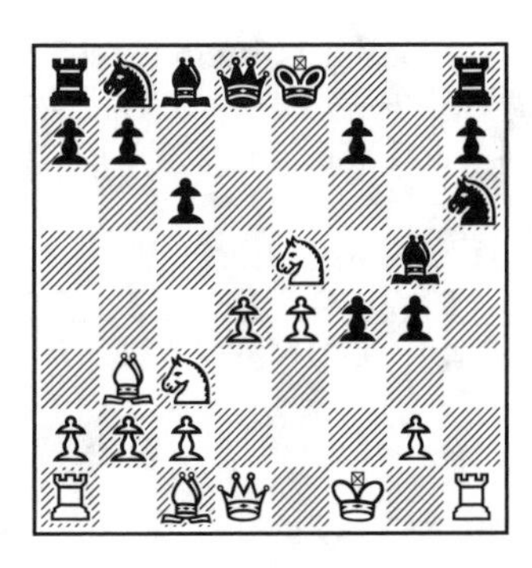

3A-8

a) **11... f6.**
b) **11... f3?**

3. Insufficient for Black is **6... f5 7 Bc4! Nf6** (for 7... Nh6 see the illustrative game on p. 12) providing White avoids 8 Nf7? Qe4 Δ ...d5−+ by playing **8 Nc3** (see Diagram 3A-9). Show that White can disrupt Black's king position to obtain a clear edge after:

a) **8... Ne4?**
b) **8... fe4.**
c) **8... d6.**
d) **8... Bg7.**

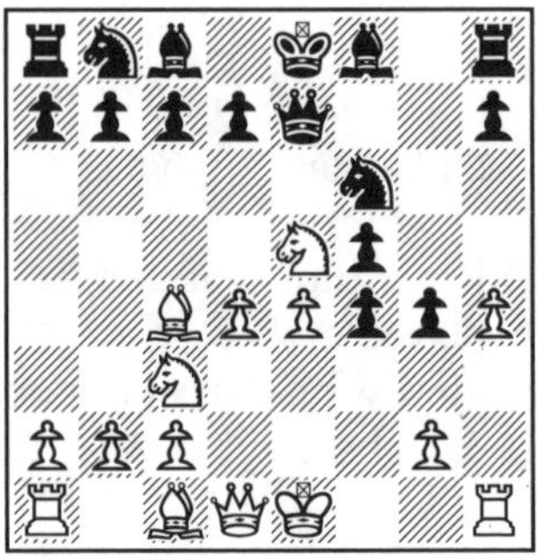

3A-9

4. Proceeding with **9... Qe2 10 Be2 Bc2 11 Nc3** (see Diagram 3A-10), deduce White's solution to:

a) **11... c6?**
b) **11... Bf5.**

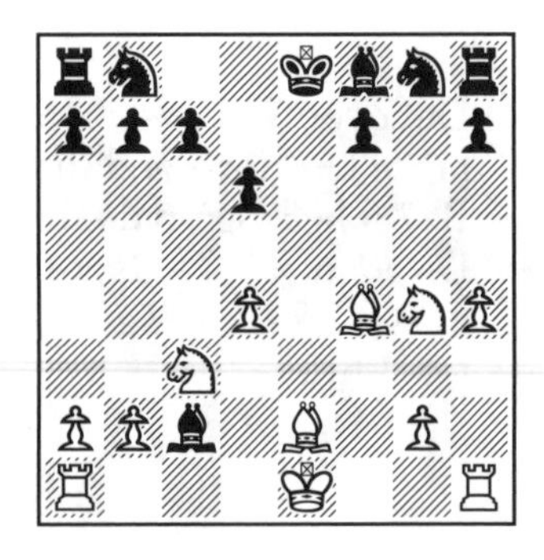

3A-10

5. **6... Be7?!** is ineffective. After **7 Bf4 Bh4 8 g3 Bf6** (8... Bg5 9 Ng4) **9 Bc4** (see Diagram 3A-11):

a) Examine **9... Qe7.**
b) Refute **9... Be5 10 de5 Qe7? 11 Nc3 Ne5.**

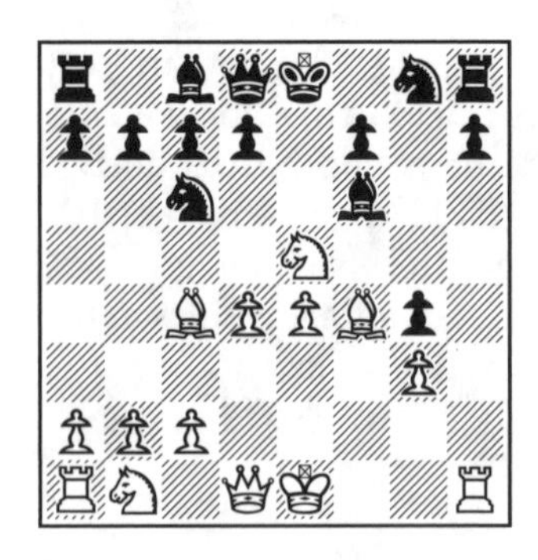

3A-11

Kieseritzky Variation (B)

The Long Whip (!), arising from 5... h5, is an outmoded continuation that deserves special mention:

1	**e4**	**e5**
2	**f4**	**ef4**
3	**Nf3**	**g5**
4	**h4**	**g4**
5	**Ne5**	**h5**
6	**Bc4**	

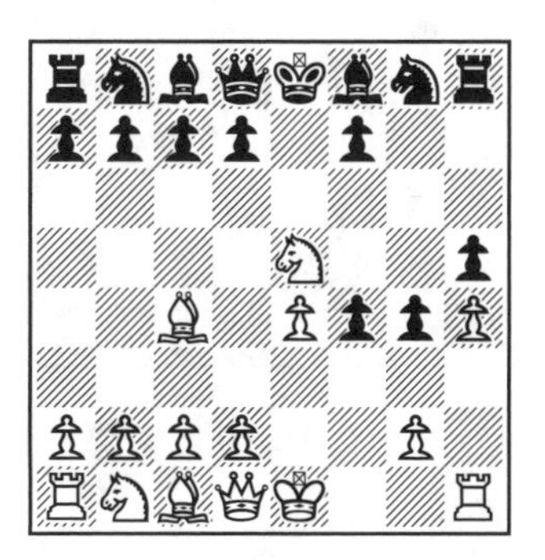

3B-1

There are two playable moves at Black's disposal here — 6... Nh6 and **6... Rh7.** Against the latter White should expand with **7 d4** after which his pieces, it seems, can hardly resist paying Black an unwelcome visit on *f7*. For instance, 7... Qf6 8 0–0 (Nc3) Qh4?![1] 9 Rf4 Bh6 invites 10 Rf7 Rf7 (10... g3 11 Nf3 Qe4 12 Bd3) 11 Bf7 Kd8 12 Bg8 Bc1 13 Qc1 g3 14 Qg5!+– [9].

The antipositional 7... Bd6 also fails tactically due to 8 Nc3 (Bf4) Nc6 9 Bf7 Rf7 10 Nf7 Kf7 11 Bf4 Bf4 when 12 0–0 gives White the advantage since 12... Qh4? can be met by 13 Rf4, e.g., 13... Kg7 14 Qd2 d6 15 Raf1± [11]. As in Problem 3A#5, doubly attacking White's P/h4 with 7... Be7[2] does not work out well for Black either. Even protecting the P/f4 with 7... Bh6 does little to halt the train. Note, however, that following 8 Nc3 Nc6 (8... d6 9 Nd3), the strategic 9 Nd5![3] (9. Nf7 Rf7 10 Bf7 Kf7 11 Bf4 [19] is an alternative) puts White clearly on top.

A more thematic line emerges from **7... d6** (7... f3 8 gf3 d6 9 Nd3 transposes, though 9 Bg5 is an option). One example is **8 Nd3** (Nf7!?) **f3** (for 8... Be7 9 Bf4 see Problem 3B#2b, while on 8... Qe7, White has 9 Nc3 Nf6 10 0–0 f3 11 Bg5) **9 gf3 Be7** (neither 9... c6? 10 Nc3 nor 9... g3 10 Bg5 Be7 11 Be7 Qe7 12 Kf1 [3] is any better) **10 Be3 Bh4 11 Kd2±**.

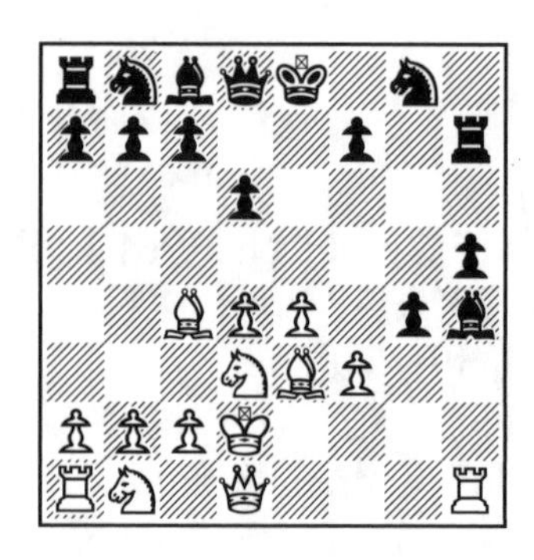

3B-2

White has achieved a significant space advantage and a huge lead in development. Both his bishops are active and his N/d3 is beautifully placed in the center, poised for play on either wing. In addition, White's queen is set to join the fray from *f1* or *e2*. After Nc3 and, say Qe2, White is ready to spring his queen rook for duty wherever needed. Finally, with **c1** available for his king, White will soon be threatening to break in the center. Thus all of White's developmental moves are at once natural and speedy.

Black, meanwhile, must try to develop without loss of position. Attempting to consolidate with 11... Bg5 leads to immediate trouble after 12 f4 (Qg1) Bh6 13 Nc3 (or 13 Nf2 but not 13 Rh5?! Nf6) Bg7 14 f5 Nc6 15 Qg1 Bd7 16 Re1 [13]. On 11... g3 White can plan Qg1-Nc3-Ne2, perhaps to be coordinated with Bf2! if Black's N/g8 remains exposed. Whether or not Black can attain general positional harmony while holding the extra pawn becomes the operative question.

Consider **11... gf3 12 Qf3 Bg4 13 Qf4 Rg7**[4] **14 Nc3 Bg5 15 Qf2 Nd7 16 Raf1 Be3 17 Qe3 Nb6 18 Bb3 Qe7 19 e5 de5 20 Ne5**± [9].

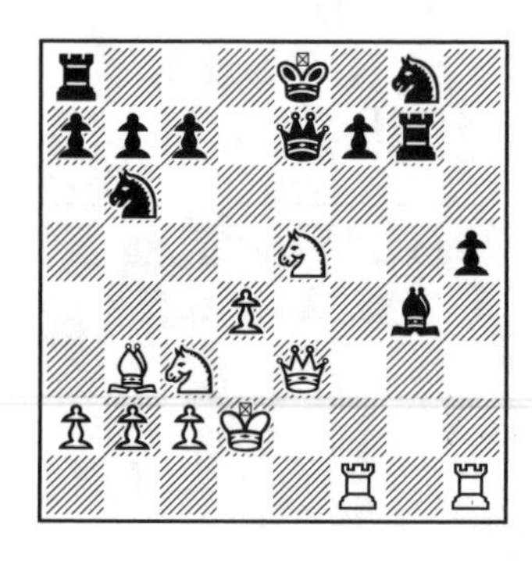

3B-3

White's advantage is clear despite the pawn deficit; it resides in his superior development combined with Black's problematical *f7* square. Next, if 20... f6, then 21 Ng4 hg4 22 Rh8! Qe3 23 Ke3 △ Ne4 is very good for White.

Returning to Diagram 3B-1, the alternative, **6... Nh6,** is also met by **7 d4.** Now with **7... d6**[5] **8 Nd3 f3** (8... Nd7 9 Bf4 Qf6 10 c3 Qg6 11 Qe2 [8]), Black deflects

White's g-pawn to win White's P/h4 and to prevent White from castling. Nevertheless, **9 gf3 Be7**[6] (9... Nc6 10 Be3 Bd7 11 Nc3) **10 Be3** (Bg5) **Bh4 11 Kd2 gf3 12 Qf3 Bg4 13 Qf4!** leads to an attractive queen sacrifice (cf. Problem 3B#4d), with **13... Nc6 14 Nc3 Nd4 15 Bd4 Bg5 16 Bh8 Bf4 17 Nf4 c6** (17... Qg5? 18 Ncd5+–) **18 Raf1 Qg5 19 Bd4**± [3].

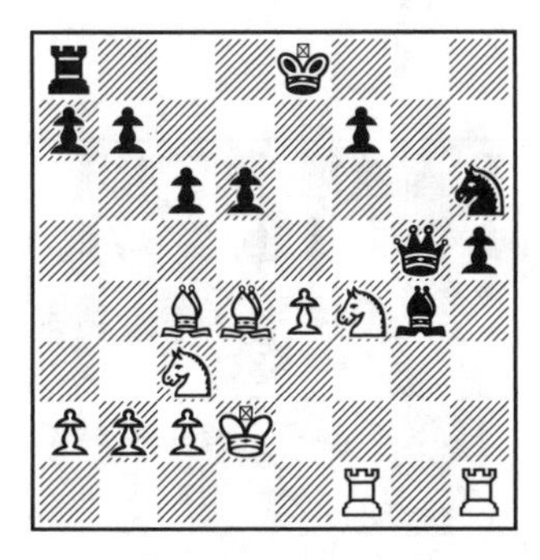

3B-4

White has secured a rook, bishop and knight for his queen and two pawns. He intends Be3 when both Black's P/h5 and N/h6 come under siege. Black lags in development and clearly faces an arduous defensive task.

ILLUSTRATIVE GAME

Morphy—McConnell
New Orleans 1849

1	e4	e5
2	f4	ef4
3	Nf3	g5
4	h4	g4
5	Ne5	h5
6	Bc4	Rh7
7	d4	d6
8	Nd3	f3
9	g3 (gf3)	Nf6
10	Nf4	Bd7
11	Nc3	Nc6
12	Be3	Ne7
13	Kf2!	c6
14	Re1	Bg7
15	e5!	de5
16	de5	Nfd5
17	Bd5	cd5
18	Bc5	Bc6
19	b4!	b6
20	Be7	Qe7
21	Nfd5	Qb7
22	Nf6	Bf6
23	ef6	Kf8
24	Qd6	Kg8
25	Re7	Qc8
26	Rc7	Qf5
27	Qc6	Qc2
28	Ke3	Rd8
29	Rd1	1-0

PROBLEMS

1. A little more tenacious is **8... Bh6,** although with **9 Nc3** (see Diagram 3B-5) White still achieves a dangerous initiative.

Analyze:

a) **9... Qh4.**
b) **9... d6.**
c) **9... Ne7.**
d) **9... c6.**

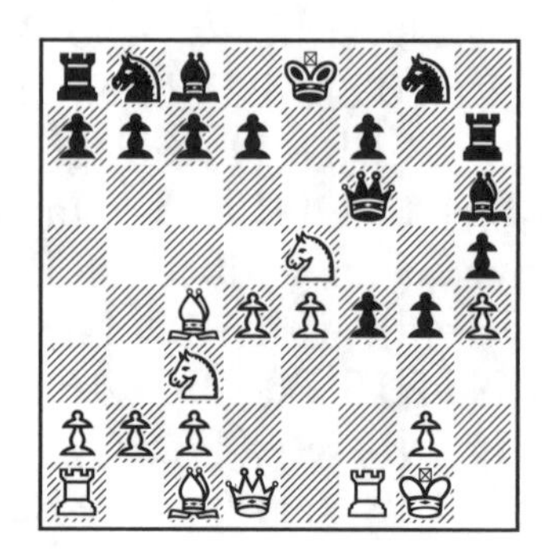

3B-5

2. After **7... Be7 8 Bf4** (see Diagram 3B-6) find White's rejoinder to:

a) **8... Bh4.**
b) **8... d6 9 Nd3 Bh4.**

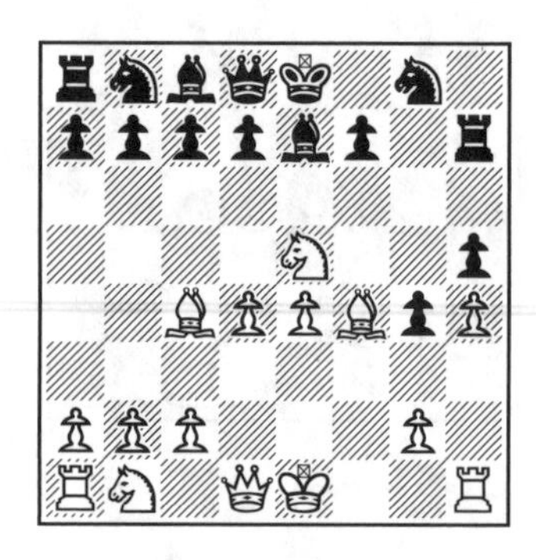

3B-6

3. Here White retains the better game by inducing Black to irreparably weaken **d6.** Following **9... Ne5 10 de5** (see Diagram 3B-7) repress:

a) **10... c6.**
b) **10... d6.**

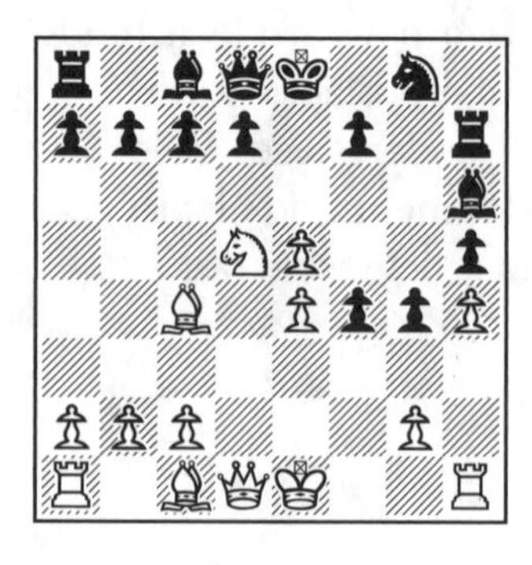

3B-7

4. From Diagram 3B-8, incorporate play against **f7** with the central break e5 to illustrate White's superiority after:

a) **13... Ne7?**
b) **13... Nd7.**
c) **13... Qf6.**
d) **13... Nc6 14 Nc3 Nd4.**

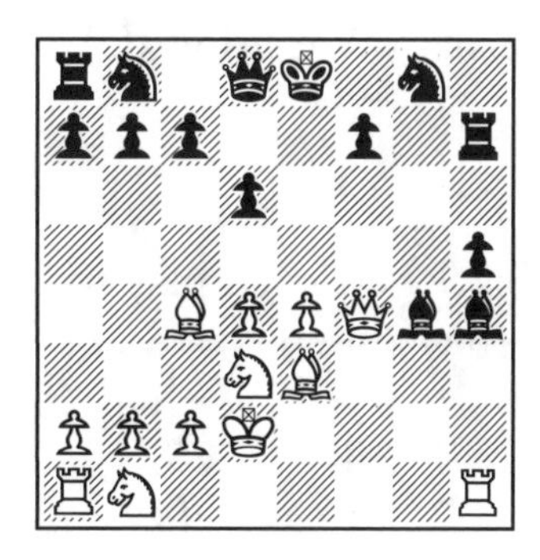

3B-8

5. Alternatives for Black here are weak. From Diagram 3B-9 prove that Black is in trouble if he tries:

a) **7... Qf6 8 Nc3 c6 9 0–0! Qh4.**
b) **7... Be7 8 Bf4 Bh4 9 g3 Bg5.**

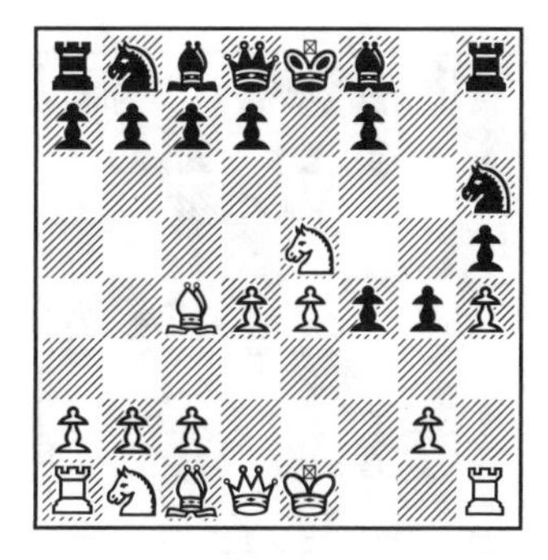

3B-9

6. No immediate improvement for Black is **9... gf3 10 Qf3 Bg4 11 Qf2** (see Diagram 3B-10):

a) Reject **11... Qd7 12 Nc3 c6.**
b) Demonstrate that **11... Qe7** gives Black no relief.

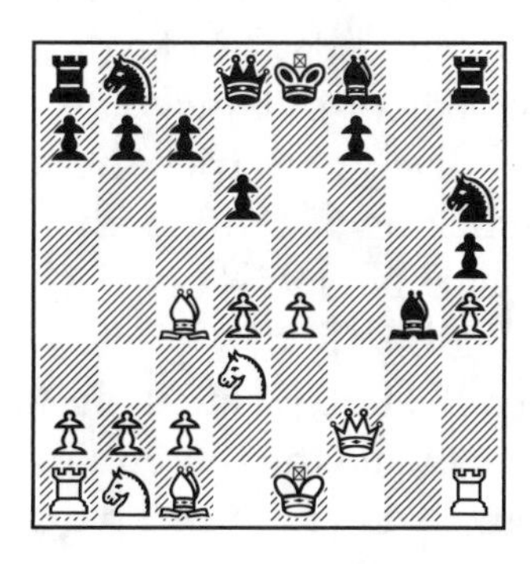

3B-10

Kieseritzky Variation (C)

Black gets good play with 5... Bg7, the Paulsen Defense:

1	e4	e5
2	f4	ef4
3	Nf3	g5
4	h4	g4
5	Ne5	Bg7
6	d4!	

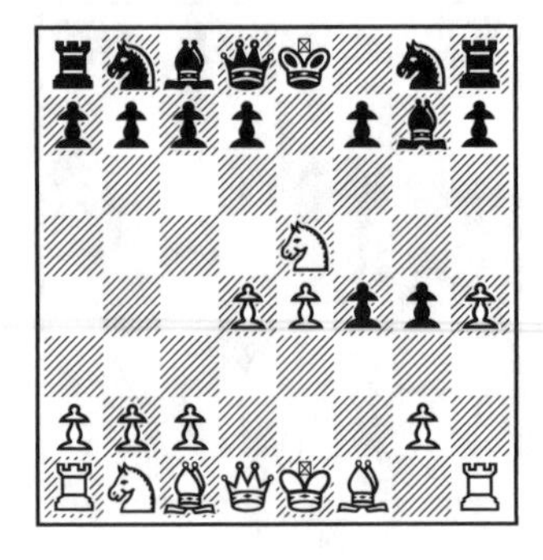

3C-1

Here White rejects the premature 6 Ng4?! d5!∓ in favor of the development-oriented 6 d4.

If Black now tries the counterattacking 6... Nf6, both 7 Nc3 d6 8 Nd3 Nh5 9 Nf4 Ng3 10 Rh2 0–0 11 Be2 Re8! [5] and 7 Ng4 Ne4 8 Bf4 0–0 [1] are in his favor. White should thus entertain 7 Bf4 when 7... d6 (7... Ne4?! 8 Qg4!±) 8 Nd3 Ne4 9 c3 transposes directly to lines of the Berlin Defense, Sections 3F through 3H.

Indigenous lines arise from the critical **6... d6**[1] (not 6... h5 7 Bc4±). Following **7 Ng4 Bg4 8 Qg4 Bd4** White should avoid the alluring 9 c3 owing to 9... Be5 10 Bf4 Nf6 11 Qf3 Bf4 12 Qf4 Qe7!∓ △ ...Rg8-Nbd7-0–0–0 and select 9 **Nc3!**, leaving Black at a crossroads. One important choice, the disruptive **9... Bc3**[2], can lead to **10 bc3 Nbd7 11 Rb1!**⩲, scrambling Black's plans for rapid consolidation.

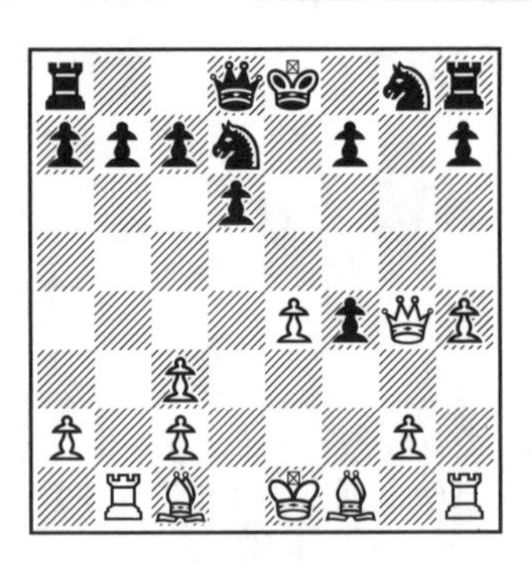

3C-2

Here it is not easy for Black to castle without creating cavernous holes on his queenside. In these lines, White's bishops — despite the splintered pawns! — appear to carry the day after both 11... b6 12 Bb5! and 11... Qf6 12 Rb7! Best, perhaps, is 11... Nb6 though Black loses control of *e5*. After 12 Bf4 Qf6 (12... Nf6 13 Qf5) 13 Rh3! △ Rf3, White's attacking chances are to be preferred.

PROBLEMS

1. The antipositional **6... Be5?!** forces **7 de5** but cedes White the bishop pair and virtual command of the kingside dark squares. After **7... Qe7** (7... f3? 8 Bg5!) **8 Bf4** (see Diagram 3C-3) discuss:

a) **8... d6?!**
b) **8... Nc6.**

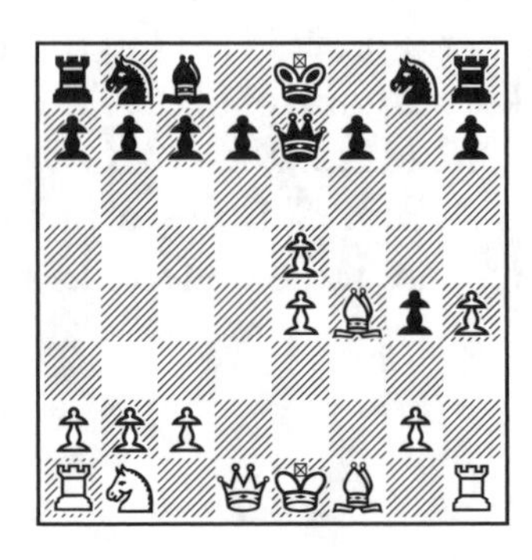

3C-3

2. From Diagram 3C-4, resolve three other choices by Black:

a) **9... Qe7?**
b) **9... Nf6.**
c) **9... Nc6.**

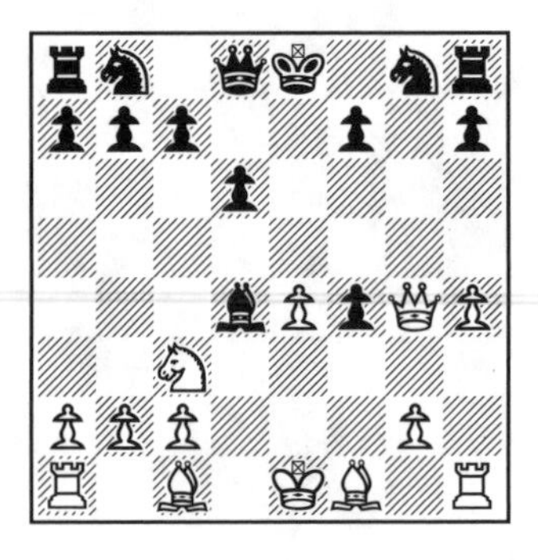

3C-4

Kieseritzky Variation (D)

The Brentano Continuation, 5... d5, appears to be an unworkable hybrid:

1	e4	e5
2	f4	ef4
3	**Nf3**	**g5**
4	**h4**	**g4**
5	**Ne5**	**d5**
6	**d4!**	**Nf6**[1]
7	**Bf4**	**Ne4**[2]
8	**Nd2!**	

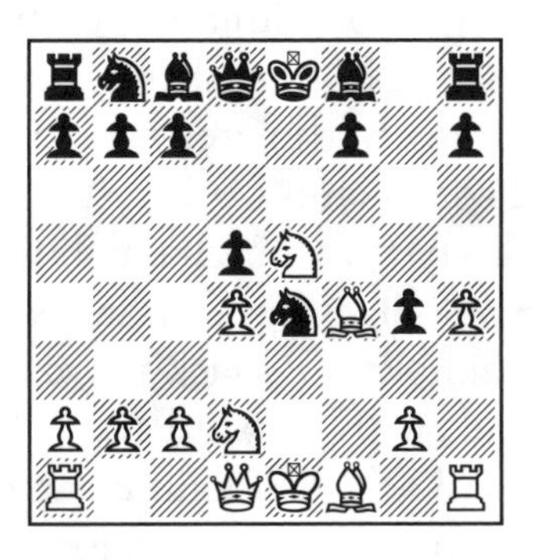

3D-1

Black has opted for the win of a pawn at the cost of development, a common theme in the Kieseritzky. In these lines White can play either to win the P/g4 or to gain an insurmountable lead in development. Raids against the White fortress only speed White's progress, although **8... Qf6**[3] (8... Bg7 9 Ne4 de4 10 Bc4 0–0 11 c3 Nd7 12 Nf7! Rf7 13 Bf7 Kf7 14 Qb3 Ke7 15 0–0–0 Nf6 16 d5!+– [13]) **9 g3 Bh6!** does seem dangerous at first sight. Here, simply **10 Ne4 de4 11 Ng4 Bg4 12 Qg4 Bf4 13 gf4** (Qf4) **Qd4 14 Rd1**± [12] bares the lie. This instructive position bespeaks the classic tradeoff of material for attack.

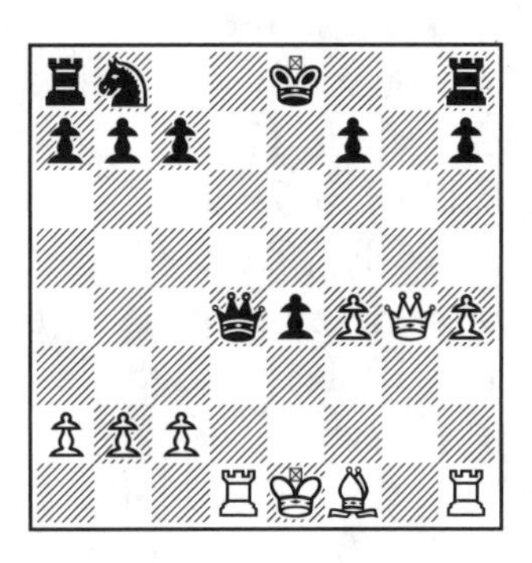

3D-2

For instance, after the greedy 14... Qb2, 15 Qc8 is winning. On the other hand, if 14... Qe3, then White does well with 15 Be2 Nc6 16 Rh3 △ Qd7.

From Diagram 3D-1, also suspect is **8... Nd2** due to **9 Qd2 Bd6**[4] **10 0–0–0 Be6 11 Bd3 Nd7**[5] **12 Rde1! Ne5 13 Be5 Be5**

14 Re5 Qd7 (14... Qe7 15 Bf5) **15 Qg5! Qe7 16 Bf5 Qg5 17 hg5**± [5].

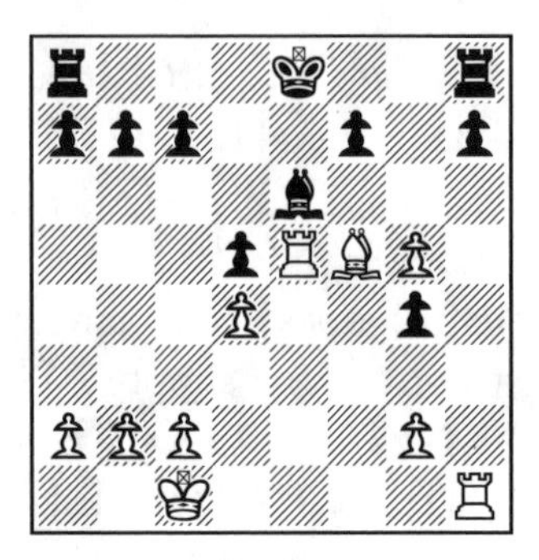

3D-3

Black must return the pawn and accept a worse ending. Examples include 17... Ke7 18 Bg4, 17... Kd7 18 Rd5 and 17... Rg8 18 Rh7. Clearly 17... 0–0–0 serves up the same evaluation after 18 Be6 fe6 19 Re6 Rdg8 20 Rh5 (Re5) [5] when White's rooks dominate the kingside files.

Finally (from Diagram 3D-1), not even **8... f5 9 Ne4 de4,** holding on to the P/g4, assures Black a reasonable game. Hardly better, however, is 9... fe4 since 10 Ng4 (Bb5) Rg8 11 Ne5 △ Qh5 presents Black with devilish defensive problems. Thus White can proceed with **10 Bc4**(±) when **10... Bg7** (Black must meet both Bf7-Bg5 and Nf7) **11 Nf7 Qd4 12 Qd4 Bd4 13 0–0–0 c5 14 c3 Bf6** is a forcible continuation.

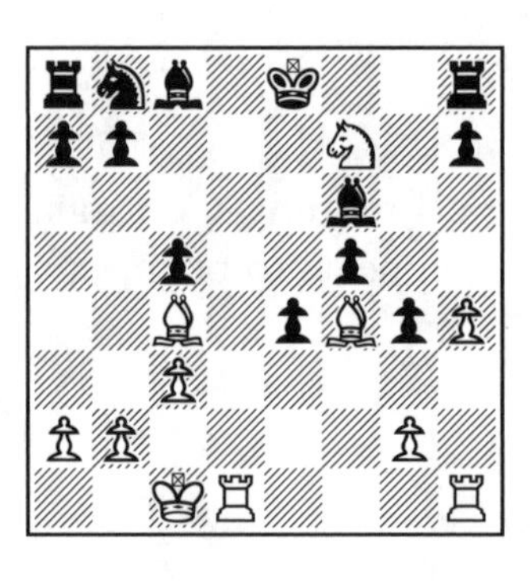

3D-4

A remarkable position — Black's king seems completely unclad! Black is anemic on the dark squares surrounding the pawn triangle on *e4*, *f5* and *g4*. White's B/f4 already threatens to invade on those squares while restraining Black's pawn umbrella. Following 15 Rd6 Nd7 16 Nh8 Bh8, White can capitalize on Black's weakened kingside with Rh6 or Rhd1. Once again, Black's difficulties can be traced to his dilatory development.

PROBLEMS

1. Other tries also fare poorly. From Diagram 3D-5, discuss White's response to:

a) **6... de4.**
b) **6... f3.**
c) **6... f6.**

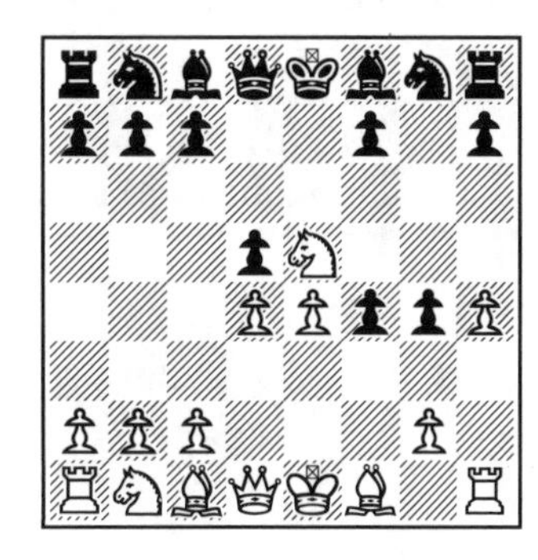

3D-5

2. From Diagram 3D-6:

a) Prove that **7... de4** prematurely concedes **c4.**
b) Resolve **7... Nh5.**

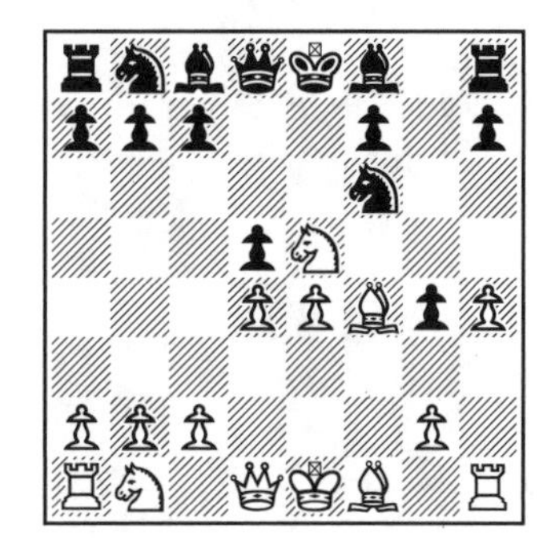

3D-6

3. Worse yet is **8... Bf5** (see Diagram 3D-7) since White can achieve an effortless plus. How?

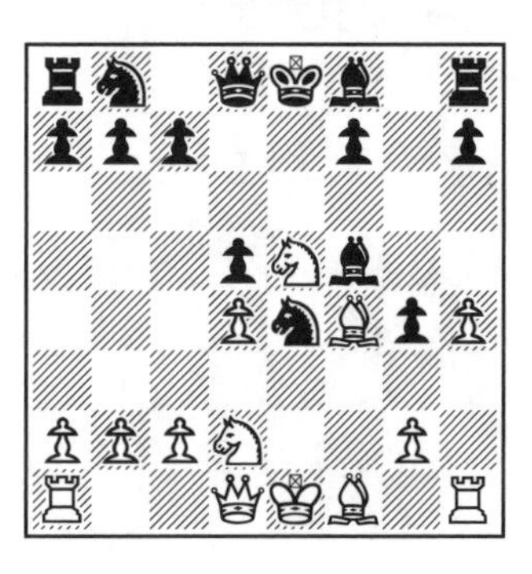

3D-7

4. It is difficult for Black to avoid defeat in other lines:

a) Show that **9... Be6 10 0–0–0 Nd7 11 Re1 Be7?!** (see Diagram 3D-8) loses material.

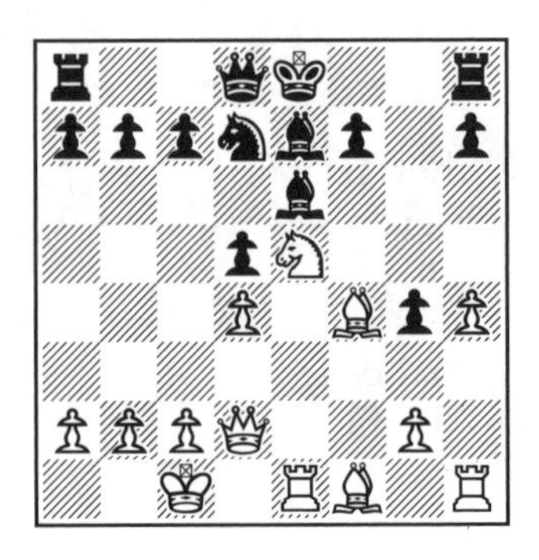

3D-8

b) An interesting miniature continued **9... Bg7 10 Bh6 Bh6 11 Qh6 Be6 12 Bd3 Nd7** (see Diagram 3D-9). Find the win.

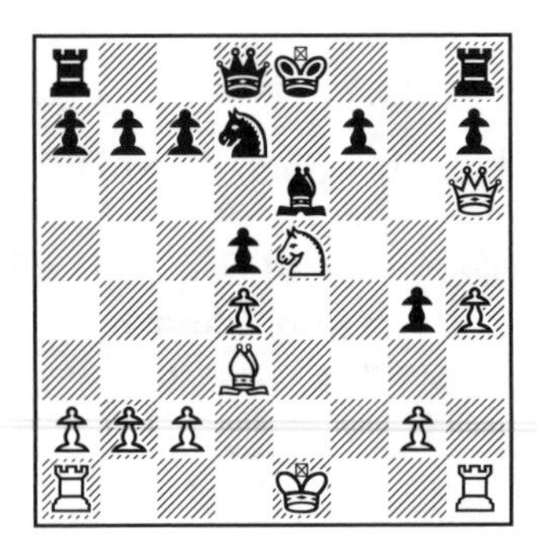

3D-9

5. Optionally, **11... f6?! 12 Rde1!** (see Diagram 3D-10) leads to a combinative success for White:

a) On **12... Be5** can White win?
b) Also refute **12... fe5.**

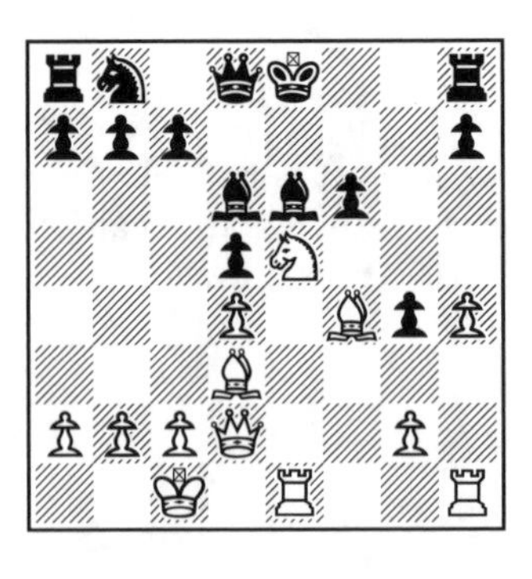

3D-10

Kieseritzky Variation (E)

Surprisingly playable is 5... d6, the Kolisch Continuation:

1	**e4**	**e5**
2	**f4**	**ef4**
3	**Nf3**	**g5**
4	**h4**	**g4**
5	**Ne5**	**d6**
6	**Ng4**	

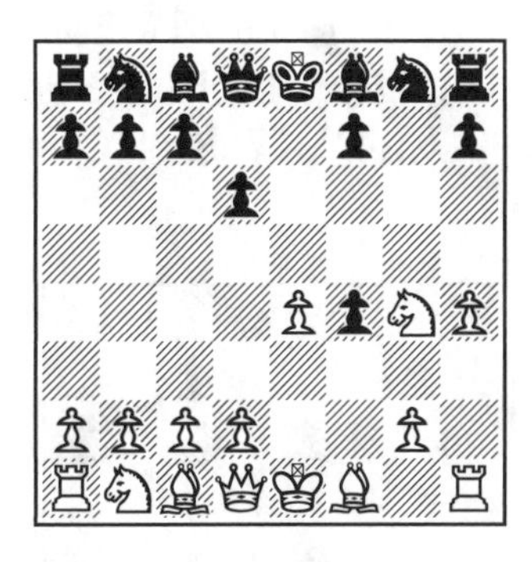

3E-1

Somewhat lax is **6... Nf6**[1] (6... Nh6 7 Nf2!) owing to **7 Nf6**[2] **Qf6 8 Nc3 c6** (8... Be6 9 Qe2 Nd7 10 b3 Rg8 11 Bb2 Bg4—11... 0-0-0 12 0-0-0 Bg4 13 Qf2 Bd1 14 Qa7 Bg4 15 Ba6! Nc5 16 Bb5 Nd7 [16... c6±] 17 Nd5 Qe6 18 Bc6+– — 12 Qf2 d5 13 Be2 Bc5 14 Qf1 Be2 15 Qe2 0-0-0 16 0-0-0 de4 17 Ne4 Qg6 18 Qc4 Nb6 [or 18... Be7 19 Ng5 and 18... Bb6 19 Ng5] 19 Qc5 Qe4 20 Rhe1± [19]) **9 Be2!?** (d4∞) **Rg8 10 Bf3 Bh6** (10... Bg7 11 d3 Be6 12 Qd2 Bh6 13 d4 Nbd7 14 Qf2 [14]) **11 d4 Na6** (△ ...Nc7-Ne6) **12 e5! de5 13 Ne4 Qe7 14 0–0**± [9].

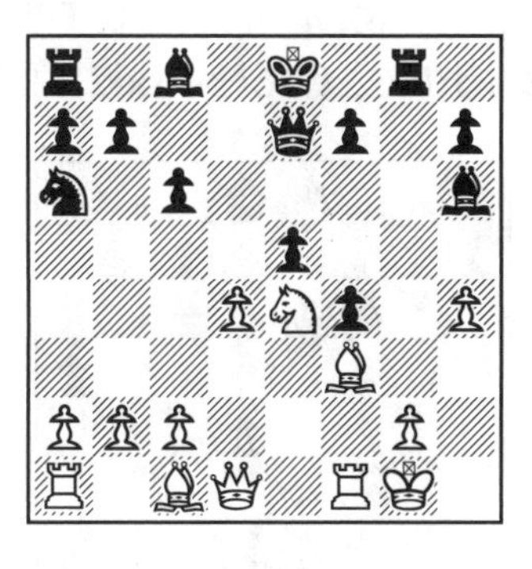

3E-2

Black's development lag again raises cause for concern despite appearances to the contrary.

After 14... Qh4 15 de5 (Nd6!?) Bg7 (15... Rg6? cedes the exchange to 16 Nf6, and 15... Kf8 16 Qd6 Kg7 17 Nf6 △ Nh5-Qh6 gives White a strong attack) 16 Re1 △ Nf6/Nd6, White would win material. On the other hand, if Black develops with 14... Be6, simply 15 de5 Rd8 16 Nf6 is destructive. Even 14... ed4 15 Qd4 Rg6 16 Bd2 Bd7 fails since 17 Rae1 is positionally crushing. In any event, White's plans should unequivocally embrace Nd6 or Nf6.

Returning to Diagram 3E-1, safer is **6... h5** in view of **7 Nf2 Nf6**[3] **8 d4 Bh6 9 Be2** (Nc3) **Nc6 10 Nc3 Ng4 11 Ng4 Bg4**[4] **12 Qd3** (thematically preparing 0–0–0 and covering the third-rank squares, while indirectly preventing ...Nb4 because of Qb5) **Be2 13 Ne2 Qf6 14 Bd2**± [1].

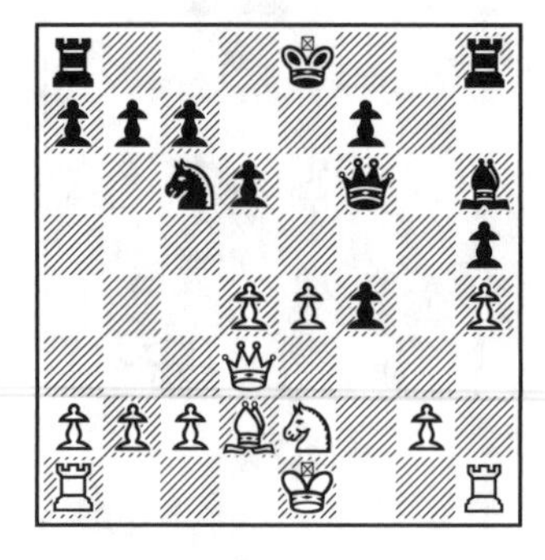

3E-3

White's position reflects a number of positive features. Though material is even, White has an ideal central pawn majority. Consequently, ...d5 can be answered tersely by e5. Moreover, White is able to castle long straight away, developing his R/a1 to the desirable d-file. Then, after Kb1 (to circumvent a discovered check along the c1-h6 diagonal) Bc3 becomes an appealing move, giving rise to powerful threats along the a1-h8 diagonal. Perhaps White would prefer c3-Qf3, intending to win Black's P/f4 or P/h5, while a glance at the f-file reveals doubled isolanis, later targets for a White rook on *f1*.

In Black's corner there is the vulnerability of the P/g2, which is currently undefended. Additionally, Black can seek to win the P/h4 or, at the very least, to tie down the R/h1 to its defense. His play, however, must be ironclad, e.g., **14... Rg8 15 Rh2 Rg4 16 0–0–0 Rh4?! 17 Rh4 Qh4 18 g3!**±.

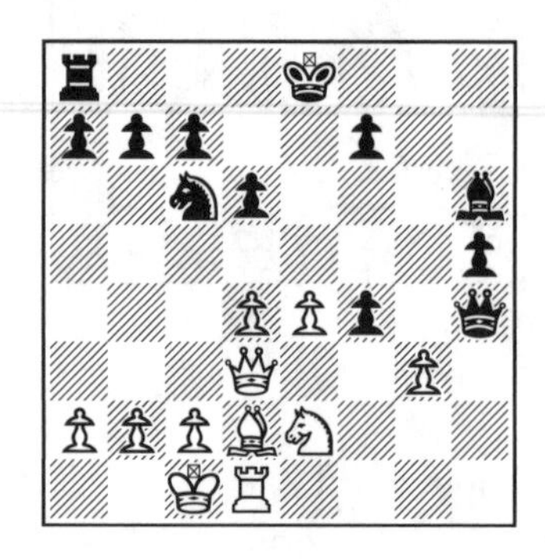

3E-4

Black's backward development has become painfully obvious. To gain the point White must win the P/h5 or create a promotable passed pawn of his own, e.g., 18... Qh2? 19 gf4 △ Qf3-Rh1-Rh5.

From Diagram 3E-1, Black

could also venture the doubly-attacking **6... Be7.** Nevertheless, after **7 d4** (to be considered is the recent idea 7 d3, e.g., 7... Bh4 8 Nf2 Qg5 9 Qd2! Bg3 10 Nc3 Nf6 11 Ne2! [19]) **Bh4 8 Nf2** Black will do well just to equalize! Inadvisable, for instance, would be 8... Bf2 9 Kf2 Nf6 10 Nc3 △ Bf4± [8].

Best play incorporates **8... Qg5** (8... Bg3 9 Qf3 is similar) **9 Nc3** (9 Qf3 Nc6 10 Qf4 Bf2 [for 10... Qf4 see the Illustrative Game] 11 Kf2 Qf4 12 Bf4 Nd4 13 Nc3! Be6 14 e5!$\overline{\overline{\infty}}$) **Nf6** (9... Bg4 10 Qd2!, 9... Nc6 10 Ne2, and 9... Bf2 10 Kf2 Qg3 11 Kg1 Bg4 12 Be2 are better for White) **10 Qf3 Bg3** (or 10... Ng4 11 Nd1 Nc6 12 c3 Nf2 13 Nf2 Bg3 14 Kd1 Be6 15 Nh3 Qg7 16 Be2! [8], e.g., 16... 0–0–0 17 Nf4 Bf4 18 Bf4 d5 19 e5 Bf5 [18] 20 Kc1 Bg6?! 21 Qh3 Kb8 22 Bg5 △ Bd8/Bf6) **11 Bd2 Nc6** (11... Bg4 12 Qg3!±) **12 Bb5 Bd7 13 Bc6 bc6**[5] **14 0–0–0 0–0–0 15 Nh3** (Nd3!?)± [9]. White can regain his pawn without making any real concessions.

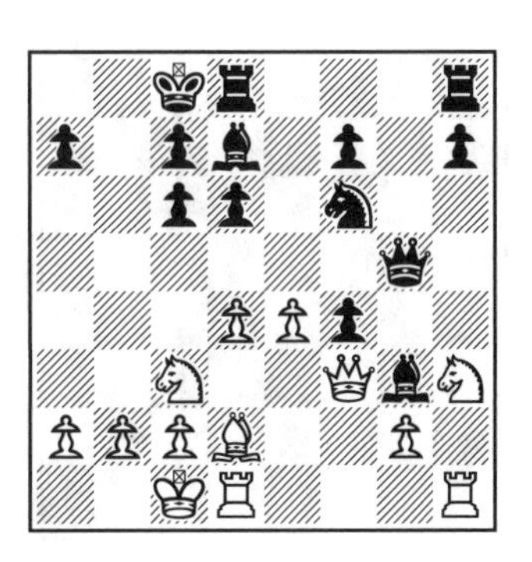

3E-5

White can intensify his f-file pressure with Rdf1 when Black will be hard-put either to maintain his N/f6 or to defend his P/f7. Clearly, White will watch for an appropriate moment to switch his attack over to Black's weakened queenside. In this regard, possible is 15... Qg7 (15... Bg4?? 16 Ng5+−) 16 Rdf1 Bg4 17 Qd3 △ Nf4 with good prospects on both wings.

Finally, on **6... Be7 7 d4 Bh4 8 Nf2,** Black may also test **8... Qf6.** In this case **9 Qf3 Bg3** (9... Bf2 10 Qf2 △ Bf4±) **10 Nc3 Qd4** (10... Ne7 11 Ne2±) **11 Bf4 Bf2**[6] **12 Qf2 Qf2 13 Kf2 Nf6** (13... Be6 14 e5±) **14 Be2 Nbd7 15 Nb5 Kd8 16 Bf3**± [6] yields White the bishop pair on an open board.

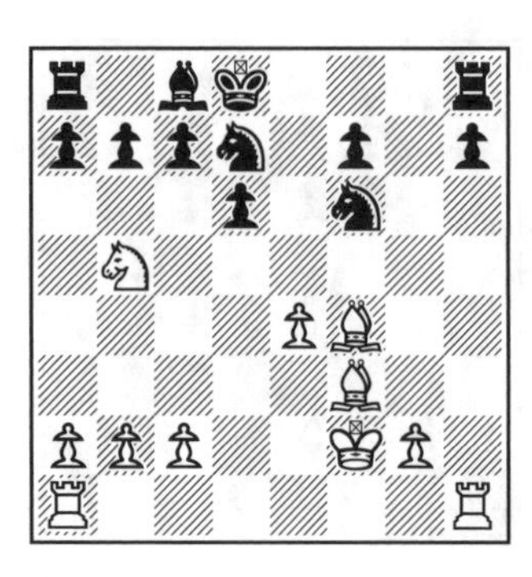

3E-6

Black has won a pawn, but he cannot castle, and his P/f7 shields White's king from direct assault by a rook. Since he is behind in development, Black will have further trouble freeing his queenside, e.g., 16... Nc5?! 17 e5! or 16... Ne5?! 17 Bg5. Mandatory may be 16... a6, though 17 Nd4 △ Rh6-Rah1-Nf5 looks good for White. Here, in particular, the nagging possibility of Bg5 is always present.

ILLUSTRATIVE GAME

A. Sanchez—Joliez
Cannes 1992

1	e4	e5
2	f4	ef4
3	Nf3	g5
4	h4	g4
5	Ne5	d6
6	Ng4	Be7
7	d4	Bh4
8	Nf2	Qg5
9	Qf3	Nc6
10	Qf4	Qf4
11	Bf4	Nd4
12	Rh4	Nc2
13	Kd2	Na1
14	Nc3	Be6
15	Bd3	Nb3
16	ab3	Bb3
17	e5	d5
18	Nb5	0–0–0
19	Bf5	Kb8
20	e6	fe6
21	Bc7	Ka8
22	Be6	Nf6
23	Bd8	Rd8
24	Nd4	Ba4
25	Rh6	Rf8
26	g4	a5
27	Bf5	Bd7
28	Ke3	Rf7
29	g5	Bf5
	(Rf6!)	
30	gf6	Bg6
31	Ng4	a4
32	Kf4	b5
33	Nb5	Rb7
34	Nd6	Rb2
35	Rg6	Rb4
36	Kg5	hg6
37	f7	Rb8
38	Ne8	a3
39	f8=Q	a2
40	Qa3	Kb7
41	Nd6	Kc6
42	Ne5	Kc7
43	Qc5	Kd8
44	Qc6	1–0

PROBLEMS

1. Unsatisfactory is **6... f5.** On **7 Nf2** (see Diagram 3E-7) briefly examine:

a) **7... fe4?**
b) **7... Qe7.**
c) **7... Nf6.**

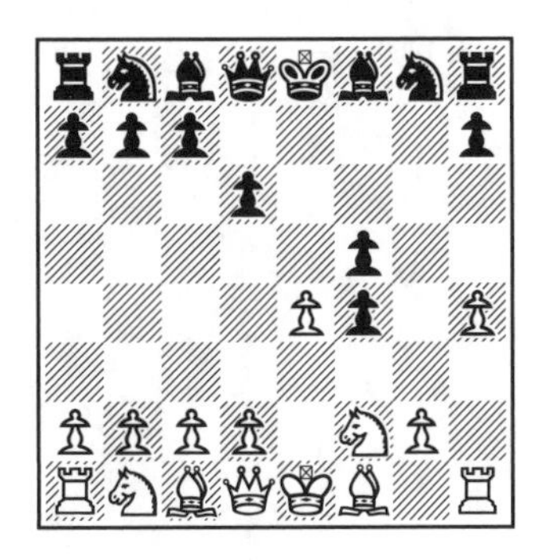

3E-7

2. The alternative **7 Nf2** incites **7... Rg8** (see Diagram 3E-8). How should White react?

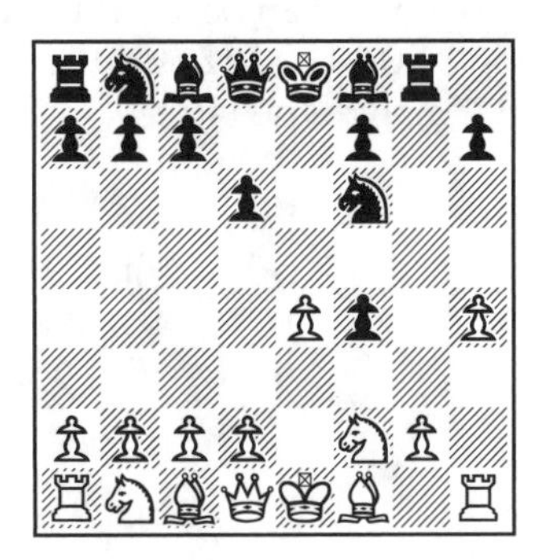

3E-8

3. The normally thematic **7... Be7** (see Diagram 3E-9) proves to be difficult for Black here. Discuss.

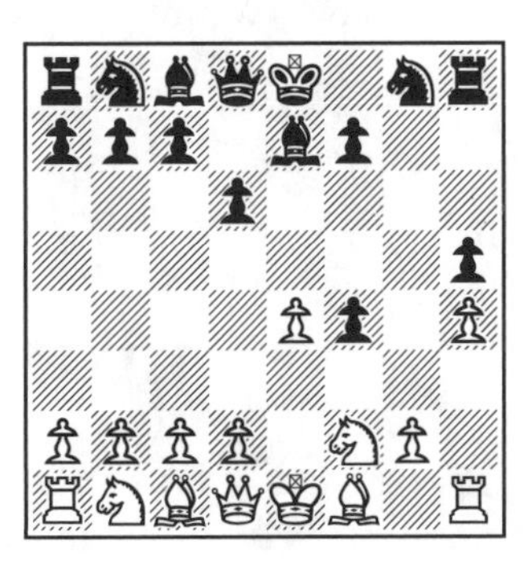

3E-9

4. Also reasonable is **11... hg4** (see Diagram 3E-10). Now which is preferable — 12 Nd5 or 12 Bg4?

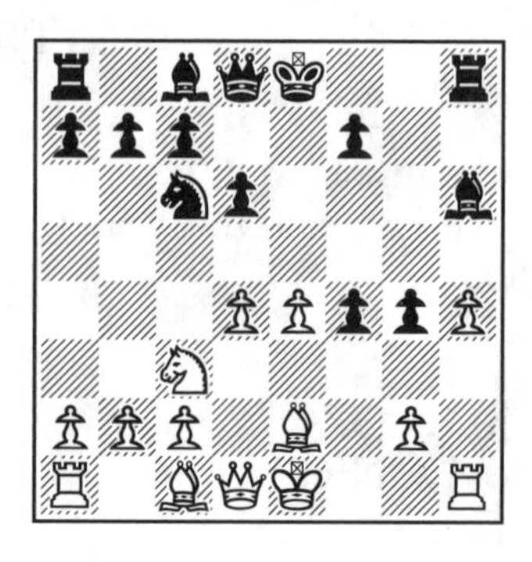

3E-10

5. Of little merit is **13... Bc6.** 14 d5 is good, but even better is the fascinating **14 0–0–0 Bf2** (see Diagram 3E-11). Analyze the latter.

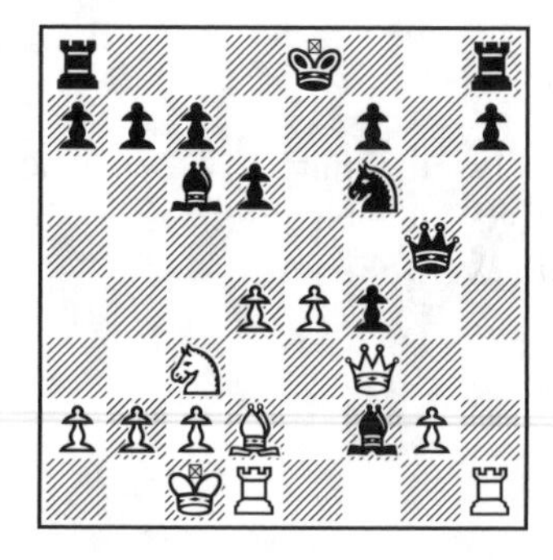

3E-11

6. Why does **11... Bf4** (see Diagram 3E-12) favor White?

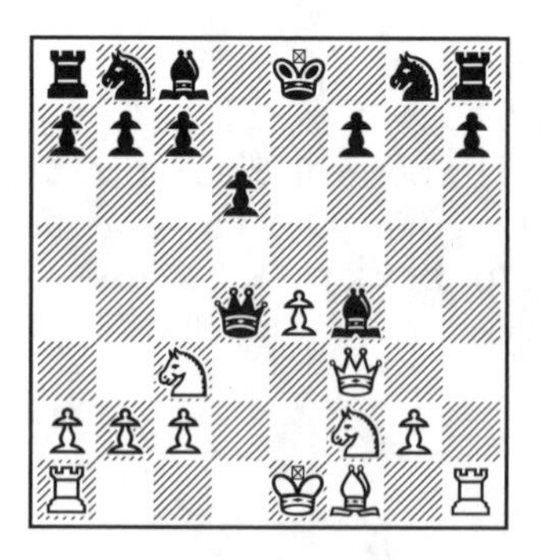

3E-12

Kieseritzky Variation (F)

One of Black's best responses from Diagram 3A-1 is 5... Nf6, the Berlin Defense:

1	**e4**	**e5**
2	**f4**	**ef4**
3	**Nf3**	**g5**
4	**h4**	**g4**
5	**Ne5**	**Nf6**
6	**d4!** (Bc4)	

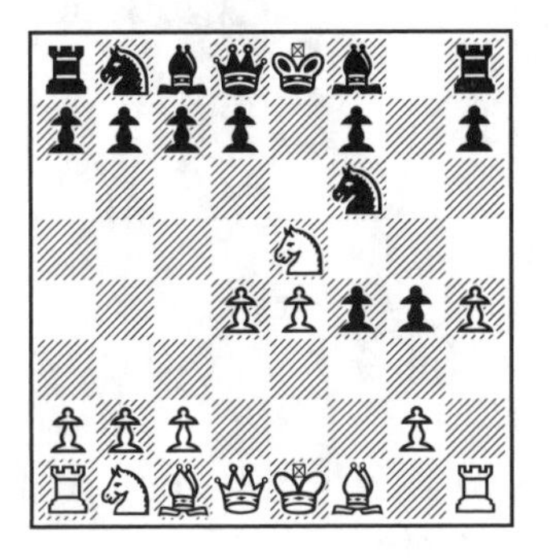

3F-1

Nothing new arises from 6... d5 7 Bf4 Ne4 8 Nd2!, transposing to Diagram 3D-1; however, **6... d6**[1] (for 6... Bg7 7 Bf4 d6 8 Nd3, cf. the lines of Diagrams 3F-7, 3F-11, 3G-2, and Section 3H) **7 Nd3 Ne4**[2] (7... f3 8 gf3[3]±, or for 7... Bg7 8 Bf4 cf. the note for 6... Bg7 directly above) **8 Bf4** uncovers fresh vistas. Black has two reliable choices here, 8... Bg7 and **8... Qe7.** The Black queen entry should be countered with **9 Qe2** (for 9 Be2 cf. the Illustrative Game) when Black can size up 9... Nc6 or 9... Bg7 (9... Bf5 arrives at Diagram 3F-4 or much of Section 3H, and for 9... Nd7 see Section 3G). Against 9... Bg7, White should turn to 10 c3 (Nd2!?) △ Nd2-0–0–0/Kd2 after which 10... Nd7 11 g3 transposes to Section 3G and 10... Nc6 11 Nd2 to Section 3H. More usual, however, is **9... Nc6 10 c3.**

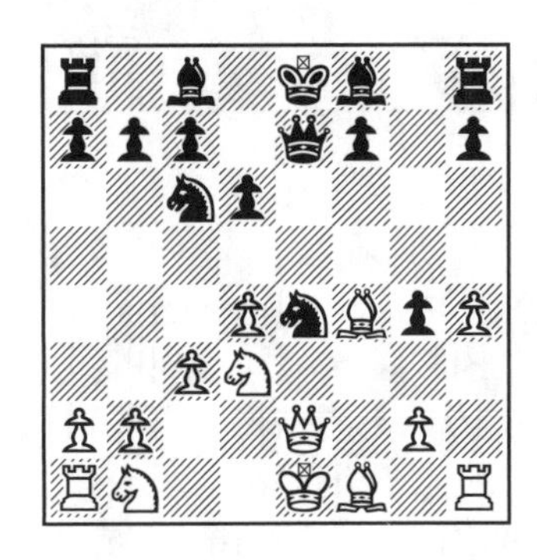

3F-2

Now, 10... Bg7 11 Nd2 Nd2 12 Kd2 Qe2 13 Be2 h5 14 Rae1 leads to Diagram 3H-2, but Black has alternatives. One possibility,

10... h6[4]**,** overprotects *g5* to prepare further support of the outpost on *e4*. Nevertheless, after **11 Nd2 d5** (11... Nd2 12 Kd2 — cf. Diagram 3H-2) **12 Ne4 de4** (12... Qe4? 13 Bc7) **13 Nc5**⩲ [12], White's N/c5 is very active and menaces both Black's P/e4 and P/b7. Thus to be anticipated is **13... f5**[5] with the plausible sequel **14 0–0–0 b6 15 Qb5 Bd7 16 Nd7 Qd7 17 d5 Na5 18 Bc7 Rc8 19 d6**±.

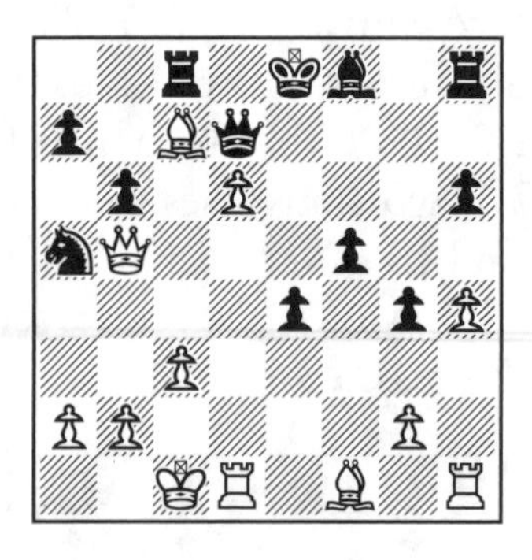

3F-3

As White threatens to play Qe5, Black may be obliged to go in for 19... Bg7 when 20 Qd7 Kd7 21 Bb5 △ d7/Ba6 is on tap.

Although this line is not conclusive, it does serve to highlight some of Black's potential hardships, including his inability to castle long. Also, after the obvious g3, restraining the P/f5 and P/g4, a familiar battle will be waged over control of the dark square around Black's pawn triangle, i.e., *f4*.

From Diagram 3F-2, Black can vary with **10... Bf5.** Next, **11 Nd2 0–0–0** (11... Nd2 12 Kd2 Qe2 13 Be2 Bg7 14 Rhf1 Ne7 15 Rae1 h5 16 Bd1! Kd7 17 Bb3 Raf8 18 Bg5 f6 19 Bf4 Re8 20 Rf2 △ Ref1 or 20 Bg3 △ Re7-Rf5 [19]⩲)

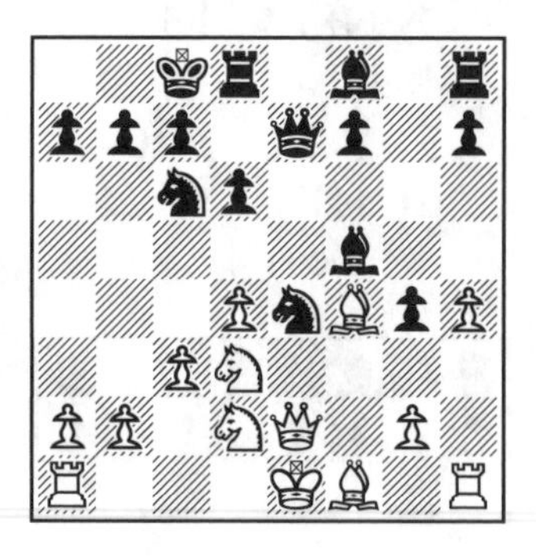

3F-4
(after **11... 0-0-0**)

leads to a critical variation of the Berlin Defense.

Usual here has been 12 0–0–0 Re8 (12... Bg7 13 d5 Nd2 14 Qd2 Ne5 15 Qf2 Nd3 16 Bd3 Bd3 17 Rd3 Kb8 18 Bg5 f6 19 Re3 Qd7—19...Qf7 20 Re6—20 Bf6 Bf6—20... Rhf8 21 Re6—21 Qf6 Rhf8 22 Qg5 Rf2 23 Re7 Qb5 24 Re2! Rff8 25 Rhe1⩲ [19]) when *ECO* has consistently espoused the highly unclear move 13 Nc4 with no supporting analysis. In particular, 13 Nc4 Qd7 14 Ne3 h5∓ [19] is good for Black. On the other hand, 13 d5 loses to the prosaic 13... Nc3 14 Qe7 Na2 15 Kb1 Ne7 16 Ka2 Nd5 [19], a sacrifice of a knight for a total of four pawns. In addition, Estrin's choice 13 Re1 is in doubt after 13... Qe6 △ Qa2.

Better would be 13 Ne4 Qe4 (13... Be4 14 Qg4 f5 15 Qh3 Qe6 16 b3 wins back the gambit pawn for White) 14 Qe4 Be4 (14... Re4 15 g3 △ Bg2) 15 Nf2 f5 16 Ne4 fe4 (16... Re4 17 g3) 17 d5 △ (c4)-g3-Bg2-Rde1$\overline{\overline{\infty}}$ or h5-Be2-Rh4 with good play for White in either case.

However, perhaps even more attractive for White from Diagram 3F-4 is the idea of exchanging knights by **12 Ne4** without taking time to castle long. This would bring on the possibility of 12... Be4 13 Qg4 (Kd2!? [14]) f5 14 Qe2 Bd3 15 Qe7 Be7 16 Bd3± whereby White has regained the pawn. Black's other main try is 12... Qe4 13 Qe4 Be4 14 Nf2 Re8 15 Kd2 f5 16 Bd3 d5 (16... Bg2 17 Bf5±) 17 Rae1 Bg7 18 Nd1 Rhf8 19 Ne3$\overline{\overline{\infty}}$ with plenty of play for White.

Finally (from Diagram 3F-1), continuing with **6... d6 7 Nd3 Ne4 8 Bf4,** a second method for Black involves **8... Bg7.** Following **9 c3 0–0** (for 9... Qe7 10 Qe2 Nd7 11 g3 consult Diagram 3G-2, and for 9... Qe7 10 Qe2 Nc6 11 Nd2 see Section 3H) **10 Nd2** (or 10 Be2 △ Nd2-Ne4-0–0) **Re8**[6] (for 10... Qe7 11 Qe2 see the discussion preceding Diagram 3H-2) **11 Ne4 Re4 12 Kf2 Qf6** (12... c5 13 Bg2) **13 g3 Bh6,** best is **14 Qd2**± [13]

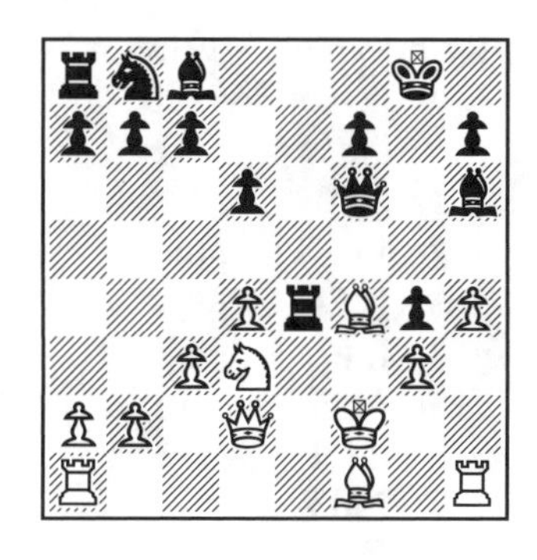

3F-5

since 14 Bg2 Bf4 (14... Rf4!?) 15 Nf4 Rf4 16 gf4 would allow 16... Qf4 with perpetual check.

Plans for White include the predictable buildup on g4, Black permitting. Certainly Bg2-Rf1-Kg1-Bd5 has a point (attack on **f7**) after which Rae1 or Rf2-Raf1 would complete an ideal deployment of White's forces. On 14... Bf4 15 Nf4 Black must be prepared to defuse the therapeutic Bg2-Rhf1-Kg1-Nd5(Nh5)-Nf6. Even 15... Bf5? 16 Bg2 and 15... Nc6 16 Bg2 Re7 17 Rf1 △ Kg1 look good for White. Black simply faces the usual problem of possessing the asset of an extra pawn, but the debt of restricted mobility. His pieces tend to trip over themselves as he strives to catch up in development.

ILLUSTRATIVE GAME

Reinderman—Winants
Wijk aan Zee 1993

1	e4	e5
2	f4	ef4
3	Nf3	g5
4	h4	g4
5	Ne5	Nf6
6	d4	d6
7	Nd3	Ne4
8	Bf4	Qe7
9	Be2	Bg7
10	Nc3 (c3!?)	Bd4
11	Nd5	Qd8
12	c3	Be6
13	cd4	Bd5
14	Bg4	Nd7
15	Nb4	c6
16	Nd5	cd5
17	0-0	Qh4
18	Bd7	Kd7
19	Qb3	Ke6
20	Rae1	f5
21	Qb7	Rab8
22	Qc7	Qe7
23	Qc3	Rhg8
24	Re2	Rg4
25	Bh2	Rbg8
26	Qf3	Qf6
27	Kh1	Rh4
28	Qa3	Qe7
29	Kg1	Rg5
30	Bg3	Rhg4
31	Rf3	Qc7
32	Rc3	Qb6
33	Qa4	Kf6
34	Be5	Ke7
35	Rc6	Qb7
36	Bd6	Kd8
37	Rc7	Rg2
38	Rg2	Rg2
39	Kg2	Qb2
40	Rc2	1–0

PROBLEMS

1. Unusual is **6... Nc6** (not 6... Nh5? 7 Qg4) **7 Bf4** (see Diagram 3F-6):

a) Combat **7.. d6?!**
b) Examine **7... Ne4 8 Ng4 Qe7.**

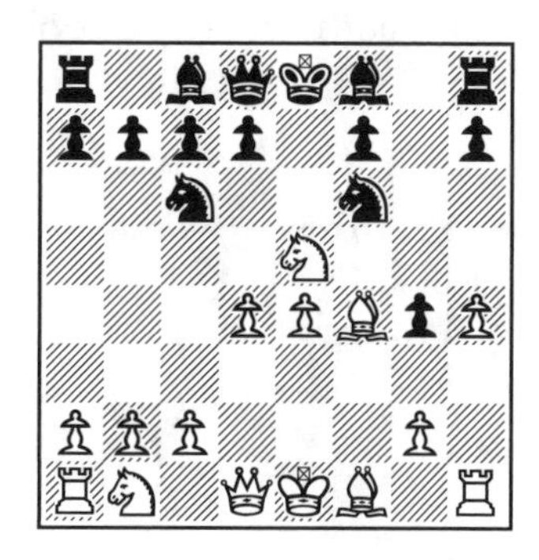

3F-6

2. Curiously, **7... Nh5,** putting pressure on *g3* and *f4*, fails to equalize. After **8 Bf4 Bg7 9 c3 Qe7 10 Nd2** — or Be2!? — (see Diagram 3F-7) analyze:

a) **10... c5.**
b) **10... f5.**
c) **10... 0–0.**
d) **10... Nf4.**

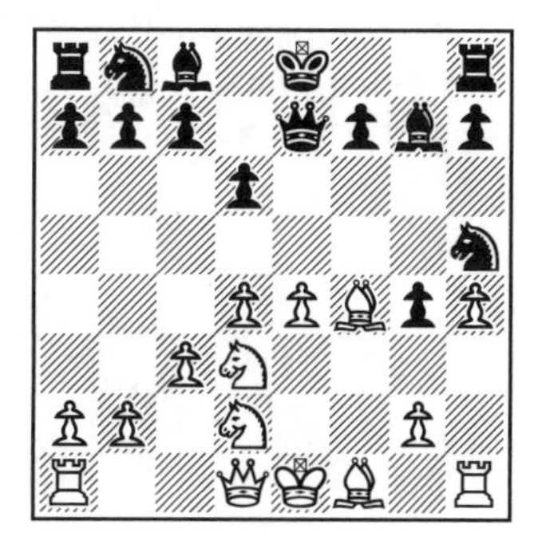

3F-7

3. Establish a convincing setup against **8... g3** (see Diagram 3F-8).

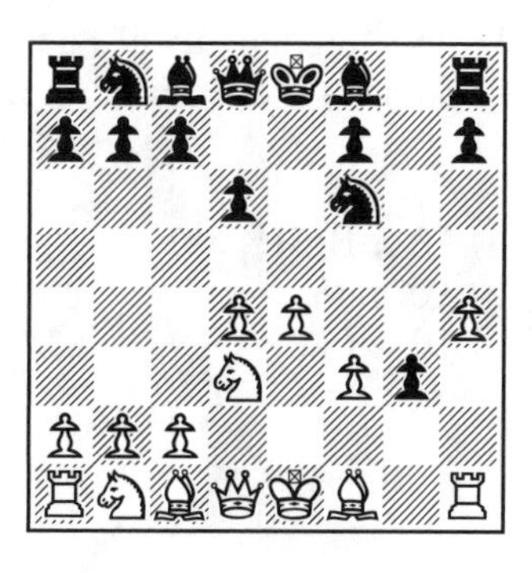

3F-8

4. The immediate **10... d5** (10... h5 11 Nd2) gives White good play on the kingside dark squares. Following **11 Nd2** (see Diagram 3F-9), survey:

a) **11... Bf5.**
b) **11... f5.**
c) **11... h5.**
d) **11... Bg7.**

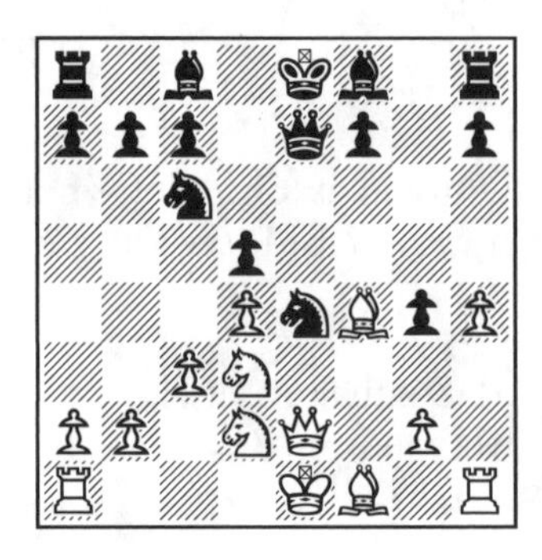

3F-9

5. **13... b6** attempts to develop with tempo, preparing ...0–0–0. After **14 Ne4** (see Diagram 3F-10), why is White to be preferred?

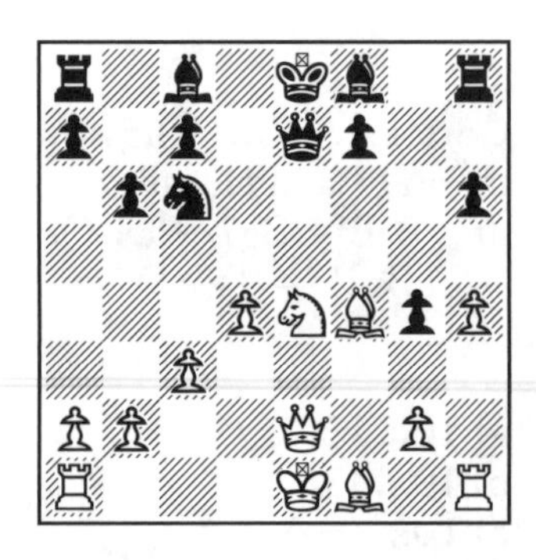

3F-10

6. From Diagram 3F-11, demonstrate that Black does not improve with:

a) **10... Bf5?!**
b) **10... d5.**
c) **10... f5.**

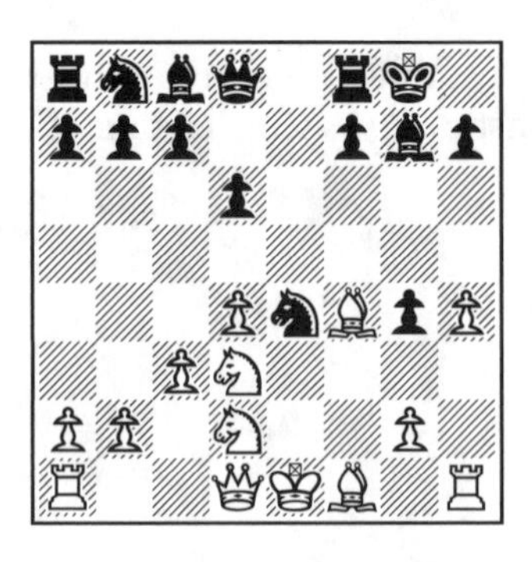

3F-11

Kieseritzky Variation (G)

An instructive variant of the Berlin Defense proper involves 9... Nd7:

1	e4	e5
2	f4	ef4
3	Nf3	g5
4	h4	g4
5	Ne5	Nf6
6	d4!	d6
7	Nd3	Ne4
8	Bf4	Qe7
9	Qe2	Nd7
10	g3	

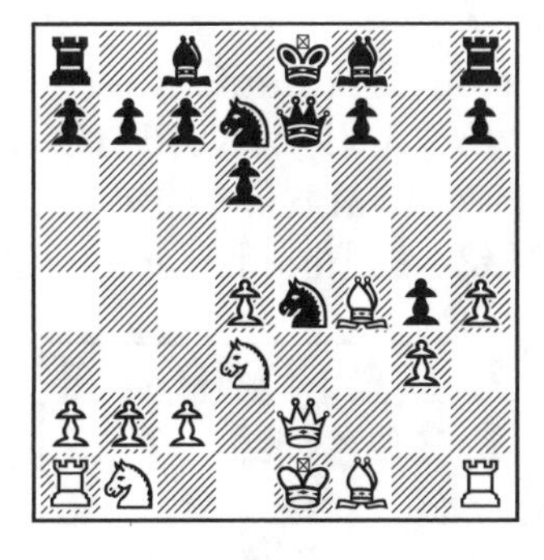

3G-1

The main point behind 10 g3 is that White can often advantageously castle short whenever Black chooses an early ...Nd7. Too slow here is 10... b6, e.g., 11 Bg2 Bb7 12 Nd2 Ndf6 13 Bg5±, and if 13... Ng5? then 14 Qe7 △ Bb7-Bc6/hg5 is winning. Also uninspired is 10... h5[1] as Black loses a tempo along with the option of posting a knight on *h5*. More significant is **10... Bg7** (10... Ndf6 11 Bg2 Bg7 12 c3 is transpositional) after which **11 c3** (Nc3!?) ± reaches Diagram 3G-2.

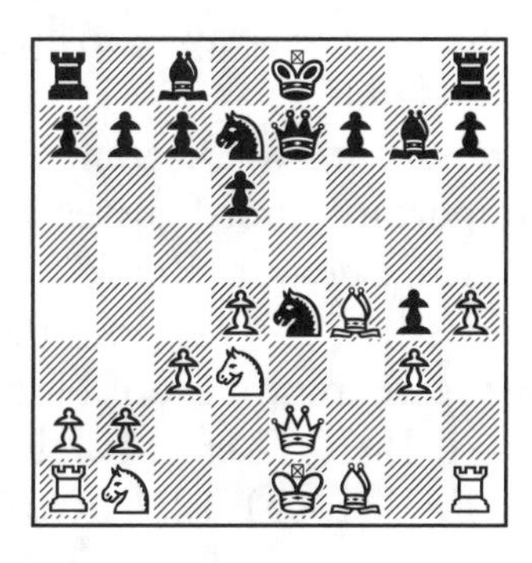

3G-2

Black has two main possibilities in this position: 11... Ndf6 and 11... f5 (11... 0–0 transposes into one of these lines). On 11... Ndf6 White can essay 12 Bg2 [1] △ 0–0-Nd2-(Rae1)-Bg5-(Bf6)-Nf4 while keeping in mind an exchange of minors on *e4*, particularly when Black must agree to ...d5-de4. Note that the attempt to castle Q-side here with 12... Bf5 lands

Black in hot water after 13 0–0 0–0–0?! 14 Bg5±.

Similarly, against 11... f5, White can again proceed with 12 Bg2. One plausible sequel is 12... 0–0 13 0–0 Ndf6 14 Nd2 d5 whereupon White can choose between Ne4 (Ne5)-Bg5-(Bf6)-Nf4 or Q-side expansion with b4-a4-Rfb1, etc. In any event, White can rely on his firm blockade of *f4*, his potential for invading Black's weakened K-side, and his prospects for Q-side activity to ensure him good play.

Going back to Diagram 3G-1, an important motif arises from **10... f5.** Because Black's king bishop still protects its queen, White can improve on 11 Nd2 with **11 Bg2.** Then **11... Ndf6** (11... Bg7 12 c3) **12 0–0 Nh5** appears to be critical, but **13 Be4±** puts an abrupt halt to Black's erstwhile initiative.

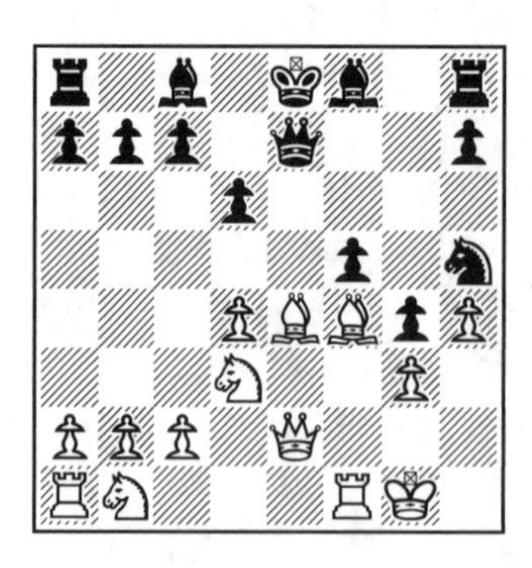

3G-3

Ill-conceived here are 13... Nf4? 14 Nf4 Qe4 (14... fe4 15 Nd5!) 15 Qd2 △ Nc3-Rae1 and 13... d5? 14 Bf3 gf3 15 Qf3 Nf4 16 Qf4± with threats all over the place. No better, however, is 13... fe4 as 14 Bg5![2] keeps Black at bay. Necessary, therefore, seems 13... Qe4, though on 14 Qf2 Nf4 (not 14... Qf3 15 Qe1 Qe4 16 Nc3 Qe1 17 Rae1 Kf7 18 Nd5 c6 19 Ne3) 15 Nf4 Qf3!? 16 Qe1 (better than 16 Qf3) Qe4 17 Nc3 Qe1 18 Rae1, Black loses too much time. His dormant bishops cut a poor figure against White's galloping steeds! For instance, after 18... Kf7 19 Ncd5 c6 20 Nc7 Rb8, the shot heard 'round the board is 21 Nfe6!

From Diagram 3G-1, after **10... f5 11 Bg2 Ndf6 12 0–0,** Black could also appraise **12... d5 13 Nd2** reaching Diagram 3G-4.

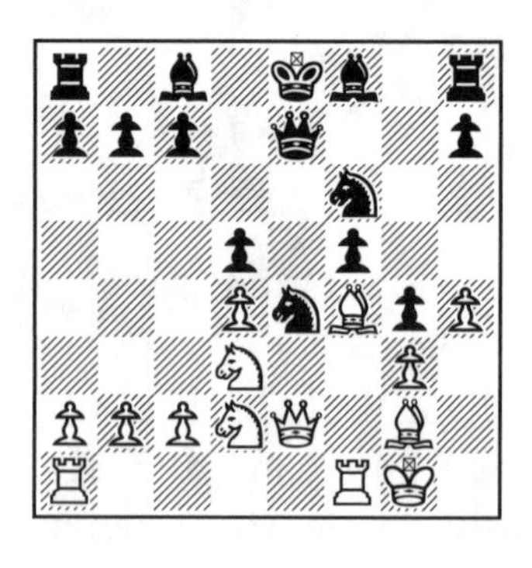

3G-4

Possible next is 13... Nd2, although following 14 Qd2 Ne4 15

Qe3±, Black's P/f5 becomes a long-term target. Instead, if 13... h5 (Δ ...Bh6-Bf4), White can plan to invade on **g6.** Even on 13... Bg7 14 Be4 fe4 (14... Ne4 15 c3 0–0 16 Ne4 fe4 17 Bg5 Δ Nf4/Ne5) 15 Rae1 0–0 (if 15... Nh5, then 16 c3 with the ultimate aim of Nf4) 16 Bg5 h6 17 Bf6 Bf6 18 c3 Δ Nf4±, Black's K-side weaknesses outweigh the gambit pawn.

PROBLEMS

1. Continuing with **11 Bg2** (see Diagram 3G-5), glean the consequences of:

   a) **11... f5.**
   b) **11... Ndf6.**

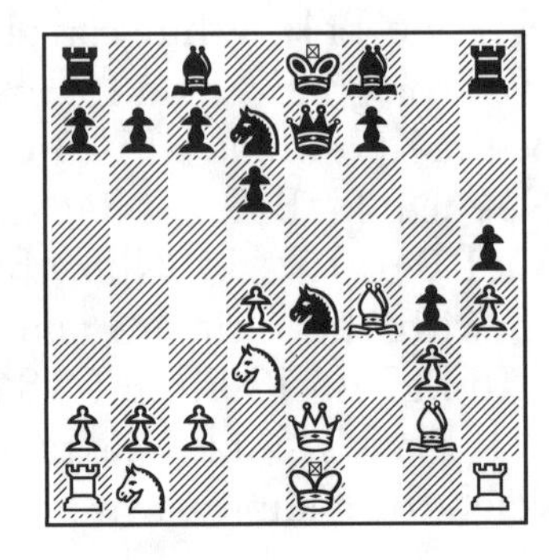

3G-5

2. Suddenly, Black is without an adequate defense. From Diagram 3G-6:

   a) Bust **14... ed3?**
   b) Profit from **14... Qe6.**
   c) Prove that the fat lady sings on **14... Ng3?**

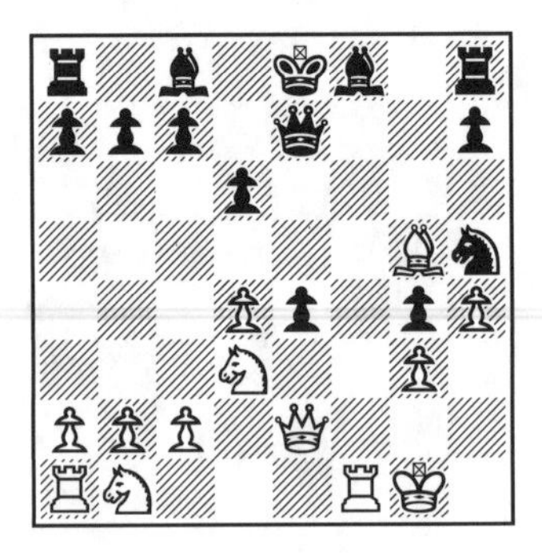

3G-6

Kieseritzky Variation (H)

In the main line of the Berlin Defense Black selects 9... Bg7:

1	**e4**	**e5**
2	**f4**	**ef4**
3	**Nf3**	**g5**
4	**h4**	**g4**
5	**Ne5**	**Nf6**
6	**d4!**	**d6**
7	**Nd3**	**Ne4**
8	**Bf4**	**Qe7**
9	**Qe2**	**Bg7**
10	**c3**	

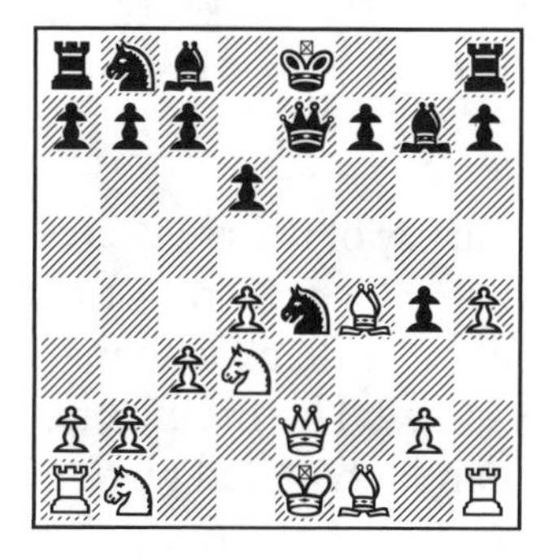

3H-1

White, as usual, has established firm control of f4 and a perennial target on *f7*. Properly timed, d5 can spearhead a queenside initiative although, in most lines, White must first prepare for ...Ne5. Whereas White's N/d3 may soon opt for *d5* or *h5* — by way of *f4* — to gain access to squares around the enemy king, Black's B/g7 bites on granite. Furthermore, after Nd2, Black may have to lose tempi in resulting exchanges while ...h5, to shore up the defense of the P/g4, may necessitate yet another delay in Black's development.

In particular, after the natural **10... Nc6** (for 10... h6 cf. the discussion following Diagram 3F-2) it transpires that **11 Nd2 Nd2** (11... Bf5 △ 0–0–0 leads to Diagram 3H-3, whereas 11... d5 12 Ne4 transposes to the discussion relating to Diagram 3F-3) **12 Kd2** (or 12 Qe7 Ke7 13 Kd2) **Qe2 13 Be2 h5** (13... 0–0 14 h5) **14 Rae1**± [5]

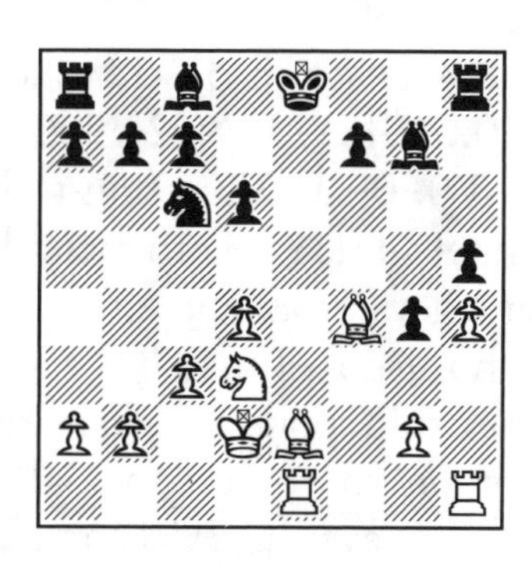

3H-2

offers White a slightly better endgame. Curiously, this position can also be reached after 10... h5 11 Nd2 Nd2[1] 12 Kd2 (Qe7) Qe2 13 Be2 Nc6 (for 13... Bf5 see the Illustrative Game) since 14 Rae1± transposes.

White's rapid and efficient development should produce a lasting spatial advantage. Because Black will have difficulty in achieving ...d5, White can already consider further expansion with an aptly conducted pawn-storm.

Black must first contend with the impending discovered attack on his king. He cannot essay the natural ...Kd7 without hemming in his light-squared bishop, and the immediate 14... Be6 △ ...0–0–0 just invites 15 b3 △ c4-d5 in combination with Be3-g3-Rhf1-Nf4. Still, Black is a pawn ahead for his trouble and he is not without chances — for instance, ...0–0 △ ...Bf5.[2]

From Diagram 3H-1, following **10... Bf5 11 Nd2 Nc6 12 0–0–0 0–0–0,** White must play accurately if he is not to incur disadvantage. For example, after 13 Nc4 h5 14 Re1 Rhe8 15 Qc2 White could soon find a kamikaze knight on c3, or, as in Gallagher–Bachmayr, *Zug 1991*, on 15... Qd7 16 g3 Bd4, a self-immolating bishop on d4. Best is **13 d5!** — a panacea which loosens the N/e4, weakens Black's king sector and disrupts the communication of Black's forces. The only palatable reply, **13... Nd2[3],** leads to **14 Qd2 Ne5** (14... Na5 and 14... Nb8 can be met by 15 Nb4 △ Bb5) **15 Re1**± [5].

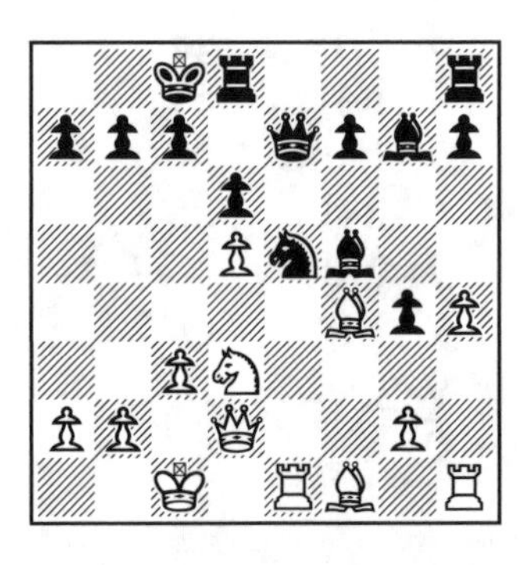

3H-3

A survey of the checkered terrain reveals a recurring twist — suddenly it is Black who may easily go astray! The indifferent 15... Rde8 can be handled by the incisive 16 Ne5. On 16... de5 (16... Be5 17 Be5 de5 18 Qf2 △ Qf5/Qa7) 17 Qf2 Kb8 18 Be3 △ Qf5/Ba7± White wins back the pawn with the better position.

Black averts these difficulties with 15... Rhe8, but abandons the defense of his P/h7 and virtually cedes White the c1-h6 diagonal (Black's king rook can no longer support ...Bh6). White has 16 Nb4 when 16... a5!? 17 Nc2 Bc2 (18 Nd4 must be prevented) 18 Qc2 Qf6 (18... h5? 19 Qf5 △ Qh5) 19 Qd2 h6 20 Bb5± △ g3-Rhf1 leaves White with the bishop pair and excellent prospects. Therefore, Black should force immediate simplifications with **15... Bd3 16 Bd3 Nd3**[4] **17 Qd3.** Here **17... Qd7**[5] **18 h5 h6 19 Rhf1 Rde8 20 Be3±** is a reasonable sequel.

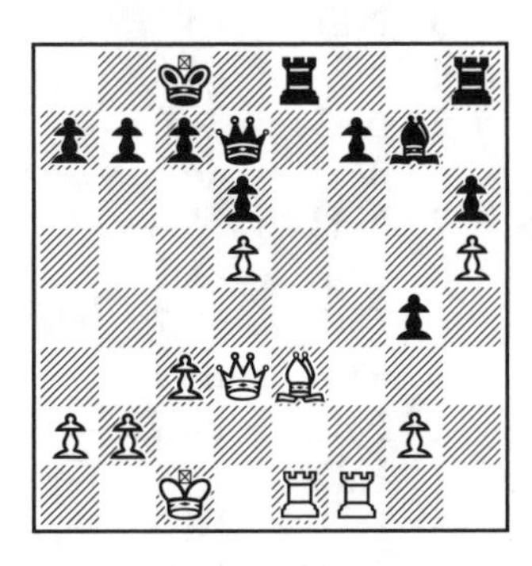

3H-4

White has obvious compensation for his pawn. He intends Rf5-Ref1, exerting pressure on the P/f7 and artificially isolating Black's P/g4. Black must defend his P/a7 if he relocates his queen to the kingside since, after Ba7, White would answer ...b6 with Qa6-Qb7. On 20... Qa4 White can play either 21 Qf5 △ Qf7 or 21 Kb1 Qe4 (else 22 Rf4) 22 Qe4 Re4 23 Rf7 with good winning chances in both cases.

Returning to **10... Bf5 11 Nd2 Nc6 12 0–0–0,** Black can try the natural-looking **12... 0–0.** Here White should trade queens with **13 Ne4 Qe4 14 Qe4 Be4** whereupon **15 Nf2 Bf5 16 h5⩲** presents his foe with annoying problems.

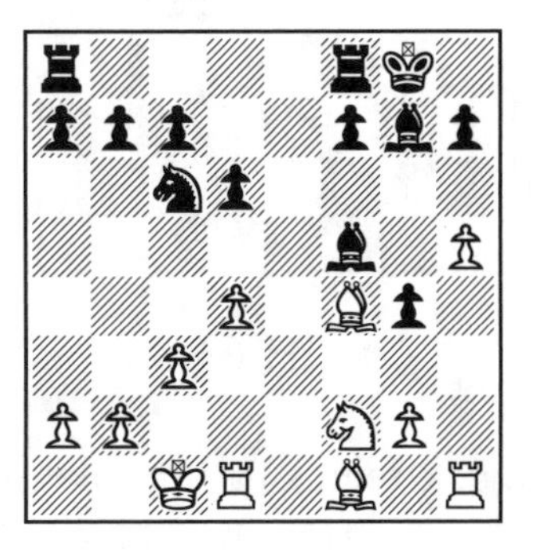

3H-5

Black cannot easily enforce ...d5, and his king position is much looser than in the line stemming from 12... 0–0–0. Furthermore, Black's king rook cannot effectively support (from g8) either the P/g4 or a bishop at g5. Sample play might now run 16... Bd7 17 h6! Bh8 18 Be2± winning back the pawn at once as 18... f5 loses to 19 Bc4. Alternatively, Black could consider 16... Rfe8 when 17 h6 Bh8 18 Kd2 Bd7 19 Be2 f5 20 Bc4 Kf8 21 Rdf1± △ Ng4-Bd6 is a possible scenario.

If again **10... Bf5 11 Nd2,** an important ending results from **11... Nd2** (11... d5 12 Ne4 de4 13 Ne5±) **12 Qe7** (Kd2!?) **Ke7 13 Kd2 Nc6 14 g3** (14 h5)±.

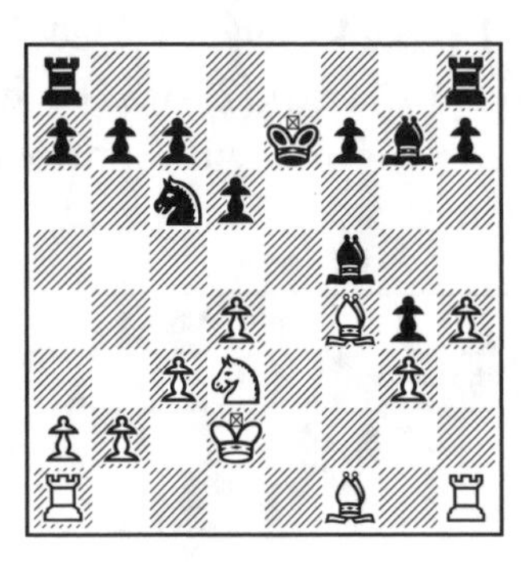

3H-6

Black seems to improve here over his position in Diagram 3H-2 since he can play ...Kd7 without blocking in his queen bishop. White, however, can complete his development while attacking Black's pieces. Thus Bg2-Rae1-Rhf1 gains time by threatening to discoverably attack the B/f5, whereas Bg2-Raf1 presages h5 in case of ...Bg6. Yet another idea is to weaken Black's P/g4 and to pile up on the square **f7,** the plan being h5-Bg2-Bd5-Rhf1-Rf2-Raf1.

ILLUSTRATIVE GAME

Black never really seems to get out of the box in this game. The unplayed finish deserves to be noticed after the rook sacrifice on Move 19.

Stoltz—Saemisch
Swinemunde 1932

1	e4	e5
2	f4	ef4
3	Nf3	g5
4	h4	g4
5	Ne5	Nf6
6	d4	d6
7	Nd3	Ne4
8	Bf4	Qe7
9	Qe2	Bg7
10	c3	h5
11	Nd2	Nd2
12	Kd2	Qe2
13	Be2	Bf5
14	Rhf1	Nd7?
15	Nb4	Nf6
16	Bb5	Bd7
17	Rae1	Kd8
18	Bg5!	Bb5
19	Rf6	1–0

PROBLEMS

1. From Diagram 3H-7, prove that Black fails to equalize with:

a) **11... d5.**
b) **11... f5.**

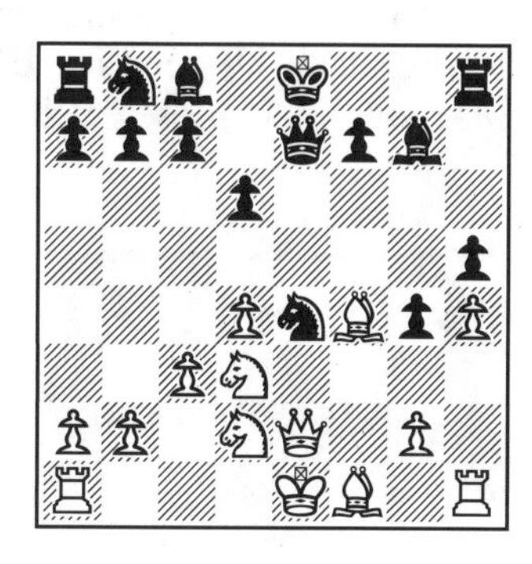

3H-7

2. On **14... 0–0** (see Diagram 3H-8), how might White proceed?

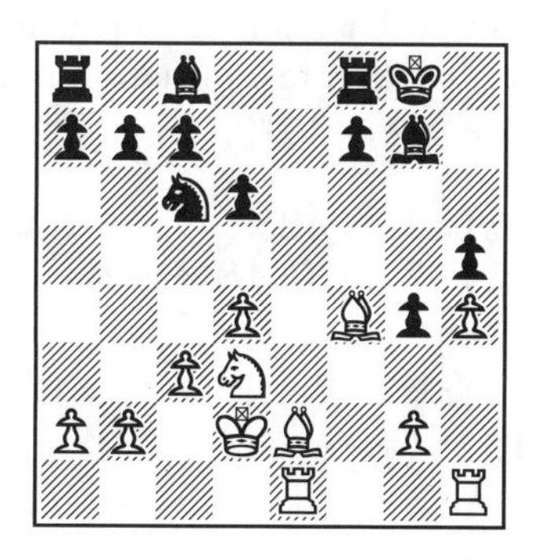

3H-8

3. No other move serves Black as well as 13... Nd2. From Diagram 3H-9, dispatch:

a) **13... Na5.**
b) **13... Nb8.**

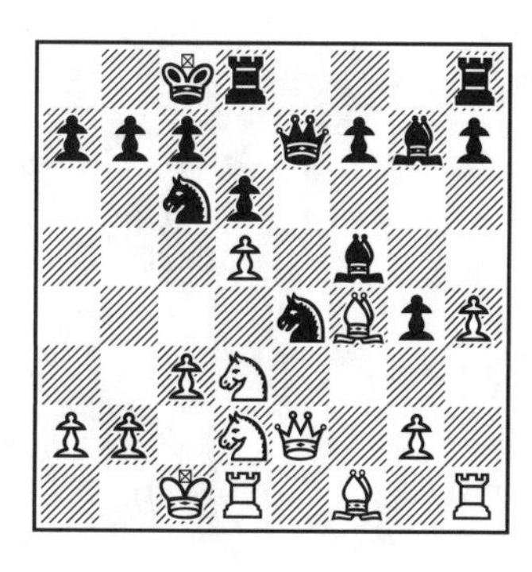

3H-9

4. Following **16... Qf6 17 Bg5** Black, with 17... Nd3, would transpose to Problem 3H#5b. **17... Bh6?** (see Diagram 3H-10) loses. Why?

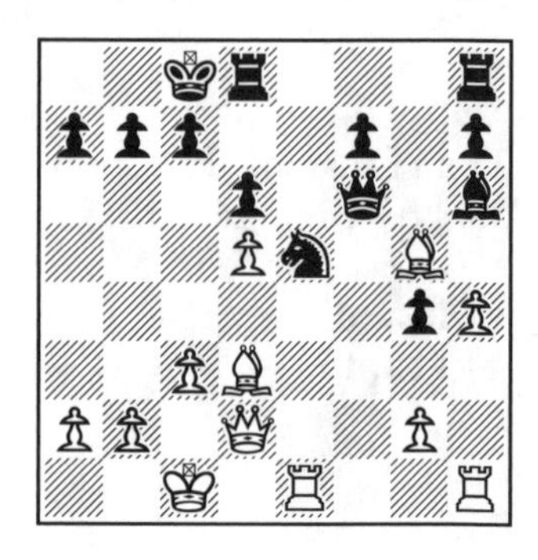

3H-10

5. From Diagram 3H-11, demonstrate that White's initiative is well worth a pawn after:

a) **17... Qf8?**
b) **17... Qf6 18 Bg5 Bh6.**

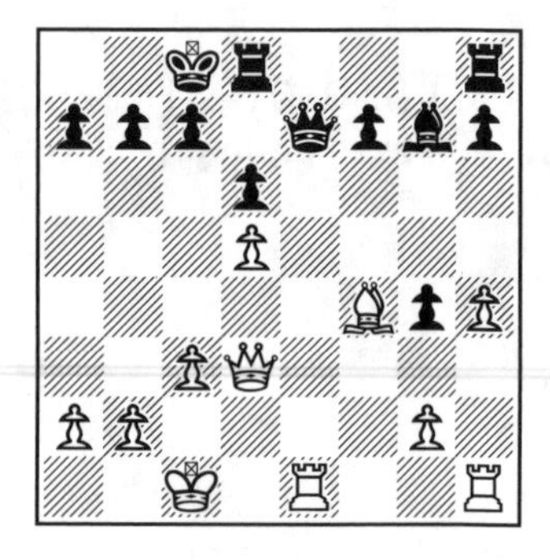

3H-11

4: FISCHER VARIATION (A)

A major alternative to the Kieseritzky Variation is the Fischer Variation, involving 3... d6:

1	**e4**	**e5**
2	**f4**	**ef4**
3	**Nf3**	**d6**
4	**d4**	
	(d3)	

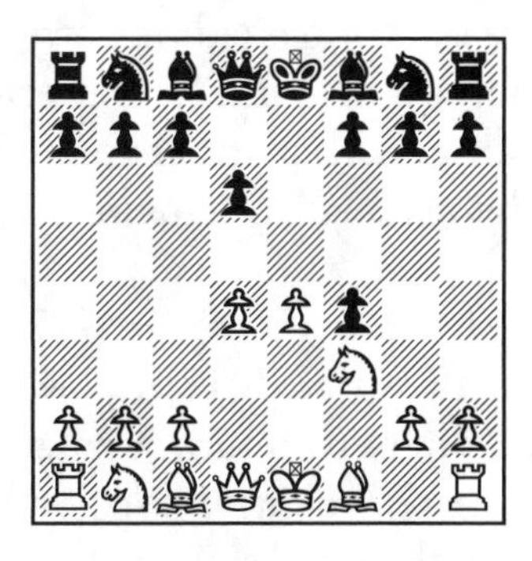

4A-1

3... d6 has been termed a "high-class" waiting move, partly because Black has not yet been forced to defend his P/f4. This move deters White from playing Ne5 after the sequence ...g5-g4, but 4 d4 is an excellent positional response.

If now 4... Qf6 then 5 Nc3 △ Nd5 leads to good positions for White (cf. Section 4C). Also promising for White is **4... Nf6 5 Nc3 Nh5** (5... Bg4 6 Bf4) **6 Be2 Bg4** (6... Be7 7 0–0 △ Nd5±) **7 0–0 g6** (7... c6 8 Ne1 Be2 9 Qe2 g6 10 Qf3± [13] or 7... Nc6 8 d5! Ne7 9 Nd4 Be2 10 Qe2 g6 11 Qb5±) **8 Ne1** (Nd5) **Be2 9 Ne2** [5] **Bg7** (9... g5 10 Nc3 Ng7 — 10... Nf6 11 Qf3 — 11 g3 △ Qf3±) **10 Nf4±.**

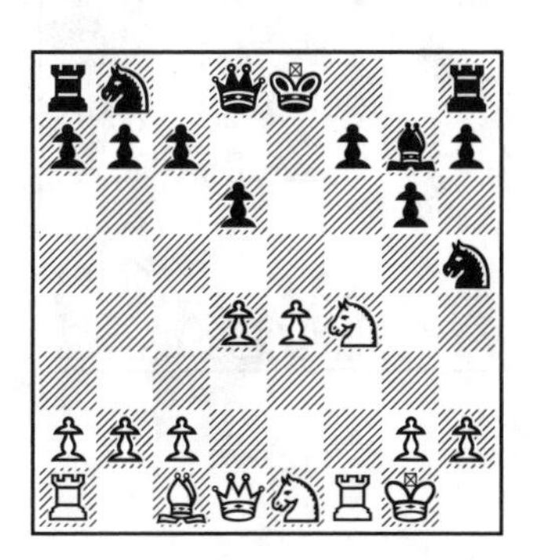

4A-2

Material is even but White enjoys the better center. Because of his potential Q-side majority, White should look for the chance to create a passed pawn in that sector. Middlegame operations along the central and f-files may also prove rewarding. Here both 10... Nf6 11 Qf3 0–0 12 Ned3 Nc6 13 c3 Qe7 14 Re1 △ Bd2-e5-Nd5 and 10... Nf4 11 Bf4 0–0 12 c3 Nc6 13 Nd3 Qd7 14 Qb3!, hitting the P/b7 and forestalling ...f5, are attractive for White.

Black's usual fourth move initiates aggressive counterplay against White's threat of Bf4, thus:

4	...	g5[1]
5	h4	g4[2]
6	Ng1	

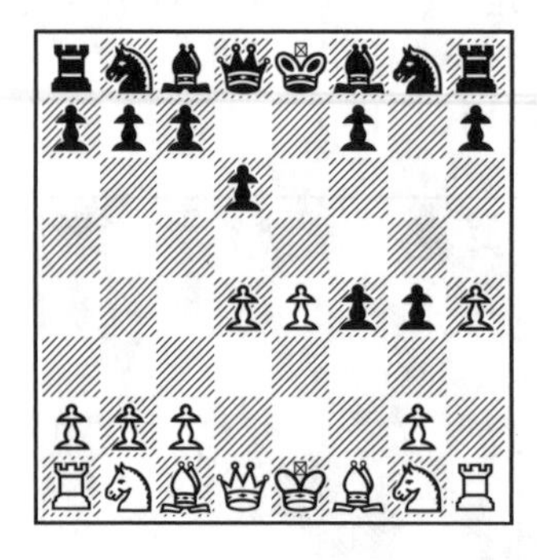

4A-3

White has attacked the base (P/g5) of the mini-pawn chain on *g5* and *f4* in accordance with Nimzovich's principle. Black, lured into attacking White's knight, passes by (cf. Diagram 3A-1), but now his advanced pawns are targets. White's "undeveloped" N/g1, by moving to *e2*, will soon assist the B/c1 in the assault on the P/f4. Furthermore, the tempo count following Nf3-Ng1-Ne2 is no different than that found in the Kieseritzky Variation after Nf3-Ne5-Nd3 (cf. Chs. 3F-H).

Black, as is already clear, must increasingly distort his position in order to hold the P/f4. Nevertheless, he can try to exploit the airy quality of White's K-side. Thus ...Be7 can be played with the idea of ...Bh4, winning a pawn and obstructing White from castling, whereas, ...Bh6 is a direct attempt to defend the P/f4. Generally speaking, both plans are premised on the attempt to remain a pawn ahead.

With **6... f5** (6... Bg7 7 Bf4 Nc6 8 Be3 △ Nc3 [17]), however, Black offers to return a pawn, to remove the central P/e4, while gaining the good square *f5* for the fast development of his B/c8. A plausible continuation is: **7 ef5** (7 Bd3) **Bf5** (7... Qe7 8 Qe2) **8 Bf4 Nf6 9 Bd3** (to challenge the light squares) **Qd7 10 Nc3 Nc6 11 Nge2 Bg7** (11... Bd3 12 Qd3 △ 0–0–0) **12 Bf5 Qf5 13 0–0**[3]± [2].

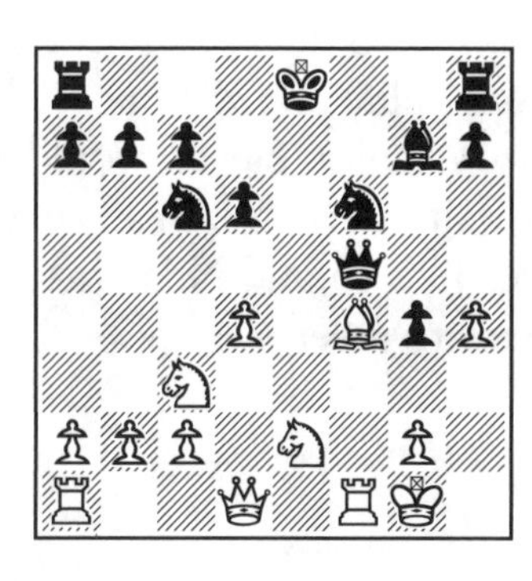

4A-4

White has regained his pawn with the better-developed game. Superficially, Black appears poised for an assault on White's K-side; however, the potential discovery on the Black queen requires immediate attention. Qd2-Rae1-Bg5-Ng3-Nf5 is a promising plan for White while g3, blockading the enemy pawns on the K-side, is solid.

Returning to Diagram 4A-3, with **6... f3,** Black improves on 6... Be7 7 Bf4 Bh4 8 g3 Bg5 (8... Bf6 9 Nc3) 9 Ne2 h5 10 Qd2 Bf4 11 Nf4 h4 12 Nc3 c6 13 0–0–0 Nd7 14 e5 d5 (14... de5 15 de5 Nh6 16 e6 fe6 17 Ne6 Qe7 [17... Qa5 18 Re1] 18 Re1) 15 e6 Ndf6 16 ef7 Kf7 17 Bd3 Ne7 18 Rdf1 h3 19 Rh2 Neg8 20 Ng6 1–0, Handoko–Thipsay, *Bangalore, 1981* by drawing off the g-pawn so that g3 may not be played to defend against ...Bh4. Now both 7 Nc3 and 7 Be3 are good choices, but after the preferred **7 gf3** (At this point 7 Bg5!? also deserves a look, e.g., 7... Be7 8 Qd2 f6 9 Bh6 Nh6 10 Qh6 Be6 11 gf3 gf3 12 Nf3 c6 13 Nc3 Qa5 14 Ng5! fg5 15 Qe6 Nd7 16 Bc4 Rf8 17 0–0–0 gh4 18 e5 d5 19 Bd5 1–0, Gallagher—Bode, Bad Worishofen 1991.), a remarkable configuration arises — neither side has a developed piece through six and one-half moves! Likely now is **7... Be7** (7... d5 8 e5 or 7... Nf6 8 Nc3 △ f4) **8 Be3 Bh4** (8... d5 9 Bf2) **9 Kd2 Nc6** (9... c5 10 Kc1 cd4 11 Qd4 Bf6 12 Qd2 Nc6 13 Nc3 Be6 14 Nd5 Bd5 15 ed5 Ne5 16 f4 Nd7 17 Rh5 Ne7 18 Be2 g3 19 a4 a6 20 Ra3 Rc8 21 Bd4 Rg8 22 Re3± [19]) **10 Nc3 Bf6**[4] (10... Bg5 11 f4±) **11 Kc1** (11 Bb5) $\bar{\bar{\infty}}$ [9].

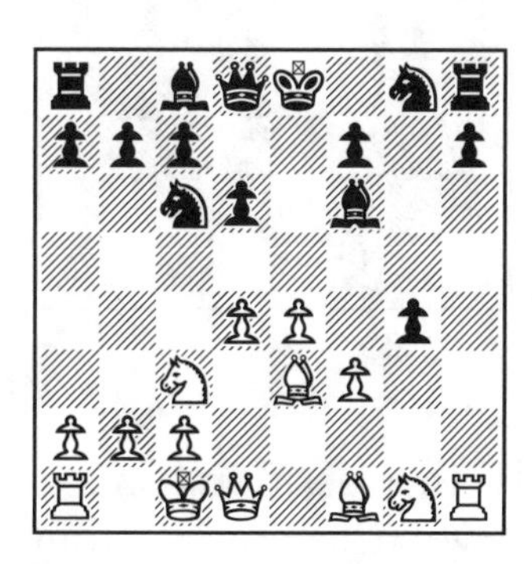

4A-5

Black is a pawn up, yet White

rules the center and his pieces possess a great deal of dynamic energy.

Although 11... h5 seems to generate a K-side pawn-roller here, at least two considerations work against such a plan: (1) fg4 would isolate the P/h5; and (2) harmonious development of Black's pieces is difficult to achieve — particularly the B/c8 and N/g8. If Black tries 11... g3, then 12 Nge2 △ Ng3 wins back a pawn at once.

More significant is **11... gf3,** though White emerges from **12 Nf3 Bg4 13 Bb5! a6**[5] **14 Ba4 b5 15 Bb3 Na5** (15... Nge7?! 16 Qf1!) **16 Qf1!**± with a strong initiative.

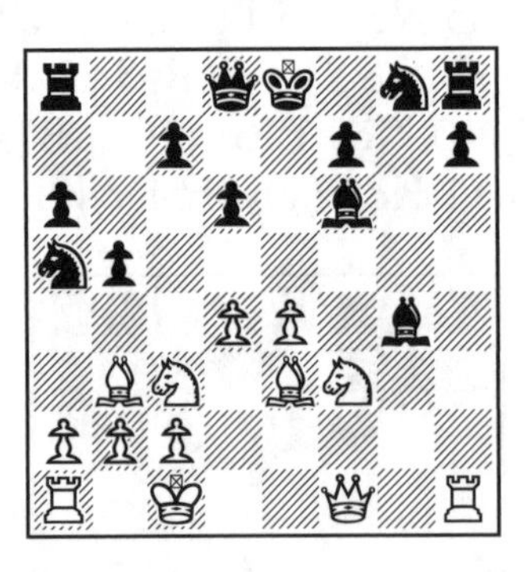

4A-6

In this position, one of the most volatile arising from the Fischer Variation, White has ample compensation for his pawn; he is ahead in development and owns a fluid pawn center. After 16... Nb3 (to thwart stock combinational play on *f7*) 17 ab3, all of White's major pieces would occupy half-open files. In any event, moves like e5 and Nd5 will soon be hard to meet.

PROBLEMS

1. Even at such an early stage, Black must choose his reply carefully:

a) Reject the poorly timed **4... f5** (see Diagram 4A-7).

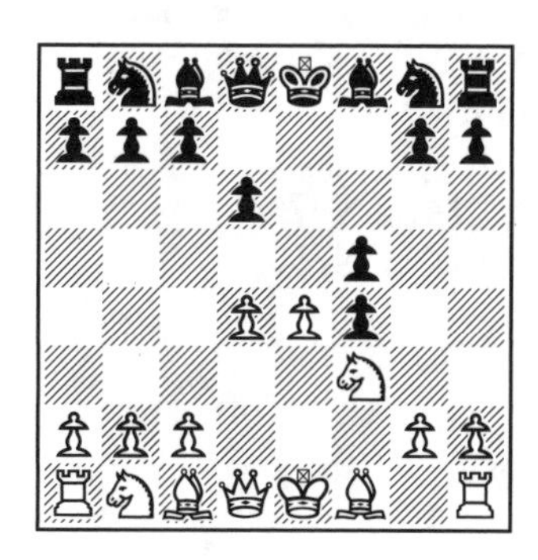

4A-7

b) On **4... Qe7 5 Nc3 g5** (see Diagram 4A-8), what positional continuation allows White to obtain a clear advantage?

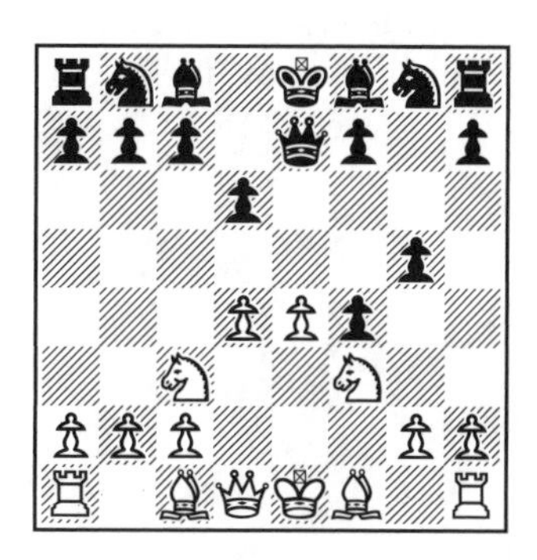

4A-8

2. If, instead, **5... f6?! 6 Nc3** (see Diagram 4A-9), what thematic response gives White the upper hand following:

a) **6... Bd7.**
b) **6... Bg4.**

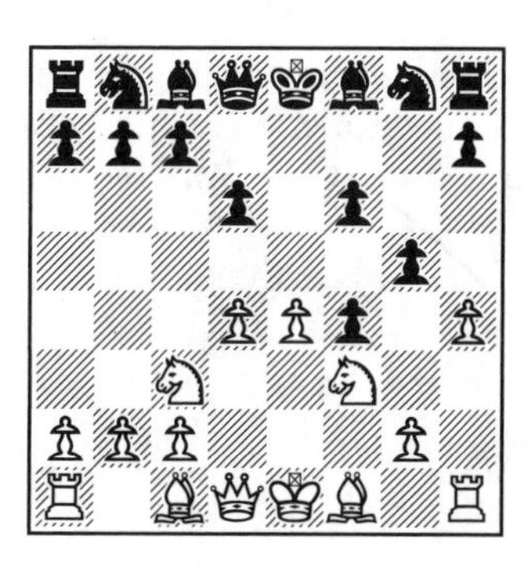

4A-9

3. Two moves suggest themselves after **13... Qg6?!** (note that 13... Qd7 14 d5 △ Nd4 is similar) **14 d5** (see Diagram 4A-10):

a) **14... Ne7.**
b) **14... Ne5.**

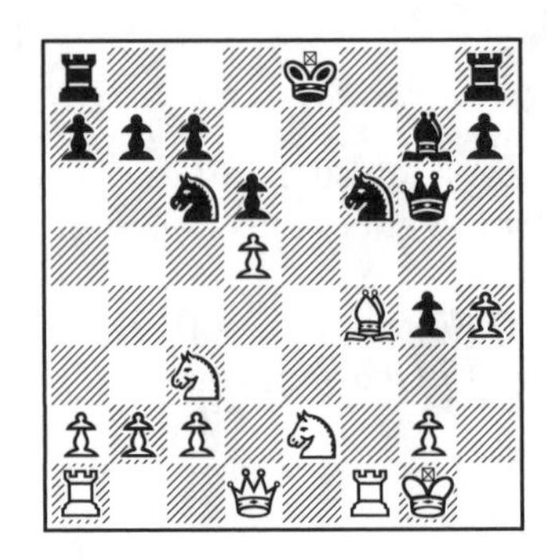

4A-10

4. **10... Qf6** (see Diagram 4A-11) is worse for Black. Why?

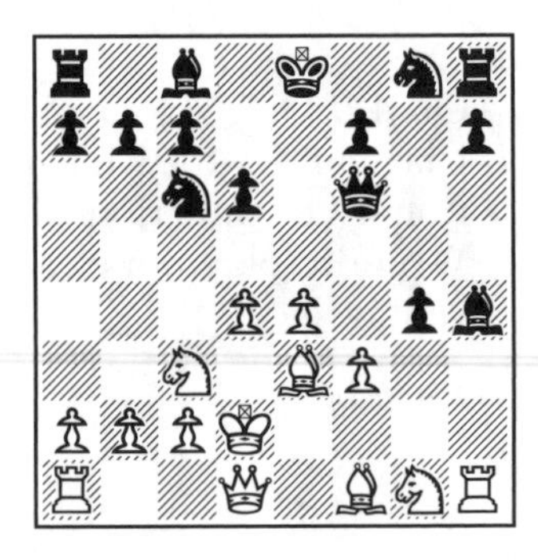

4A-11

5. Besides threatening to disrupt Black's queenside, White has set some cunning traps. On **13... Nge7?** (13... Qd7?? 14 d5+−) **14 Nd5!** (see Diagram 14A-12) analyze:

a) **14... Bg7?**
b) **14... Nd5.**

4A-12

Fischer Variation (B)

A common theme in the Fischer Variation is simply to defend the P/f4 by way of natural development of Black's pieces. There are two main methods employed to achieve this result — **6... Bh6** and 6... Qf6 (cf. Chap. 4C):

1	**e4**	**e5**
2	**f4**	**ef4**
3	**Nf3**	**d6**
4	**d4**	**g5**
5	**h4**	**g4**
6	**Ng1**	**Bh6**
7	**Nc3**	

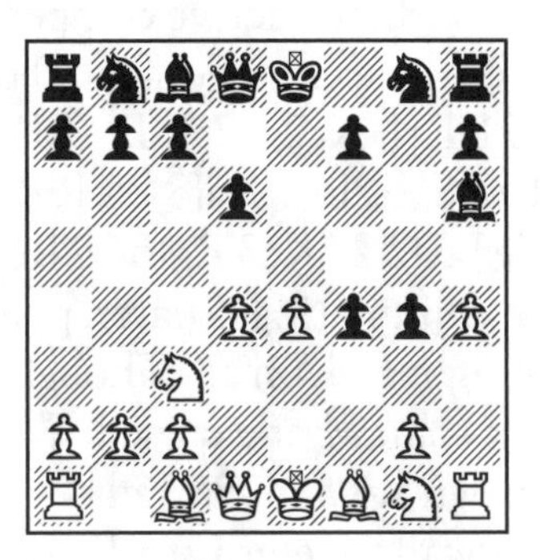

4B-1

Less flexible is 7 Ne2 Qf6 8 Nbc3 f3 9 Ng3 f2 10 Ke2 Nc6!∞; the text prevents 7... Qf6 because of 8 Nd5. Black now has three main options: **7... c6**[1]**,** 7... Nc6, and 7... f5. The first of these disallows Nd5 whereupon **8 Nge2 Qf6** (8... f3 9 Nf4 [Ng3!?] transposes) **9 g3** leaves Black with a dichotomy of choices. Here the headstrong 9... fg3 can lead to 10 Ng3 Bc1 (10... Qf3 11 Qf3 gf3 12 Kf2) 11 Rc1 h5 (or 11... Qf4 12 Nce2 Qe3 [12... Qf3 13 Rh2, and 12... Qf6 was tried in Illustrative Game II] 13 Qd2 [or 13 c4 △ Rc3] as in Christiansen—Lobo, *San Jose, 1980)* 12 Qd2 Qh6 13 Nce2 Qd2 14 Kd2 Nf6 15 Nf4 Nbd7 16 Re1± [5], but even the usual **9... f3 10 Nf4**± [9] besets Black with an inferior center and limited lines of maneuverability for his pieces.

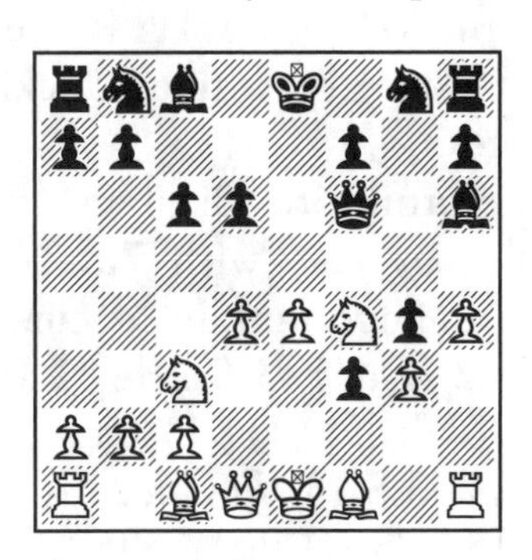

4B-2

White, who can comfortably

station his king on *f2*, threatens to rout Black's forces with a timely e5. Parrying this thematic central thrust repeatedly emerges as Black's chief headache in this position.

Thus 10... Ne7 (10... Bg7 11 Be3 h5 12 Qd2 Nd7 13 0–0–0 Nf8 14 e5! de5 15 de5 Qe7 16 Bc5 Qc7 17 Ne4 Be5 18 Bd6 Bf4 19 Bf4 Qb6 20 Nd6+–) leads to trouble due to 11 e5! Qg7[2] 12 Ne4±, and 10... Bd7 11 Kf2 Na6? 12 e5 crosses Black up as well. On 10... Nd7 11 Kf2 (Be3) both 11... Nb6 12 a4 a5 13 Be3± and 11... Ne7 (11... Bg7 12 Be3 or 12 e5!? de5 13 Ne4 Qe7 14 Nh5! cf. Problems 4B#2 and 4B#3) 12 e5![3] reveal the awkwardness of Black's setup. Even 10... Qe7 11 Qd3 (or 11 Kf2. For 11 Bd3 see Illustrative Game V.) Nf6 12 Kf2 Bf4 13 Bf4 Nh5 14 Qd2 (or Bg5) △ Re1-e5± offers White bona fide attacking chances.

Returning to Diagram 4B-1, Black may vary with **7... Nc6.** Then an important line occurs on **8 Nge2** (Qd3) **f3 9 Nf4 f2** (9... Qf6 10 Ncd5! Qd4 11 Qd4 Nd4 12 Nc7 Kd8 13 Na8 Nc2 14 Kd1 Na1 15 Nd5± [17]; 9... Nf6 10 Be3 is better for White since 10... Qe7 loses to 11 Nfd5 [5]) **10 Kf2 g3 11 Kg3 Nf6 12 Be2 Rg8 13 Kf2 Ng4 14 Kf1** (Bg4) [7] ⩱∞.

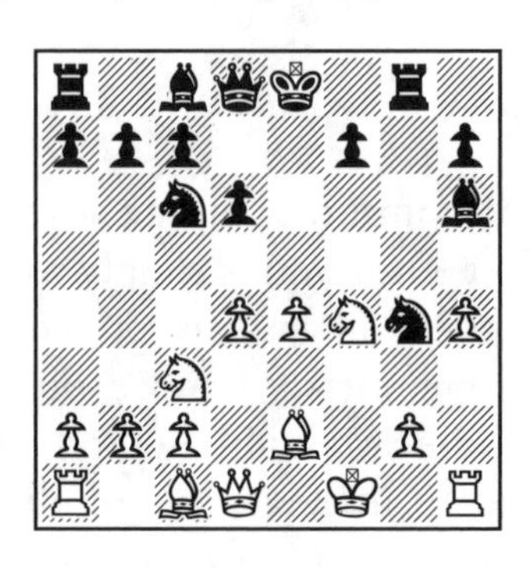

4B-3

Here White eschews 14 Ke1 (not 14 Kg1? Bg7!∓) Qf6 15 Ncd5 Qd4 16 Bg4 Bg4 17 Qd4 Nd4 18 Nf6 Kf8 19 Ne6 (19 Ng8 Kg8 20 Nd5 Nc2 21 Kf2 Bg7! — clearly preferable to Kastner's suggested 21... Bc1? 22 Rc1, etc. — 22 Rb1 Re8 gives Black active compensation for the exchange) fe6 20 Bh6 Kf7 21 Rf1 Nc2 22 Kd2 Na1 23 Ng4 Kg6 24 Bg5 Raf8 25 Ra1 h5 26 Ne3 Rf2 27 Kc3 Rgf8 28 Rc1∞ while eliminating a later potential knight fork on *c2*. Though his king is somewhat exposed, White is a pawn up and can rely on his center wall to retard any Black offensive.

Thus 14... Bf4 15 Bf4 Qf6 can be handled by 16 Qd2 (not 16 Nd5?? Ne3–+) since 16... Qd4 (16... Nd4?? 17 Nd5) 17 Qd4 Nd4 18 Bg4 Bg4 19 Nd5+– wins an exchange. Even fewer tricks arise from 14... Qf6 15 Ncd5 Qd4 16 Bg4! Bg4 (16... Rg4 17 Qd4 △ Nf6) 17 Qd4 Nd4 18 Nf6+−, while on 14... Qe7 the immediate 15 Qd3 △ Ncd5± works well. Black also has 14... f5!?, but 15 Qd3, once again, is a strong retort. After 14... Ne7 (△ ...Ng6) White can turn the tables with 15 Nh5! Bc1 16 Qc1± [7]. If Black reacts slowly with 14... Bd7, then 15 Ncd5, preparing c3-Bf3, is logical. Against other tries, an eventual Ncd5 can serve to over-protect the N/f4 and to permit Qd3, shoring up the third-rank squares.

A good question arises (from Diagram 4B-1) after **7... f5:** How does White uphold his vaunted center and hinder the bolstering of Black's K-side pawn structure? Undeniably best for White is the all-purpose **8 Nge2!,** doubly attacking the P/f4. One sequel is **8... f3**[4] (or 8... Qe7 9 Qd3[5]) **9 gf3 Bc1**[6] **10 Qc1** (Nc1) **gf3 11 Ng3 f2** (11... Nc6 12 Qe3 fe4 13 Nge4 Nce7 14 Bc4±) **12 Kf2 Qf6 13 Qg5! Qd4 14 Kg2**±.

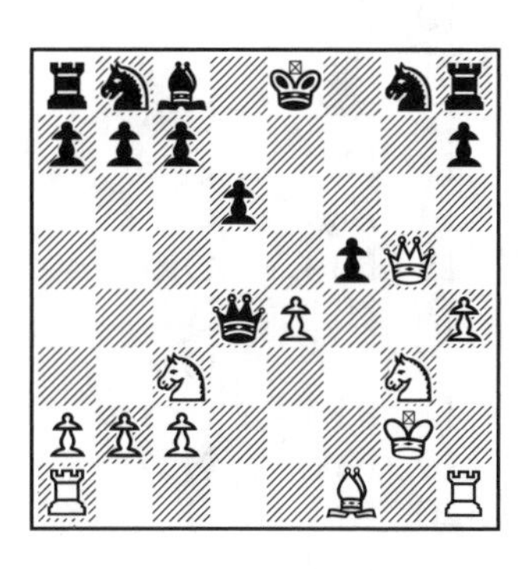

4B-4

Both sides appear loose, but the impending Rd1 followed by Nd5 or ef5 should clarify the issue in White's favor. Examples include 14... fe4 (14... Ne7 is similar) 15 Rd1 Qf6 16 Nd5 Qg5 17 hg5 Kd8 18 g6 h6 19 Ne4 △ Ng5± and 14... Nf6 (14... Nc6 15 Rd1 Qf6 16 ef5) 15 Rd1 Qe5 16 Bc4 (threatening ef5) fe4 17 Rhe1±.

ILLUSTRATIVE GAME I

Maser—McCrary
1978

1	e4	e5
2	f4	ef4
3	Nf3	d6
4	d4	g5
5	h4	g4
6	Ng1	Bh6
7	Nc3	f5
8	Nge2	Qe7
9	Nf4 (Qd3)	Bf4?

10	Bf4	Nf6
11	Bg5	h6
12	Bf6	Qf6
13	Nd5	Qd8
14	Bd3	c6
15	Nf4	Qf6
16	ef5	Bf5
17	0–0	Qd4
18	Kh1	Bd3
19	Nd3	Nd7
20	Rf4	Qe3
21	Qg4	0–0–0
22	Re1	Qd2
23	Rf2	Qa5
24	Re7	Rhg8
25	Qe6	Qc7
26	Rff7	Rh8
27	Nf4	1–0

ILLUSTRATIVE GAME II

Bogner—Beelby
Los Angeles 1985

1	e4	e5
2	f4	ef4
3	Nf3	d6
4	d4	g5
5	h4	g4
6	Ng1	Qf6
7	Nc3	c6
8	Nge2	Bh6
9	g3	fg3
10	Ng3	Bc1
11	Rc1	Qf4
12	Nce2	Qf6
13	Qd2	Na6
14	Bg2	Bd7
15	Qa5	Qd8
16	Qa3	Qe7
17	Qa5	Qd8
18	Qc3	Qb6
19	0–0	h5
20	Qe3	0–0–0
21	Rf7	Qb2
22	Qf4	Qa2
23	c4	Qa3
24	c5!	dc5
25	Nf5	Be6
26	Nd6	Rd6
27	Qd6	Bf7
28	Qf8	Kc7
29	Qf7	Kb6
30	Rb1	Ka5
31	Qb7	Rh6
32	Qa7	Qe3
33	Kh1	Qe2
34	Qb6	Ka4
35	Ra1	1–0

ILLUSTRATIVE GAME III

John—Hurtlen
World Open 1985

1	e4	e5
2	f4	d6
3	Nf3	ef4
4	d4	g5
5	h4	g4
6	Ng1	Bh6
7	Nc3	c6
8	Nge2	Qf6
9	g3	fg3
10	Ng3	Bc1
11	Rc1	Qf4
12	Nce2	Qe3
13	Qd2	Qd2
14	Kd2	Ne7
15	Nf4	Nd7
16	Bc4	b5
17	Bd3	a6
18	Nfh5	c5
19	c3	Kd8

20	Rcf1	Rf8
21	Nf6	Nf6
22	Rf6	c4
23	Bc2	d5
24	e5	a5
25	Rhf1	Ke8
26	Bh7	Ra6
27	Ra6	Ba6
28	Nh5	Rh8
29	Nf6	Kf8
30	h5	Kg7
31	Bc2	Bc8
32	Rg1	Kh6
33	Bd1	b4
34	Bg4	bc3
35	bc3	Bg4
36	Rg4	Rb8
37	Kc2	a4
38	Rg1	a3
39	Rb1	Rd8
40	Rb6	Kg5
41	Ra6	Nf5
42	Ra3	Ne3
43	Kd2	Nf1
44	Kc2	Ne3
45	Kc1	Ng2
46	Ra6	Nf4
47	h6	Nd3
48	Kd2	Kh6
49	Nd5	Kg5
50	Ne3	Ne5
51	Ra5	f6
52	Ke2	Kf4
53	de5	fe5
54	Rc5	Rh8
55	Rc4	e4
56	Nf1	Rg8
57	Kf2	Rd8
58	Rd4	Rf8
59	Nd2	Ke5
60	Ke3	1–0

ILLUSTRATIVE GAME IV

Bishop—Lubarsky
Sunnyvale 1990

1	e4	e5
2	f4	ef4
3	Nf3	d6
4	d4	g5
5	h4	g4
6	Ng1	Qf6
7	Nc3	c6
8	Nge2	Bh6
9	g3	f3
10	Nf4	Ne7
11	e5!	de5
12	Ne4	Qg7
13	Nh5	Qg6
14	Nef6	Kf8
15	de5	Nd5
16	Bd3	Bf5
17	Bf5	Qf5
18	Bh6	Ke7
19	Kf2	Nd7
20	Bg5	Kf8
21	Qd3	Qd3
22	Nd7	Ke8
23	Nhf6	1–0

ILLUSTRATIVE GAME V

Gallagher—Jackson
Blackpool Ch-GB 1988

1	e4	e5
2	f4	ef4
3	Nf3	d6
4	d4	g5
5	h4	g4
6	Ng1	Bh6
7	Nc3	c6

8	Nge2	Qf6
9	g3	f3
10	Nf4	Qe7
11	Bd3	Bg7
12	Be3	h5
13	Qd2	Nd7
14	0-0-0	Nf8
15	Rhe1	Bd7
16	e5	de5
17	de5	Ne6
18	Ne4	Be5
19	Ne6	Be6
20	Bc5	Qc7
21	Nd6!	Bd6
22	Re6	Be7
23	Bd6!	Qd6
24	Rd6	Bd6
25	Ba6	0-0-0
26	Qc3	Ne7
27	Rd6	ba6
28	Rf6	Rhf8
29	Qc5	Rd7
30	Qh5	Rfd8
31	Qg4	Kb7
32	Qf3	Nd5
33	Rf7	Nb6
34	b3	a5
35	h5	a4
36	Kb2	ab3
37	ab3	a5
38	h6	a4
39	h7	ab3
40	cb3	Ka7
41	Rd7	1-0

ILLUSTRATIVE GAME VI

Popovich—Wysocki
US Open, 1989

1	e4	e5
2	f4	ef4
3	Nf3	d6
4	d4	g5
5	h4	g4
6	Ng1	Bh6
7	Nc3	Nf6
8	Nge2	Qe7
9	Qd3	c6
10	Bf4	Bf4
11	Nf4	Bf5
12	0-0-0	Ne4
13	Re1	d5
14	Rfd5!	cd5
15	Nd5	Qd6
16	Nc3	Qf4
17	Qe3	Qe3
18	Re3	Nc6
19	Ne4	Nd4
20	Nd6	Kd7
21	Nf5	Nf5
22	Bb5	Kc7
23	Rc3	Kd6
24	Rd1	Ke5
25	Rc5	Kf4
26	Rf1	Kg3
27	Rcf5	Kg2
28	h5	g3
29	Bd3	Kh2
30	Be4	g2
31	R1f2	Rag8
32	h6	Rg4
33	Bb7	Rhg8
34	Rf7	Kh3
35	Bg2	Rg2
36	Rg2	Rg2
37	Rh7	1-0

PROBLEMS

1. **7... Nf6?!** (7... Ne7 8 g3; or 7... Be6 8 Qd3 [8 Nge2] a6 9 Bd2 Nc6 10 Nd5! Bd5 11 ed5 Nce7 12 0–0–0 [17]) strands the B/h6 and fails to meet the requirements of the position. Thus **8 Nge2 Nh5** (8... f3? 9 Bh6; or 8... d5 8 Bf4 Bf4 10 Nf4 de4 11 Bc4!± [19] for 8... Qe7 see Illustrative Game VI) **9 g3!** (see Diagram 4B-5) puts White on top. Analyze:

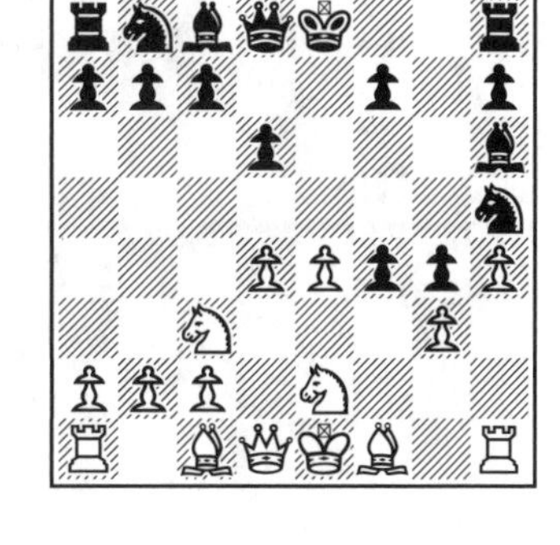

4B-5

a) **9... Nc6.**
b) **9... fg3.**
c) **9... 0–0.**
d) **9... Qe7.**

2. One try on Black's eleventh move was used in a major microcomputer program, since corrected. Show why **11... de5?** (see Diagram 4B-6) actually loses devastatingly.

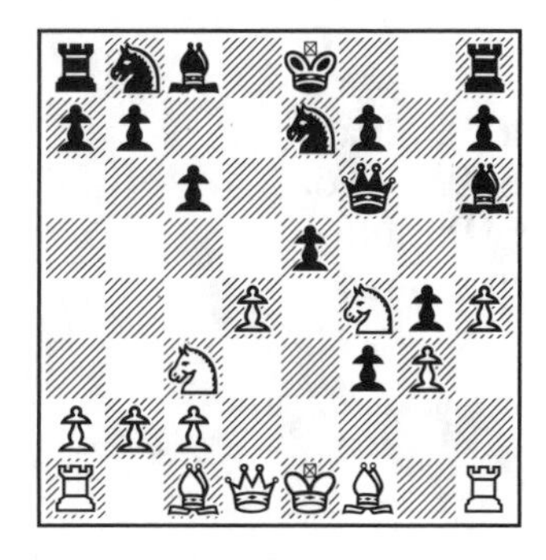

4B-6

3. Following **12... de5 13 Ne4 Qg7,** White establishes his superiority with **14 de5!** (see Diagram 4B-7). Investigate:

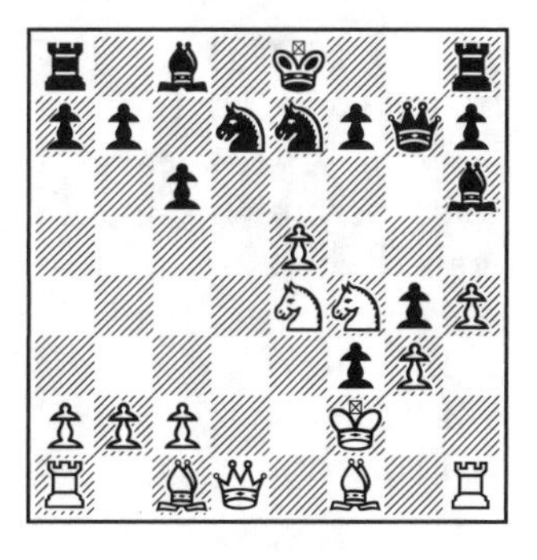

4B-7

a) **14... Ne5?**
b) **14... Qe5?**
c) **14... 0–0.**
d) **14... Bf4.**

4. **8... fe4** only looks impressive as **9 Nf4** (see Diagram 4B-8) provides a comfortable retort. Find White's strategy against:

a) **9... Nf6.**
b) **9... Bf4.**
c) **9... Bf5.**

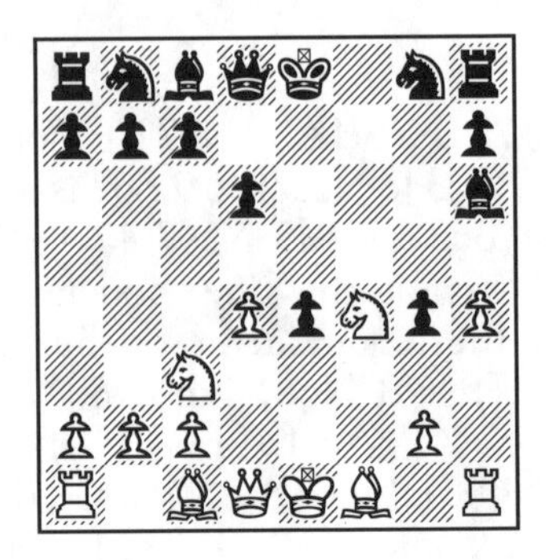

4B-8

5. From Diagram 4B-9, elaborate on:

a) **9... Na6.**
b) **9... Nc6.**
c) **9... Nf6.**
d) **9... fe4.**

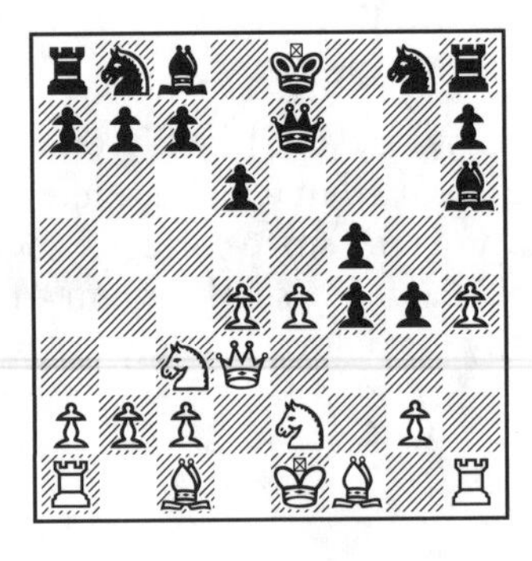

4B-9

6. **9... gf3 10 Ng3 fe4 11 Nge4 Bg4 12 Qd3** (Kf2!?) **Bc1 13 Rc1** (see Diagram 4B-10) leaves White for choice despite his inability to castle long. Rebuff:

a) **13... Ne7??**
b) **13... Nc6.**
c) **13... Nf6.**

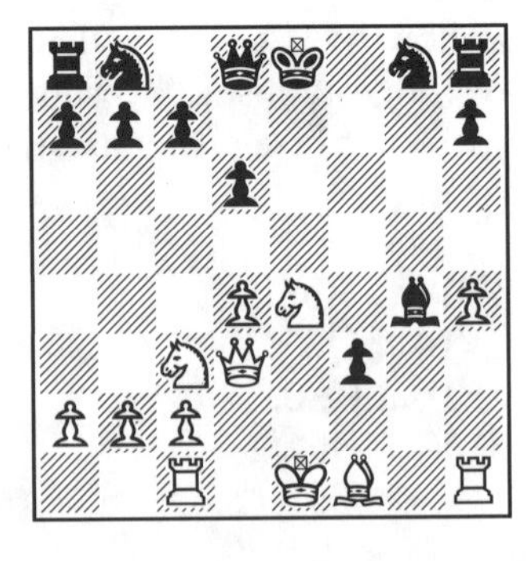

4B-10

Fischer Variation (C)

White obtains good prospects when Black supports his P/f4 with **6... Qf6:**

1	**e4**	**e5**
2	**f4**	**ef4**
3	**Nf3**	**d6**
4	**d4**	**g5**
5	**h4**	**g4**
6	**Ng1**	**Qf6**
7	**Nc3**	

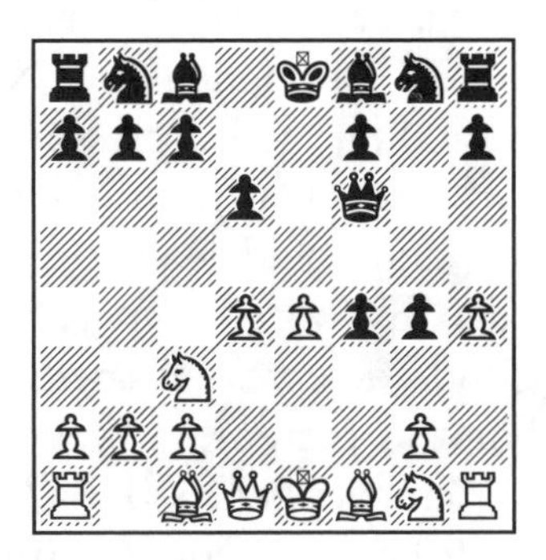

4C-1

Black is obliged to defend against Nd5; the alternative 7... f3 loses a pawn for no reason. Logical, therefore, is **7... c6** or 7... Ne7. In case of the former, a number of major sources of the King's Gambit Fischer Variation give 8 e5 here, which initiates a double pawn sacrifice. The trouble is that the sacrifice probably fails flat out on 8... de5 9 Ne4 Qe7 10 de5 Qe5 11 Qe2 Be6[1] (or even 11... Be7). More prudent after 7... c6, therefore, is the thematic **8 Nge2** when possible next is **8... f3** (8... Bh6 9 g3 transposes to lines of Diagram 4B-1) **9 Ng3 f2 10 Ke2±.** (See Diagram 4C-2.)

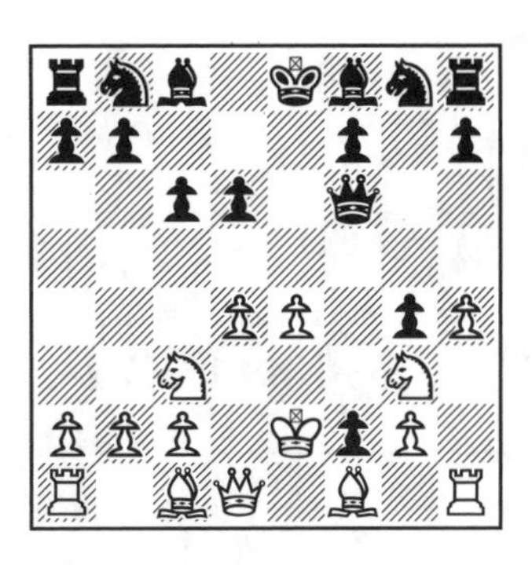

4C-2

White has apparently begged for some trouble by permitting his king to be buffeted around in the center, though Black's cross-fire bishop moves on 10... b6 11 Bg5 Ba6 12 Ke3 Bh6 (12... Qe6 13 Kf2) run aground after 13 Qg4±.

Offering Black improved chances is 10... Bh6 as seen in the follow-up 11 Bh6 Nh6 12 Qd2 Na6 13 Qg5 Qg5 (or 13... Qe6 14

Kf2) 14 hg5 Ng8 15 Kf2 h6 16 gh6 Rh6 17 Rh6 Nh6 18 Be2±, e.g., 18... Ng8 19 Ke3 Be6 20 a3 0–0–0 21 Rh1 Ne7?! 22 Rh4 f5 23 ef5 Nf5 24 Nf5 Bf5 25 Kd2 Rg8 26 Nd1 △ Ne3-Ng4 when White is better.

Black improves with **7... Ne7,** but **8 Nge2 Bh6** (8... f3 9 Ng3 f2 10 Ke2 b6 11 Bg5 Ba6 12 Ke3 Bh6 13 Qg4—cf. discussion of Diagram 4C-2 or 9 Nf4!?) **9 Qd2** (g3) **Bd7** (9... Nbc6 10 Nb5! Kd8 11 d5 Ne5 12 Qc3 or 12 Qa5) **10 g3 Nbc6** (10... f3 11 Qh6± or 10... fg3 11 Qh6±) **11 gf4 0–0–0 12 Bg2 Qg7** (12... Bg7 13 d5 [13 e5] Nd4 14 Nd4 Qd4 15 Qd4 Bd4 16 Bd2 △ 0–0–0 or 16 Ne2 △ f5) **13 d5 Ne5 14 Qe3 Kb8 15 Qf2**[2]± [1]

4C-3

leaves White in control of *f4* with material parity. White has obtained a panoply of central pawns, a spatial advantage, good lines for his bishops, and castling potential on the Q-side. Ideas for White include: (1) invading Black's kingside by Ng3-Nh5-(Nf6); (2) playing f5-f6 to fork the N/e7 and Q/g7; and (3) ultimately opening the center with e5 to activate the B/g2 in the direction of the square *b7*.

Black, though cramped, can attempt to crack open the center (with ...f5) before the White king reaches safety. Another plan is to obtain a tripled attack on the P/f4 beginning with ...N5g6, though White currently has h5 as a counterstroke. The maneuver ...Ng8-Nf6 would put added pressure on both *d5* and *e4*, while the enterprising ...c6 could lead to ...Bc6 after dc6. Even ...c5, a try to close the Q-side, deserves consideration.

For the present, however, if White achieves Be3, both Ba7 and Bd4 will be threatened. Sensible then is 15... Nc4, but 16 b3 △ Bb2-Na4 is a convenient response. More challenging is the counterattacking 15... g3[2] when 16 Qg1 Ng4 17 Rh3 Qf6 18 Rg3±, as in Illustrative Game I, offers White an enduring initiative in an exciting tactical melee.

ILLUSTRATIVE GAME I

Planinc—Portisch
Ljubljana 1973

1	e4	e5
2	f4	ef4
3	Nf3	d6
4	d4	g5
5	h4	g4
6	Ng1	Qf6
7	Nc3	Ne7
8	Nge2	Bh6
9	Qd2	Bd7
10	g3	Nbc6
11	gf4	0-0-0
12	Bg2	Qg7
13	d5	Ne5
14	Qe3	Kb8
15	Qf2	g3
16	Qg1	Ng4
17	Rh3	Qf6
18	Rg3	Rhg8
19	Bd2	Ng6
20	Bh3	Qh4
21	0-0-0	Ne7
22	Be1	Qh5
23	Kb1	Nf6
24	Qd4	Bh3
25	Qf6	Nc8
26	Bf2	Bd7
27	Rdg1	Rge8
28	Nd4	Bf8
29	Nf3	Qh6
30	Qd4	Be7
31	Be3	Bf6
32	e5	Bh8
33	Qd3	Qh5
34	Rg5	Qh6
35	R5g2	Qh5
36	Ne4	Ka8
37	Bd2	Qf5
38	Rg5	Qh3
39	Nf2	Qh6
40	Rh1	Qf8
41	Rh7	de5
42	fe5	f6
43	Rgh5	Bg7
44	Qg6	fe5
45	Rg7	Qf3
46	Rd7	Qf2
47	Bc1	Qb6
48	Qf5	a6
49	Rd8	Rd8
50	Qe5	Qd6
51	Qe4	Nb6
52	c4	Nc4
53	Rh7	Nb6
54	Bf4	Qd5
55	Qd5	Nd5
56	Bc7	Nc7
57	Rc7	½-½

ILLUSTRATIVE GAME II

Bangiev—Mayr
1986

1	e4	e5
2	f4	ef4
3	Nf3	d6
4	d4	g5
5	h4	g4
6	Ng1	Qf6
7	Nc3	Ne7
8	Nge2	f3
9	Nf4	fg2
10	Bg2	c6
11	e5	de5
12	Ne4	Qg7
13	Nh5	Qg6
14	Nef6	Kd8
15	de5	Bd7

16	Be4	Nf5
17	Nd7	Nd7
18	Nf6	1–0

ILLUSTRATIVE GAME III

Raingruber—Tiffin
Modesto, CA 1989

1	e4	e5
2	f4	ef4
3	Nf3	d6
4	d4	g5
5	h4	g4
6	Ng1	Qf6
7	Nc3	c6
8	Nge2	Bh6
9	g3	fg3
10	Ng3	Bc1
11	Rc1	h5
12	Qd2	b6
13	Nce2	Ba6
14	c4	Nd7
15	Qf4	0–0–0
16	Bg2	c5
17	Qf6	Ndf6
18	0–0	Bb7
19	Rf4	Re8
20	Rcf1	Rh6
21	Nf5	Ne4
22	Nh6	Nh6
23	dc5	Nc5
24	Bb7	Kb7
25	Nc3	Nd3
26	Rf6	Rh8
27	Rd6	Nb2
28	Rff6	Nc4
29	Rh6	Rc8
30	Rd7	Ka6
31	Nd5	Ne5
32	Nb4	Kb5
33	Rh5	Rc5
34	Re5	Re5
35	Rd5	Rd5
36	Nd5	Kc6
37	h5	Kd5
38	h6	f5
39	h7	Ke4
40	h8=Q	1–0

PROBLEMS

1. From the diagrammed position does 12 Bd2 △ Bc3 salvage this oft-recommended but apparently flawed line for White? Show a line.

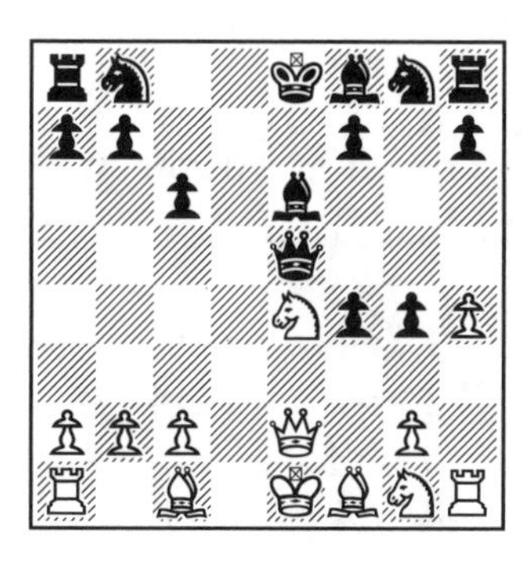

4C-4

2. With **15... Nf3 16 Bf3 gf3 17 Qf3 f5!?** Black sacrifices a pawn to disrupt White's position. Following **18 Rg1 Qf6** (see Diagram 4C-5) what thematic ploy makes White's superiority apparent?

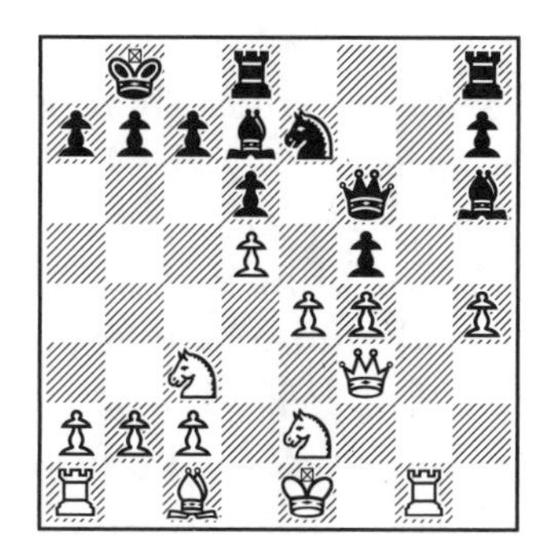

4C-5

Fischer Variation (D)

A crucial line occurs with **6... Nf6:**

1	**e4**	**e5**
2	**f4**	**ef4**
3	**Nf3**	**d6**
4	**d4**	**g5**
5	**h4**	**g4**
6	**Ng1**	**Nf6**
7	**Bf4**[1]	

Begging attention here is the problematical 7 Qd3 Qe7 (7... Nh5?? 8 Qb5+− or 7... d5!? 8 e5 Nh5∞) 8 Nc3 Bh6 9 g3 (or Nge2) 0–0. Another idea by Black in response to 7 Qd3 is ...b6-Ba6 when c4 may be required. The reader is nevertheless advised to give the 7 Qd3 lines a closer look.

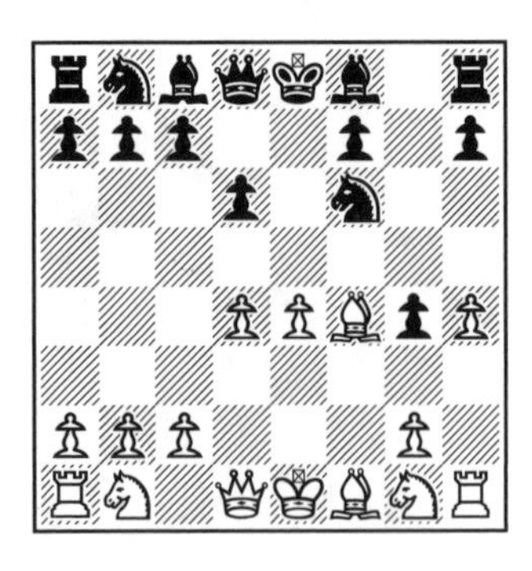

4D-1

Now if **7... Ne4** (7... Nh5 8 Ne2), **8 Nd2** (to be admired as well is 8 Bd3!?, e.g., 8... Qe7 9 Ne2 Bg7 10 0–0 0–0 11 Be4 Qe4 12 Nbc3 Qc6 13 Qd2 d5 14 Ng3 Qf6 15 Be5 Qh4 16 Bg7 Kg7 17 Nd5 f5 18 Qf4 Nc6 19 Nc7 Rb8 20 Rae1 Kg8 21 d5 Ne7 22 Nh5 Qh5 23 Re7 b5 24 Rfe1 Rb6 25 d6 Qh4 26 g3 Qf6 27 Ne8 Qb2 28 Qg5 Kh8 29 Rh7 Kh7 30 Re7 Kh8 31 Qh6 Kg8 32 Qh7 mate, Hebden—Borm, *Toulon Open 1987)* **Qe7** (8... d5 9 Ne4 de4 10 Bc4±) **9 Qe2 Nd2**[2] **10 Kd2 Qe2 11 Ne2**$\bar{\bar{\infty}}$ [9]

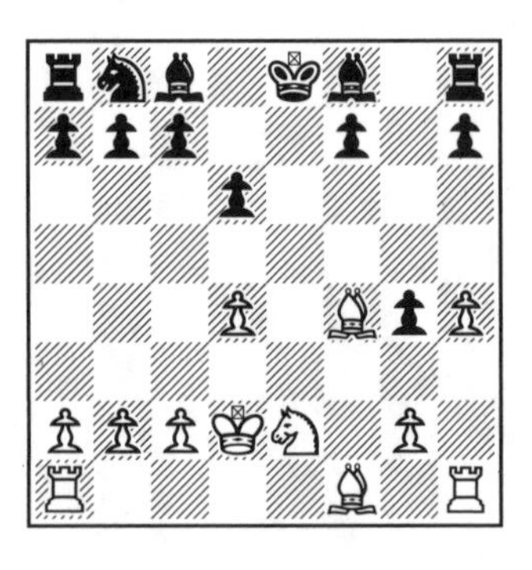

4D-2

White's development is superior and his pieces will have very good squares (compare this position with that of Diagram 3H-2).

Especially promising here is g3-Bg2 followed by bringing the rooks to the e- and f-files. Black's extra pawn (on *f7*) is often more of a hindrance than a plus. It can be blockaded and is not usually telling in the endgame.

Other ideas for White include: (1) h5-(h6), semi-isolating the P/g4 since ...f5 would blunt some of the effectiveness of the B/c8; (2) c4-b4-c5, indirectly hitting the P/c7; (3) Ng3-Bc4-Raf1-Rf2-Rhf1 intending the obvious discovery on *f7*; and (4) Ng3-Bd3-Bg5-Bf6 with a view to winning the P/h7. If Black tries to neutralize Bc4 by ...c6-d5, then plans (1) and (4) gain force.

ILLUSTRATIVE GAME I

Shevelev—Klovan
SSSR 1980

1	e4	e5
2	f4	ef4
3	Nf3	d6
4	d4	g5
5	h4	g4
6	Ng1	Nf6
7	Nc3 (Bf4)	Nh5
8	Qd3	Nc6
9	Nge2	Bd7?! (Be7!?)
10	Nd5!	Be7
11	Bf4	Bh4
12	g3	Nf4
13	Nef4	Bg5
14	Be2	Ne7
15	Ne3	c6?
16	Qa3	Qc7
17	0–0–0	Ng6
18	Rdf1	a6
19	Bg4	Bg4
20	Ng4	0–0–0
21	Kb1	Rde8
22	Nh3	Bd8
23	Qf3	Qe7
24	Nh6!	f6
25	Nf5	Qd7
26	Nf4	Kb8
27	Rh6	Nf4
28	Qf4	Re6
29	Rfh1	Bc7
30	Qf3	d5?
31	ed5	Qd5
32	Qd5	cd5
33	a3	Rg8
34	Rh7	Re2
35	Rd7	Rf2
36	Rhh7	1–0

ILLUSTRATIVE GAME II

Gallagher—Sanz
Gijon 1988

1	e4	e5
2	f4	ef4
3	Nf3	d6
4	d4	g5
5	h4	g4
6	Ng1	Nf6
7	Qd3	d5
8	e5	Nh5
9	Ne2	Be7
10	Bf4	c5
11	dc5	Nc6
12	Nbc3	Nf4
13	Nf4	Ne5
14	Qe3	Bf6
15	Ncd5	0–0
16	0–0–0	Bg7
17	Nh5	Nd7
18	Ne7	Kh8
19	Ng7	1–0

ILLUSTRATIVE GAME III

Berthelot—Lamoureux
Torcy 1991

1	e4	e5
2	f4	ef4
3	Nf3	d6
4	d4	g5
5	h4	g4
6	Ng1	Nf6
7	Bf4	Ne4
8	Bd3	Qe7
9	Ne2	Nc6
10	0–0	Bg7
11	Be4	Qe4
12	Nbc3	Bd4
13	Kh1	Bc3
14	Nc3	Qc4
15	Nd5	Ne7
16	Nf6	Kd8
17	Bd6	Be6
18	Rf4	Qc6
19	Ba3	Kc8
20	Be7	h5
21	Rd4	b6
22	Qe2	1–0

PROBLEMS

1. White has an interesting alternative in **7 Nc3.** On **7... Nh5 8 Nge2** (for 8 Qd3 see Illustrative Game I) **f3** (see Diagram 4D-3), what is a reasonable follow-up?

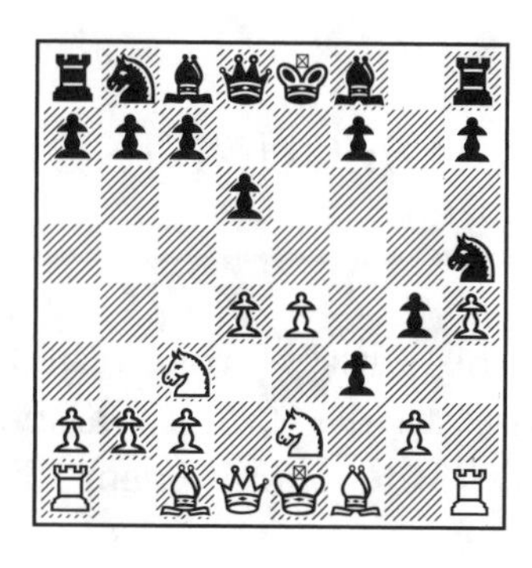

4D-3

2. From Diagram 4D-4, demonstrate the inadequacy of:

a) **9... Bf5.**
b) **9... f5.**

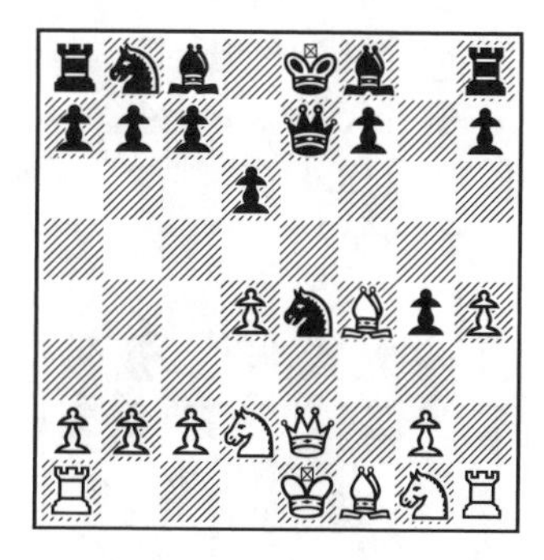

4D-4

5: CUNNINGHAM VARIATION (A)

One of Black's time-tested responses to the King's Gambit is 3... Be7, the Cunningham Variation:

1	**e4**	**e5**
2	**f4**	**ef4**
3	**Nf3**	**Be7**
4	**Nc3*** (Bc4)	**Bh4**
5	**Ke2**	

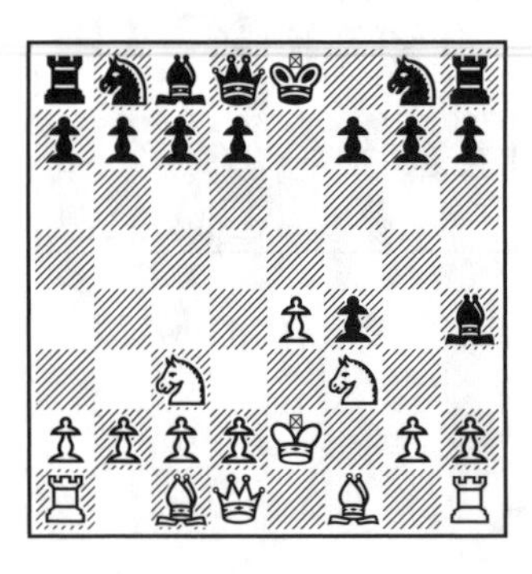

5A-1

With his surprising fourth move, the Spassky Continuation, White reserves the placement of his king bishop for a more propitious moment. Black's check on *h4* (for 4... d6 and 4... Nf6 see Sections 5B and 5C, respectively) appears to refute this brazen idea, as (1) White cannot castle, (2) his king obstructs his B/f1, and (3) his entire first rank is practically frozen! Nevertheless, by utilizing his central pawns as a shield, White can continue to mobilize rapidly without rushing to clarify his king's ultimate intentions. If White succeeds in castling by hand while retaining his lead in development, Black's position may even become critical!

Black, of course, will be looking for a weak link in White's defensive pawn chain. One direct challenge involves **5... f5 6 d3 fe4 7 de4 d6**[1] **8 Bf4±.**

---

* 4 Be2 can lead to Diagram 8-2.

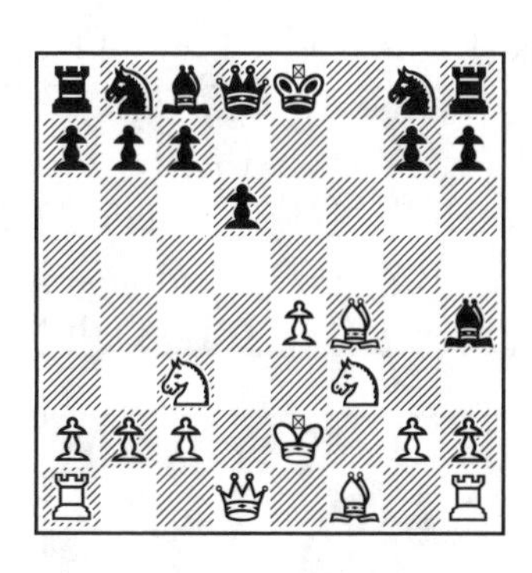

5A-2

White has regained his pawn and has increased his lead in development. The half-open d-file gives White considerable longitude for his queen, and either wing can provide a haven for his king, e.g., 8... Bg4 9 Qd3 Nc6 10 Kd2 [13]. Alternatively, after playing a subsequent g3 with tempo White can play Kf2 with the follow-up Kg2-Bc4-Rf1 or Bg2-Rf1-Kg1 in mind.

A new idea by Black from Diagram 5A-1 is 5... c6!? △ ...d5 to try to break up the center with an attack on White's king. The tempo thus expended allows 6 d3 (6 d4 d5 7 Bf4 or 7 Qd2!?) when possible are: **a)** 6... Bg5 7 g3 d5 8 gf4 Bh6 9 e5 f6 10 d4 c5 11 Be3 cd4 12 Qd4 △ (Rd1)-Qd5/ef6; **b)** 6... g5 7 Nh4 gh4 8 Bf4 d5 9 Kd2 Qf6 (9... h5 10 h3) 10 Qf3 d4 (10... de4 11 Qe4 △ Re1/Be5) 11 Ne2 Nd7 12 Qh5 c5 13 Bg5 Qb6 14 Kc1⩲ △ Qh4/Bh4 and/or a4-Ra3-Rb3; and **c)** 6... d5 7 Bf4 d4 8 Nb1 Bg4 (8... Qb6 9 Qc1) 9 g3 Bg5 10 Qc1⩲, e.g., 10... Bf4 11 Qf4 Nf6 12 Nbd2 0–0 13 Kf2 Na6 14 a3 △ (h3)-Kg2-Be2-Rhf1.

From Diagram 5A-1, another attempt to expose White's king incorporates **5... d5,** but **6 Nd5 Nf6** (6... f5 7 d3 and 6... Bg4!? 7 d4 f5 8 Qd3 Ne7 9 Nf4 Nbc6 10 c3 Qd7 11 e5 g5 12 Nh3⩲) **7 Nf6 Qf6 8 d4** (for 8 e5!? see Illustrative Game I) **Nc6**[2] (8... Bg4 9 c3 [9 Qd2!?] c5 10 dc5 Qe7 11 Qd5 Nd7 12 Bf4 Nf6 13 Qe5 Ne4 14 Ke3 Bf3 15 Bb5 Kf8 16 Qe7 Be7 17 Kf3 Nc5 18 Rad1 a6 19 Bc4 Rc8 20 Rhe1 g5 21 Bd6± [19]) **9 c3 Bg4 10 Qd2 g5** (10... 0–0 11 Kd1 Rfe8 12 Bd3 Rad8 13 Kc2± [13] or 10... Bg5 11 Kd1 0–0–0 12 Kc2 Bf3 13 gf3±, e.g., 13... Nd4? 14 cd4 Rd4 15 Qa5!+–) **11 Kd1 0–0–0 12 Kc2 Qh6 13 Nh4 Qh4 14 g3!±** [1] produces an amusing paradox. (See Diagram 5A-3.)

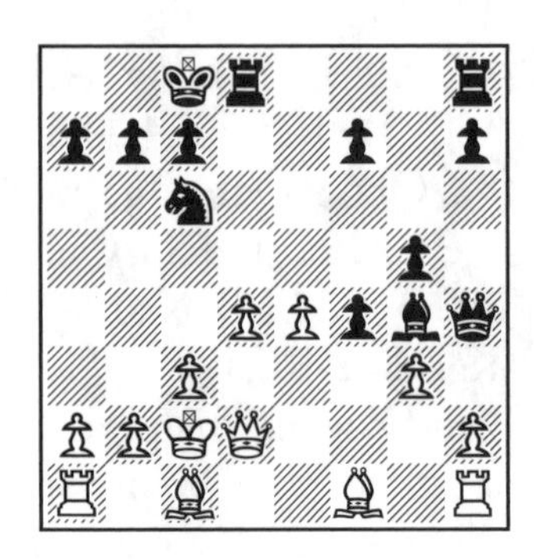

5A-3

The initiative belongs to White even though his development has been neglected and his king has been sent to flight! White possesses the center, whereas Black's queen and queen bishop are offside. Black is already embarrassed to find that his kingside pawn play has been excessive. A typical sequel could run 14... fg3 15 Qg5 (Qg2) Qg5 16 Bg5 Rde8 17 Bg2 Rhg8 18 Bf4 gh2 19 Rh2 △ Rf1-Kd3, whereupon White's mobile center and bishop pair begin to dictate the future course of events.

Returning to Diagram 5A-1, a line that bears some interest stems from **5... d6.** Here **6 d4 Bg4**[3] (6... Bg5 7 g3) **7 Bf4 Nc6**[4] (7... Bg5 8 Qd2) **8 Qd3 Bg5** (8... Nge7 9 Kd2 Bf3 10 gf3 Qd7 11 Rd1 0–0–0 12 Kc1 Kb8 13 Qe3 [13] and 8... Nf6 9 Kd2 Bf3 10 gf3 0–0 11 Be3 Qd7 12 Rg1 Kh8 13 Rd1 a6 14 Kc1 b5 15 Qd2 Rg8 16 Bg5 Bg5 17 Rg5 h6 18 Rg3 Rae8 19 Bh3 Qd8 20 Rdg1 Nh5 21 R3g2 Na5 22 Bf5 Nc4 23 Rg7 1–0, Mourges–Maumey, *French Ch.)* **9 Bg3**± [9]

5A-4

already favors White, as after Kf2, to decamp the pin, his middlegame plans should flow quite smoothly.

One buildup, Re1(Rd1)-Be2-Rhf1-Kg1, aims at a solid position with an ideal center. Black must develop apace if he is not to incur an insurmountable disadvantage.

Finally (from Diagram 5A-1), White also secures some advantage if Black redeploys his king bishop. Easy for White is 5... Be7 6 d4 Nf6[5] 7 Bf4 d5 8 ed5 Nd5 9 Nd5 Qd5 10 Kf2, but **5... Bg5 6 d4** (d3) **Bh6**[6] **7 Kf2** (g3) hardly improves Black's chances. Now on 7... g5 8 Bc4 d6 9 h4! g4 10 Ng5± [9], White can answer 10... Bg5

11 hg5 Qg5 by 12 Nd5 △ Bf4. Even on **7... Nf6 8 Bc4 Ng4** (8... 0–0 9 Re1) **9 Kg1 0–0 10 h3 Ne3 11 Be3 fe3 12 Kh2 d6 13 Rf1**± [1],

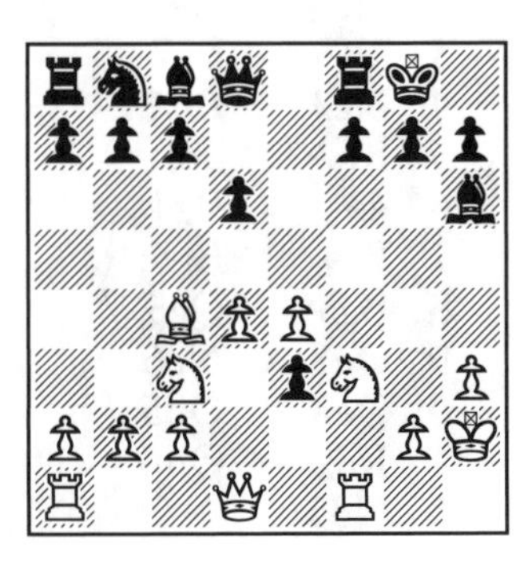

5A-5

it is improbable that Black can retain his extra pawn.

White can work to capture Black's P/e3 by employing a plan such as Qd3 (keeping an eye on the P/e4)-Nd5(Nd1)-Ne3. Once again, White has a clear advantage which is traceable to his edge in development and central pawn majority.

ILLUSTRATIVE GAME 1

Prins-Zuidema
Prvenstvo 1965

1	**e4**	**e5**
2	**f4**	**ef4**
3	**Nf3**	**Be7**
4	**Nc3**	**Bh4**
5	**Ke2**	**d5**
6	**Nd5**	**Nf6**
7	**Nf6**	**Qf6**
8	**e5!?** (d4)	**Qe7?!**
9	**d4**	**0–0**
10	**g3**	**Bg5**
11	**gf4**	**Bh6**
12	**Qe1**	**f6**
13	**Qh4**	**Qe8**
14	**Rg1**	**Kh8**
15	**Kf2**	**fe5**
16	**fe5**	**Bc1**
17	**Rc1**	**Bf5**
18	**Rg3**	**Nc6**
19	**c3**	**Ne7**
20	**Kg1**	**h6**
21	**Re1**	**Bh7**
22	**Qg4**	**Nf5**
23	**Rg2**	**Qe7**
24	**Rf2**	**Rad8**
25	**Bc4**	**c6**
26	**a4**	**Bg8**
27	**Bg8**	**Kg8**
28	**Nd2**	**Nd6**
29	**Ref1**	**Rf2**
30	**Rf2**	**Ne8**
31	**Ne4**	**1–0**

ILLUSTRATIVE GAME II

Eade—Valentine
Corres. 1988

1	e4	e5
2	f4	ef4
3	Nf3	Be7
4	Nc3	Bh4
5	Ke2	d6
6	d4	Bg4
7	Bf4	Nc6
8	Qd3	Qd7
9	Kd2	Bf3
10	gf3	Nge7
11	Rd1	0–0–0
12	Kc1	f5
13	d5	Ne5
14	Qe3	Kb8
15	Nb5	Nc8
16	Nd4	fe4
17	Be5	de5
18	Ne6	Qe7
19	Rg1	Rdg8
20	fe4	g5
21	c4	g4
22	Qc3	Bg5
23	Kb1	Bf4
24	Rg2	h5
25	c5	Rh6
26	Nf4	ef4
27	e5	h4
28	Rgd2	Rd8
29	Qd4	Qg5
30	d6	cd6
31	ed6	a6
32	Qb4	Ka8
33	Rd5	Qf6
34	c6	bc6
35	Ba6	1–0

ILLUSTRATIVE GAME III

Ermenko—Kulmanovsky
USSR Corres. 1983

1	e4	e5
2	f4	ef4
3	Nf3	Be7
4	Nc3	Bh4
5	Ke2	d6
6	d4	Bg4
7	Bf4	Bg5
8	Bg5	Qg5
9	Qd3	Nc6
10	Qe3	Qh5
11	Kd2	Qh6
12	Nd5	0–0–0
13	c3	f5
14	ef5	Re8
15	Qh6	Nh6
16	f6	Bf3
17	gf3	gf6
18	Nf6	Ref8
19	Ng4	Nf5
20	Be2	Nh4
21	Raf1	Rf4
22	Rf2	Rhf8
23	Rhf1	Ne7
24	a3	h5
25	Ne3	d5
26	Ng2	Ng2
27	Rg2	c6
28	Rff2	Nf5
29	Rg5	Nd6
30	Rfg2	h4
31	R5g4	Rg4
32	Rg4	Rh8
33	Rf4	Kd7
34	Bf1	Ke6
35	Ke1	Nf7
36	Rg4	Kf6
37	Kf2	Ng5
38	Bd3	1–0

PROBLEMS

1. Black has several seventh-move alternatives. From Diagram 5A-6, explore:

a) **7... g5.**
b) **7... Be7.**
c) **7... Bg5.**
d) **7... b6.**

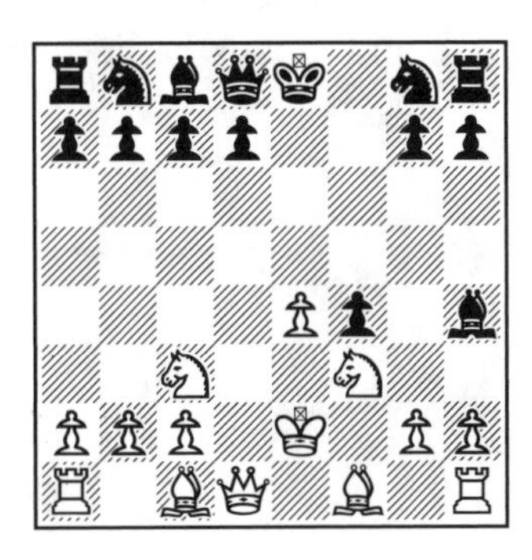

5A-6

2. Also bleak is **8... 0–0** (see Diagram 5A-7). Discuss.

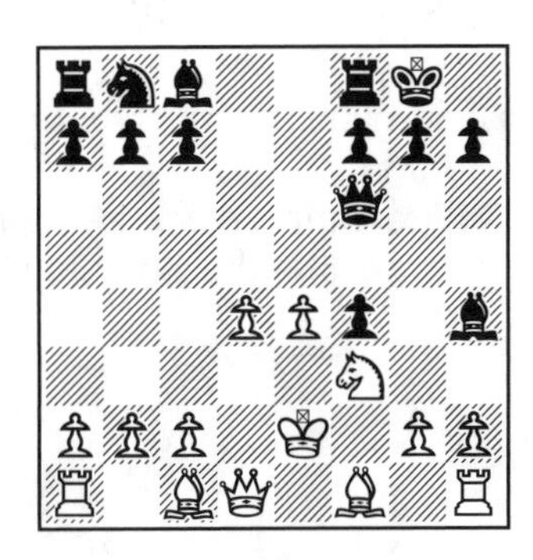

5A-7

3. **6... f5** (see Diagram 5A-8) can be rejected by what thematic response?

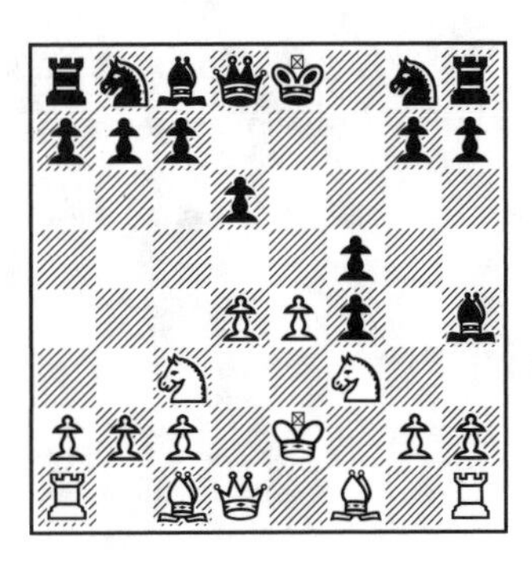

5A-8

4. After **7... f5** (see Diagram 5A-9), how can White demonstrate that knights should usually be developed before bishops?

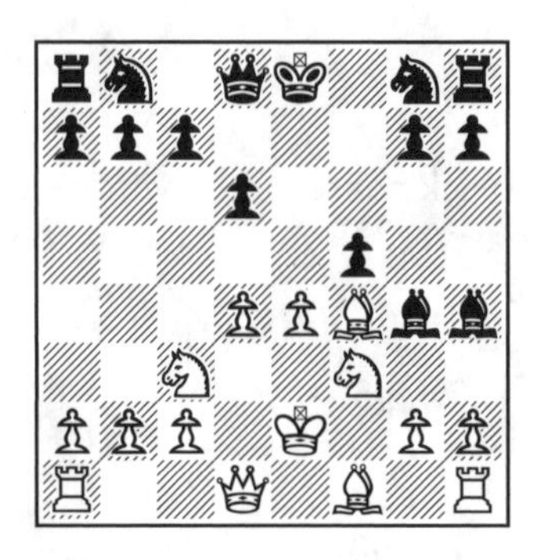

5A-9

5. From Diagram 5A-10:

a) Find an effective rebuttal to **6... f5.**
b) Undermine Black's kingside pawns after the loosening **6... g5.**

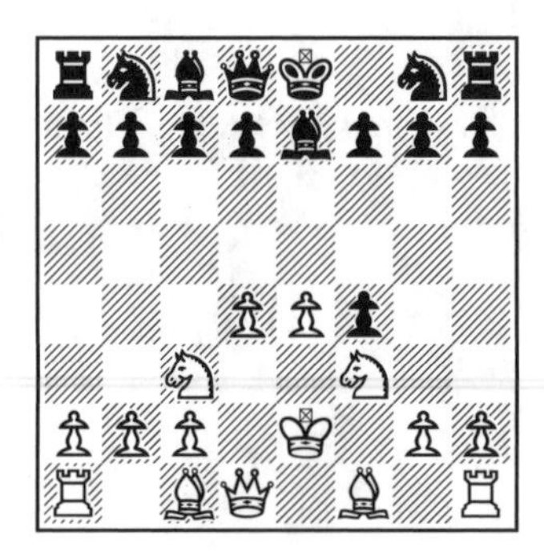

5A-10

6. Prove that **6... f5** (see Diagram 5A-11) only helps White.

5A-11

Cunningham Variation (B)

In the Spassky Continuation (4 Nc3), dazzling pyrotechnics can erupt from 4... d6:

1	**e4**	**e5**
2	**f4**	**ef4**
3	**Nf3**	**Be7**
4	**Nc3**	**d6**
5	**d4**	**g5***
6	**Bc4!**	
	(g3!?)	

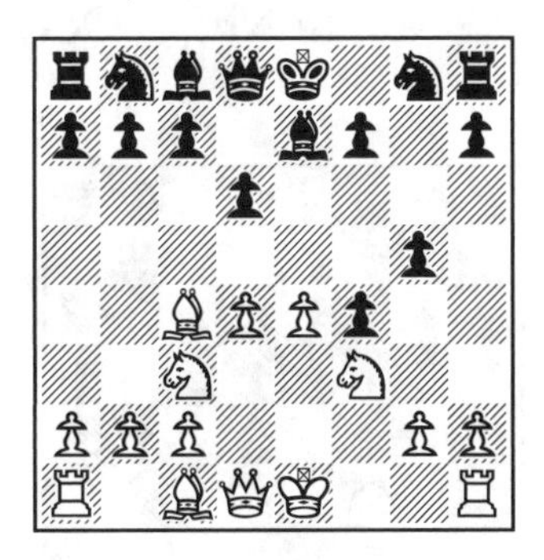

5B-1

White's aggressive development has already limited Black's options. Thus 5... f5 could have been swiftly dismissed with 6 Bf4 fe4 7 Ne4 d5 8 Neg5 △ Bd3± since 8… h6? 9 Nf7! Kf7 10 Ne5+− unleashes a decisive attack, e.g. 10… Kf6 11 Qh5 Bb4 (what else?) 12 c3 Qf8 13 Ng6 Qf7 (13… Qe8 14 Be5 is similar) 14 Bd3 Bc3 15 bc3 Qe8 16 Be5. Instead on 10… Ke6 Black loses his queen at a minimum after 11 Qg4 Kd6 12 Nf7 Kc6 13 Nd8†.

Now White squashes 6... f5? with 7 Ng5![1] and handles **6... Bg4** by **7 Qd3 Nc6 8 Nd5 Na5** (8... Nf6 9 Bd2 △ Ng5/0–0–0) **9 Bd2 Nc4 10 Qc4 c6 11 Ne7 Qe7** (11... Ne7? 12 Ng5) **12 0–0!**±.

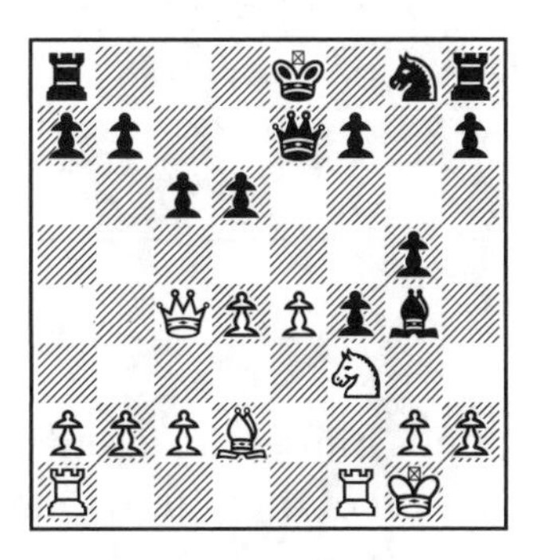

5B-2

How will Black shelter his king? On 12... Nh6 (△ ...0–0) White has 13 Ng5! when 13... Qg5 14 Bf4 Qg6 15 Bh6 Bh3 (not 15... Qh6? 16 Qf7 Kd8 17 Rae1! △ Rf6/Qb7) 16 Rf2 0–0–0 (16... Bg2 17 Rg2 Qh6 18 Raf1) 17 Bf4 Rg8 18

* For 5… Nf6 cf. the Illustrative Game.

Bg3± gives Black little for his pawn. Even the immediate 12... 0–0–0 fails due to 13 d5! c5 14 b4 Bf3 15 bc5! dc5 16 Rf3 △ Bc3-Re1.

Returning to Diagram 5B-1, Black might also reply with the radical **6... g4?!** White, however, can merely ignore the "threat" with **7 0–0!** — an explosive offer of a knight! Here on **7... gf3** (7... Nf6 8 Ng5) **8 Qf3±**

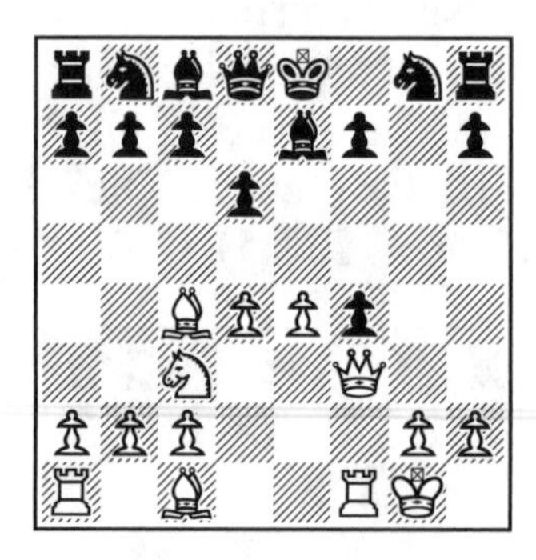

5B-3

Black finds himself in an unfavorable version of the Muzio Gambit because his misplaced king bishop hinders his queen from supporting the beleaguered *f7* square.

In spite of Black's material superiority, both 8... Nc6 9 Qh5! Nd4 (9... Qd7 10 Rf4! Nd8 11 Bf7 △ Rf7-Bg5-e5) 10 Qf7 Kd7 11 Rf4 Qe8 (11... Nc2? 12 Qf5) 12 Qg7+– and 8... Be6 9 d5 Bd7 (9... Bc8 10 Bf4!) 10 Qf4! Nf6 11 e5 △ Qe5+– are unavailing. 8... Nf6 seems steadier, yet 9 Qf4![2] still launches a fearful attack which Black must somehow palliate.

To circumvent these trying complications, Black can consider **6... Be6.** Nonetheless, after **7 Be6 fe6 8 h4! g4** (8... h6 9 hg5 Bg5 10 g3 Qf6 11 e5) **9 Ng5 Bg5 10 hg5 Qg5 11 0–0!,** White leads in development and will recover at least one pawn. In particular, **11... Qg7[3] 12 Rf4 h5** (12... Nh6 13 e5! threatening Rf6 △ Rh6/Re6) **13 d5 e5** (13... ed5 14 ed5 Nd7 15 Qe2 Ne7 16 Nb5 △ Qc4) **14 Rf5±**

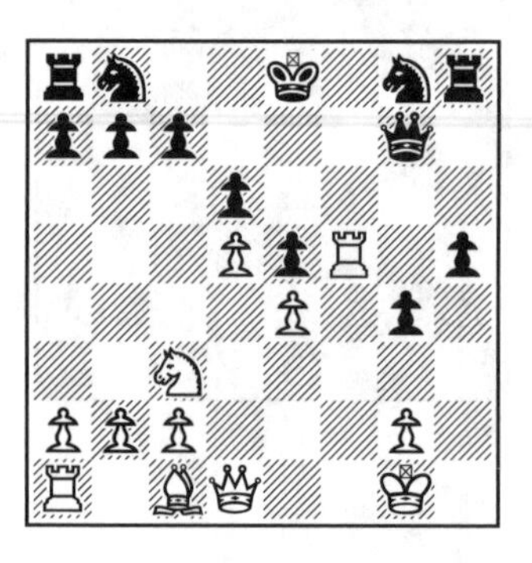

5B-4

dashes Black's hopes for a kingside pawnstorm. White's rook on *f5* stifles Black's counterplay and is even more vexing than a knight; for instance, on 14... Ne7, simply 15 Rg5 maintains the pressure. Apparently, Black should accede to 14... Nd7 (14... Na6 15 Bg5), though 15 Qe2 △ Be3-Nb5-Qc4-Raf1 requires him to assume a defensive posture while struggling to complete his development.

ILLUSTRATIVE GAME

Raingruber—Rizzo
1973

1	e4	e5
2	f4	d6
3	Nf3	ef4
4	d4	Nf6
5	Nc3	Be7
6	Bc4	Bd7
7	Bf4	c5
8	dc5	dc5
9	0-0	0-0
10	Ne5	Bc6
11	Nd5	Ne4
12	Nc7	Qc7
13	Nf7	Qb6
14	Bd6!	Nd6
15	Nd6	Kh8
16	Rf8	Bf8
17	Nf7	Kg8
18	Nh6	Kh8
19	Qf1	Nd7
20	Qf7	Nf6
21	Qg8	Ng8
22	Nf7 mate	

PROBLEMS

1. Following the forced **7... Bg5 8 Qh5 Kd7** (see Diagram 5B-5), find the clincher that clears the smoke!

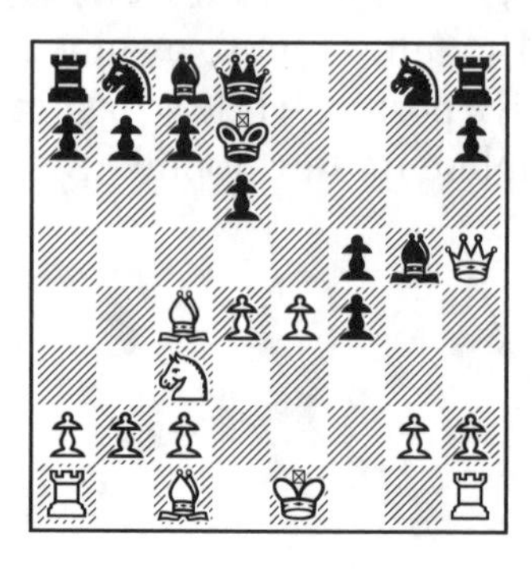

5B-5

2. From Diagram 5B-6, display a convincing initiative if Black turns to:

a) **9... Be6.**
b) **9... Nc6.**

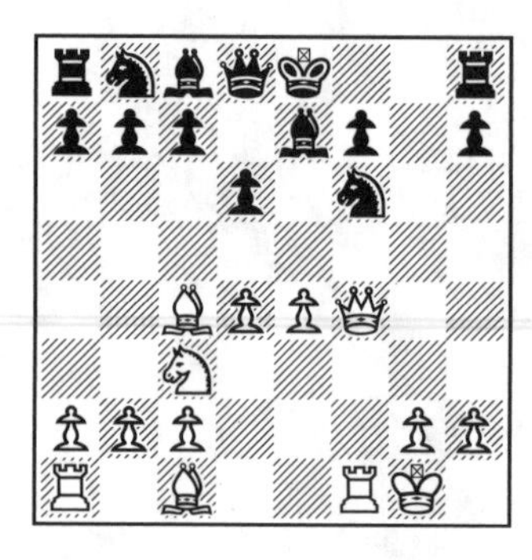

5B-6

3. Plot White's course, from Diagram 5B-7, if Black embarks on:

a) **11... g3.**
b) **11... e5.**

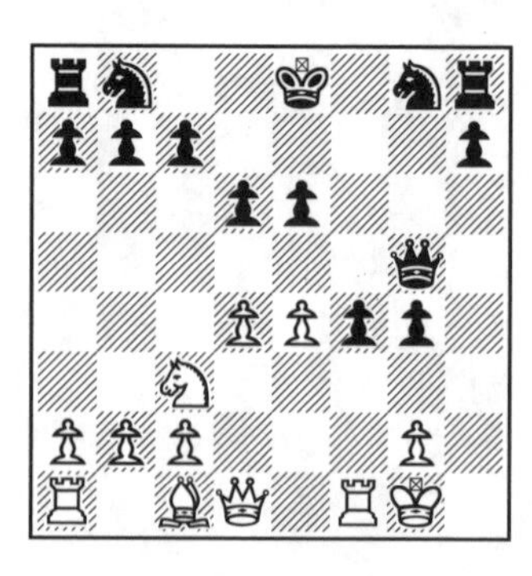

5B-7

Cunningham Variation (C)

Black's preferred choice in the Spassky Continuation involves 4... Nf6:

1	e4	e5
2	f4	ef4
3	**Nf3**	**Be7**
4	**Nc3**	**Nf6**
5	**d4**	

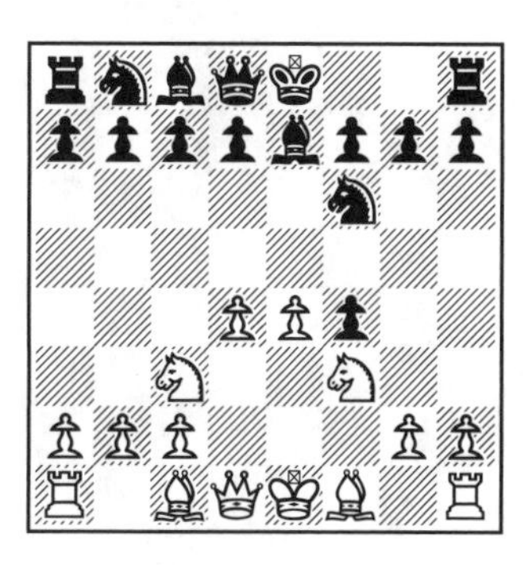

5C-1

White has a cogent but perhaps optimistic alternative here in 5 e5, but 5... Ng4 6 d4 (6 Bc4!?) Bh4 7 Ke2 Nf2 8 Qe1 Nh1 9 Qh4 Qh4 10 Nh4 g5 11 Nd5 Kd8 12 Nf3 h6 yields a complicated position with unclear play. The reader is invited to look for improvements here for White.

Instead, the text forces Black to reach an immediate decision regarding his P/f4. Since 5... Bb4?! fails to 6 Bd3 d5 7 e5 Ne4 8 0–0 Nc3 9 bc3 Bc3 10 Rb1 Nc6 11 Bf4 Nd4 12 Ng5 Nf5 13 Nf7± [1] with a king hunt by White in the wings, e.g., 13... Kf7 14 g4 Bd4 15 Kh1 Kg8 16 gf5 b6 17 Qg4 Bc5 18 Qg2 is good for White (how does Black prepare for f6 ?). Black's only worthy rejoinder is **5... d5.**[1]

Untested next is 6 e5 Ne4 7 Bd3! f5∞, but **6 ed5** (not to be undervalued is 6 Bd3 de4 7 Ne4 Ne4 8 Be4 Bd6 9 0–0 0–0 [for 9... Nd7 cf. Illustrative Game II] 10 Ne5 Be5 11 de5 Qd1 12 Rd1 Nc6 13 Bf4± [1]) offers White known chances for obtaining a plus. Now the obligatory **6... Nd5** can lead to **7 Bc4** (a good option is 7 Nd5 Qd5 8 Be2 0–0 9 0–0 g5 10 b3 arriving at Diagram 8-2) **Be6**[2] (7... Bh4 8 g3 Nc3 9 bc3 fg3 10 Qe2 Be6 11 0–0 gh2 12 Nh2 △ Ba3 is unclear) **8 Qe2 Nc3 9 bc3 Bc4 10 Qc4 Bd6 11 Qb5 Nd7 12 Qb7 Qe7**[3] **13 Kf2 0–0 14 Re1 Qf6 15 Bd2±** [12].

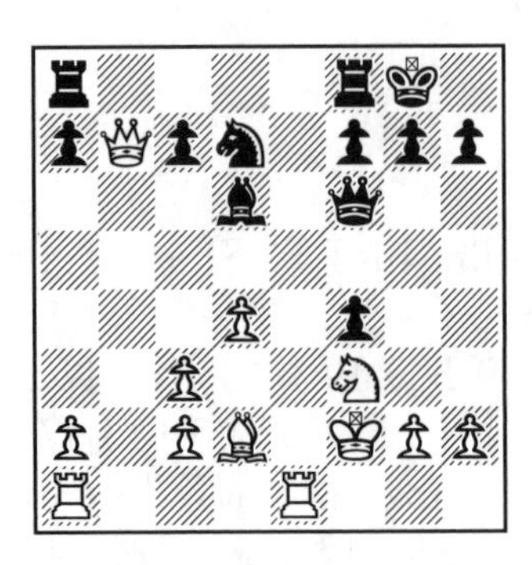

5C-2

Besides having reestablished material equality, White possesses his usual edge in the center. While considering the prophylactic Kg1, White can concentrate on c4-c5, hitting Black's B/d6, followed by c4-Bc3-d5-d6 when appropriate. Black must challenge this plan resourcefully if he is to prevent White from creating a duo of passed pawns. In addition, Black is hampered by the rather awkward placement of his undefended N/d7. On 15... Rfb8?!, for example, the simple 16 Qc6 △ Qd7/Rab1 quickly contravenes the notion that Black will have time to penetrate on the b-file. Even 15... Qf5 (△ ...Qc2) 16 Qe4 or even 16 c4 △ c5 leaves White unruffled.

Ideally, Black should activate his pawn majority to strive for level play, but here he would expose his own king in the process. The thrust ...g5-g4, therefore, must be carefully prepared, as 15... g5? 16 Qb5! g4 17 Qd7 gf3 18 Qg4 △ Qf3± just hands White a big advantage. In some lines h4 can also interfere with Black's plans, though White will need to monitor the resulting weakness on g3. Thus Black may have to resort to a game of restraint while looking for the right moment to march his kingside pawns.

ILLUSTRATIVE GAME I

Spassky—Liberzon
USSR Ch
Leningrad 1960

1	e4	e5
2	f4	ef4
3	Nf3	Be7
4	Nc3	Nf6
5	d4	d5
6	ed5	Nd5
7	Bc4	Be6
8	Qe2	Nc3
9	bc3	Bc4
10	Qc4	Bd6
11	Qb5	Nd7
12	Qb7	Qe7
13	Kf2	0–0
14	Re1	Qf6
15	c4 (Bd2)	Rab8
16	Qc6	Bb4
17	Qd7	Rbd8
18	Qc7	Be1
19	Ke1	Rd4
20	Kf2	Re4
21	Rb1	Qc3
22	Rb8	Qc2
23	Bd2	g6
24	h4	Qc4
25	Qa7	Rfe8
26	Re8	Re8
27	a4	h6
28	Qd7	Re2
29	Kg1	Qc5
30	Kh2	Qf2
31	Qc8	Kh7
32	Qg4	Rd2
33	Nd2	Qd2
34	h5	½–½

ILLUSTRATIVE GAME II

Castedo—Pulg
Spanish Corres. 1982

1	e4	e5
2	f4	ef4
3	Nf3	Be7
4	Nc3	Nf6
5	d4	d5
6	Bd3 (ed5)	de4
7	Ne4	Ne4
8	Be4	Bd6
9	0–0	Nd7
10	Qd3	Nf6
11	c4	c5
12	b4	cd4
13	c5	Bc7
14	Bb7!	Rb8
15	Bc8	Qc8
16	Re1	Kf8
17	Qd4	Qf5
18	Bb2	Rd8
19	Qc4	h5
20	Ne5	Nd5
21	Rad1	Ne3
22	Rd8	Bd8
23	Qd4	Qg5
24	Ng6	fg6
25	Qg7	Ke8
26	Qh8	Kd7
27	Qd4	Kc8
28	Qe4	Qh4
29	Re2	Qg4
30	Qa8	Kd7
31	Rd2	1–0

PROBLEMS

1. On **5... Nh5** (see Diagram 5C-3), what thematic reply virtually refutes Black's setup?

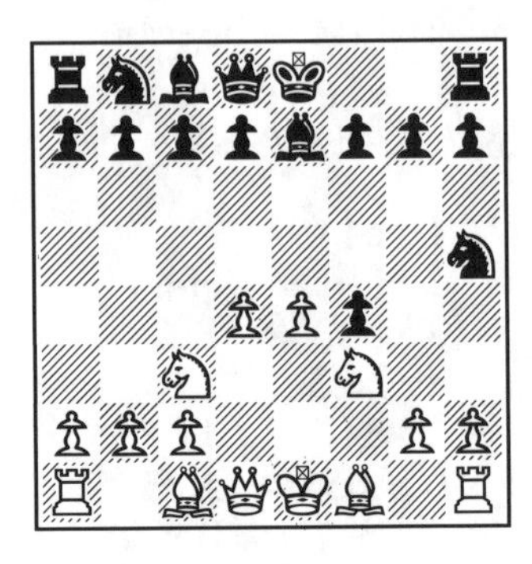

5C-3

2. Show that Black loses time with **7... Nc3 8 bc3 Bd6** (see Diagram 5C-4).

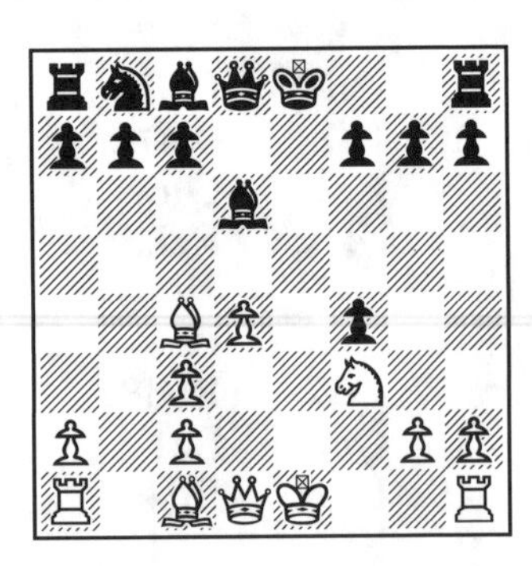

5C-4

3. Black might also adopt **12... 0–0.** After **13 0–0 Qf6** [12] (see Diagram 5C-5), prove that White is for choice.

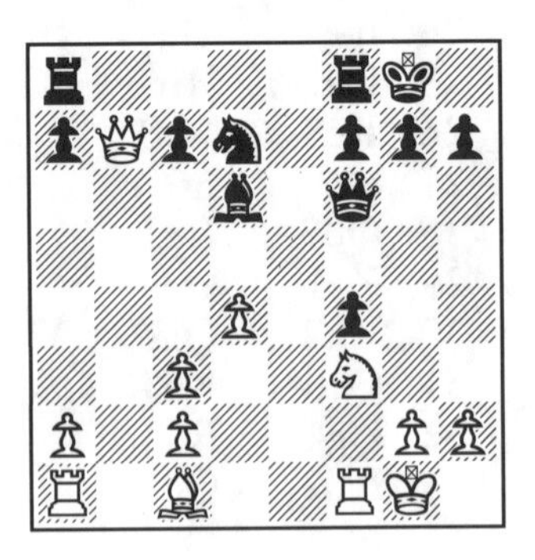

5C-5

6: BECKER VARIATION

One of Black's more salient Kingside pawn methods for holding the extra pawn is 3... h6, the Becker Variation:

1	**e4**	**e5**
2	**f4**	**ef4**
3	**Nf3**	**h6**
4	**d4**	

(For the interesting 4 b3 see Illustrative Game I.)

4	**...**	**g5**
5	**h4**	
	(g3)	

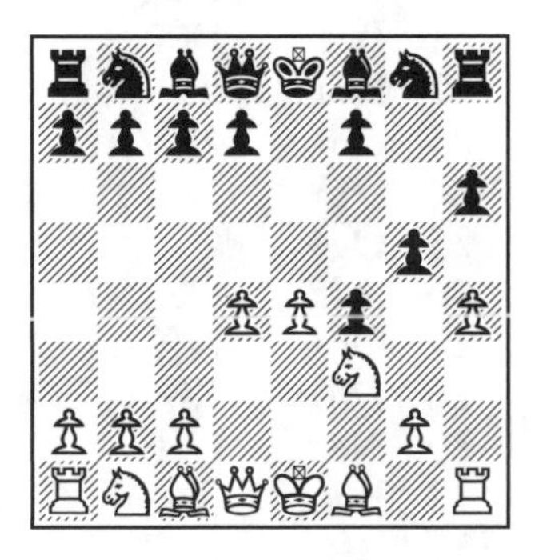

6-1

With his fifth move, White ducks 5 Nc3 Bg7 6 g3 d6! 7 gf4 g4 8 Ng1 Qh4 9 Ke2 Ne7! (Gallagher [19] is big on 5 Nc3 but only Trevor Hay mentions this possibility for Black here) 10 Be3 d5 11 e5 Be6 12 Qe1 Qe1 13 Re1 Nbc6∓ [5] and immediately puts pressure on g5.

Inconsistent now would be 5... g4?! 6 Ne5±, as Black would too easily relinquish his main objective — the support of his P/f4 by a pawn. Thus **5... Bg7** is more natural, refusing to enter the Kieseritzky Variation while hoping for 6 Bc4?! d6 which transposes into the Philidor Gambit. White, of course, need not be so obliging. With **6 g3** (6 hg5 hg5 7 Rh8 Bh8 8 g3 d6! 9 gf4 g4 10 Ng5 f6 11 Nh3 f5!∓), he can continue to derail Black's pawn train by not giving his opponent enough time to consolidate.

Misguided next is 6... d5[1] since 7 gf4 de4 (7... g4 8 Ne5) 8 Ne5 culminates rapidly into an advantage for White, so Black should opt for **6... g4** instead. Interesting here is the piece sacrifice line 7 Ne5 d6 8 Nf7 (see Illustrative

Game II); however, **7 Nh2** exploits the undefended advanced Black pawns without incurring such risks. There follows **7... fg3**[2] (7... h5 8 Bf4± when the N/h2 can go to *e3* via *f1*) **8 Ng4 d6** (8... h5 9 Ne5 △ c3-Qf3 and 8... d5 9 e5 h5 10 Bg5 f6 11 ef6 Nf6 — 11... Bg4 12 fg7 Rh6 13 Be2 or 12... Rh7 13 Qd3 — 12 Ne5 0–0 13 Be2) **9 c3 Nf6**[3] **10 Nf6 Qf6** (10... Bf6 11 Qh5) **11 Be3 Nc6 12 Nd2 Bd7 13 Qb3 0–0–0**⩲ [9].

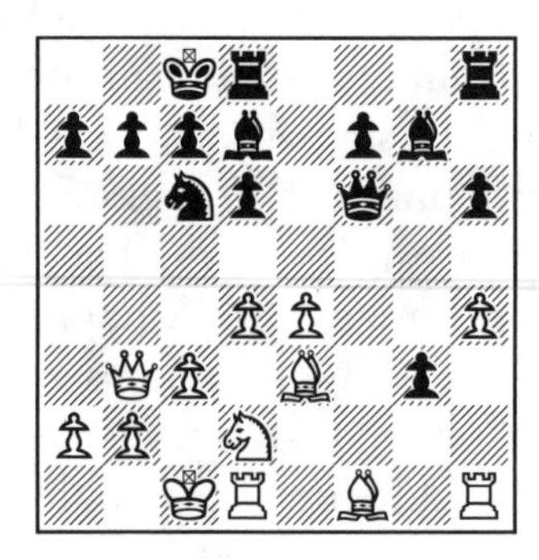

6-2

Black is a pawn up, but such a pawn! How does he defend it or return it in exchange for a good position? 14... Na5?, for instance, fails to 15 Qa3 Nc6 16 d5! △ Qa7. In fact, White's well-disposed pieces can discomfit Black on either wing. After Bg2, indirectly attacking *b7*, Rdf1 △ Bf4-Bg3 will also pressure *f7* and can quickly drive Black into an uphill battle.

ILLUSTRATIVE GAME I

Bangiev—Karolyi
Kecskemet (Teams) 1987

1	e4	e5
2	f4	ef4
3	Nf3	h6
4	b3	d6
5	Bb2	Nf6
6	Nc3	Be7
7	Qe2	0–0
8	0–0–0	Nc6
9	g3	Bg4
10	Qf2	Ne5
11	Be2	fg3
12	Qg3	Nh5
13	Qf2	Bf3
14	Bf3	Bh4
15	Qf1	Nf4
16	Rg1	c6
17	Bg4	Nfg6
18	Bf5	Bg5
19	Kb1	Ne7
20	d4	N5g6
21	Bc1	Bc1
22	Kc1	d5
23	e5	Nf5
24	Qf5	Ne7
25	Qg4	g6
26	Rdf1	Qc8
27	Qh4	Nf5
28	Qf6	Kh7
29	Ne2	Qe6
30	Rg6!	Qf6
31	Rf6	Ng7
32	Rf7	Kg8
33	Rf8	Rf8
34	Rf8	Kf8
35	Kd2	Ne6
36	Ke3	Kf7
37	c4	Nc7

38	Nf4	b5
39	Kd3	a5
40	cd5	cd5
41	a4	b4
42	Ke3	Ke8
43	Nd3	Ne6
44	Nc5	Nd8
45	Nd3	Nc6
46	Nf4	Ne7
47	Ne2	Kf7
48	Kf4	Kg6
49	Ng1	Nc6
50	Nf3	Kf7
51	Kf5	Ne7
52	Kg4	Ke6
53	Nh4	Nc8
54	Nf5	Nb6
55	Nd6!	Nd7
56	Nb5	Nb8
57	Kf4	Nc6
58	h4	Ne7
59	Nd6	Nc6
60	Nf5	h5
61	Kg5	Ne5
62	Ng7	Kd6
63	de5	Ke5
64	Nh5	Kd4
65	Nf4	Kc3
66	h5	Kb3
67	h6	Ka2
68	h7	b3
69	Nd3	1–0

ILLUSTRATIVE GAME II

Cheremisin—Volovich
Moscow 1964

1	e4	e5
2	f4	ef4
3	Nf3	h6
4	d4	g5
5	h4	Bg7
6	g3	g4
7	Ne5 (Nh2)	d6
8	Nf7	Kf7
9	Bc4	d5?
10	Bd5	Ke8
11	Bf4	Ne7
12	Nc3	Rf8
13	0–0	c6
14	Be5	Be5
15	Rf8	Kf8
16	Qf1	Nf5
17	de5	Qb6
18	Kh2	cd5
19	ef5	Qb2
20	Qf4	Qc2
21	Kg1	Qf5
22	Qh6	Ke8
23	Rf1	Qe5
24	Qf8	1–0

PROBLEMS

1. From Diagram 6-3, several alternatives should be examined:

a) **6... h5?**
b) **6... fg3.**
c) **6... d6.**
d) **6... f5.**

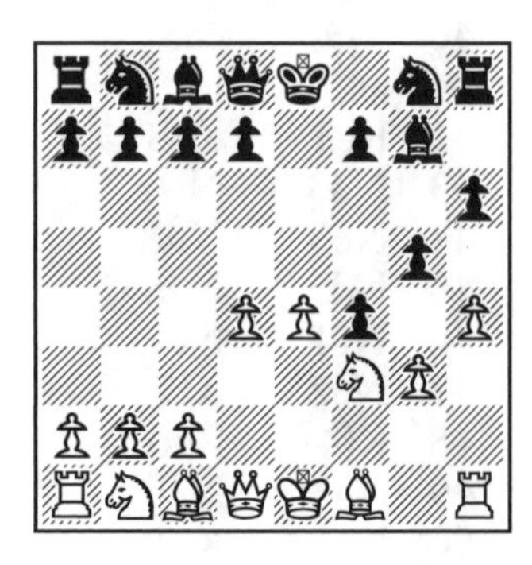

6-3

2. Reveal **7... f5** (see Diagram 6-4) as a premature sally.

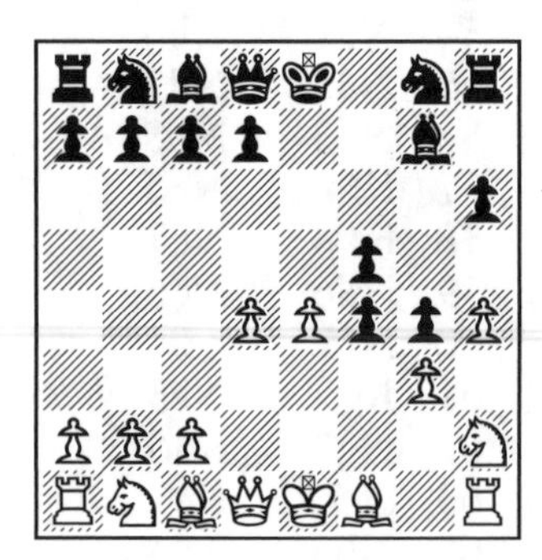

6-4

3. With **9... f5** (see Diagram 6-5) Black tries to neutralize White's center and to gain control of the b1-h7 diagonal. How should White react?

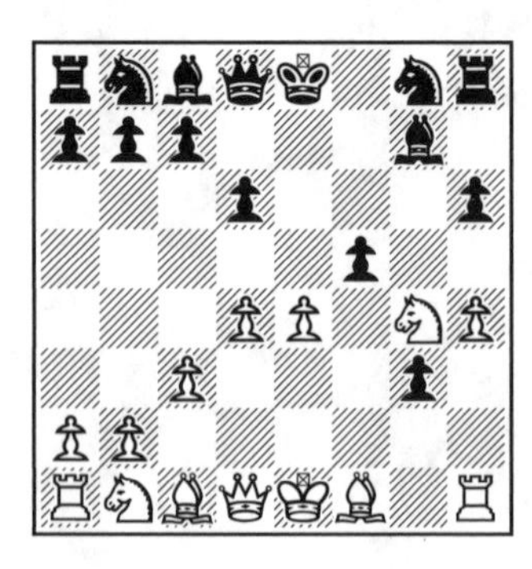

6-5

7: ALAPIN VARIATION

Sharp counterplay by Black is injected from the earliest moves with 3... f5, the Alapin Variation. Theory has shown this move to be insufficient, but not without a passel of poison!

1	e4	e5
2	f4	ef4
3	Nf3	f5
4	e5!	

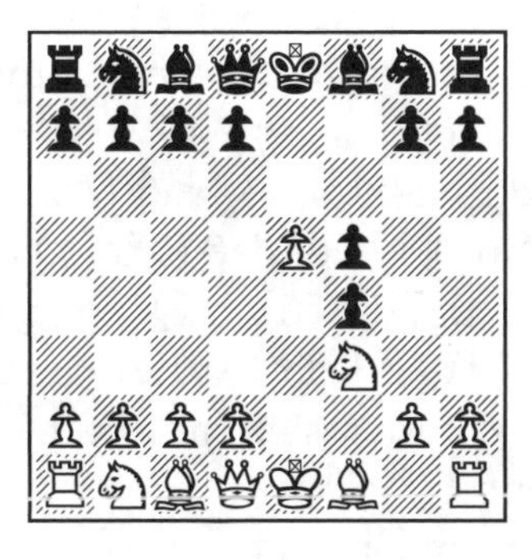

7-1

On 3... f5 Black threatens to disband White's center, and thus invites the first player to agree to a symmetrical pawn position with 4 ef5. White rightly demurs. Instead, by selecting 4 e5!, White maintains his influence in the center, prevents the natural ...Nf6-(Nh5), and prepares to restore material equality with d4-Bf4. Apparently, Black can easily support his advanced soldier on *f4* with **4... g5?;** however, following **5 d4 g4**[1] thematic sacrificial play quickly ensues from **6 Bf4! gf3 7 Qf3.** One typical sequence is **7... Qh4**[2] **8 g3 Qg4 9 Qe3 Nc6 10 Be2 Qg6 11 Nc3 Bb4 12 d5** (establishing a powerful central bind) **Nd8 13 0–0–0 (0–0)±** [12].

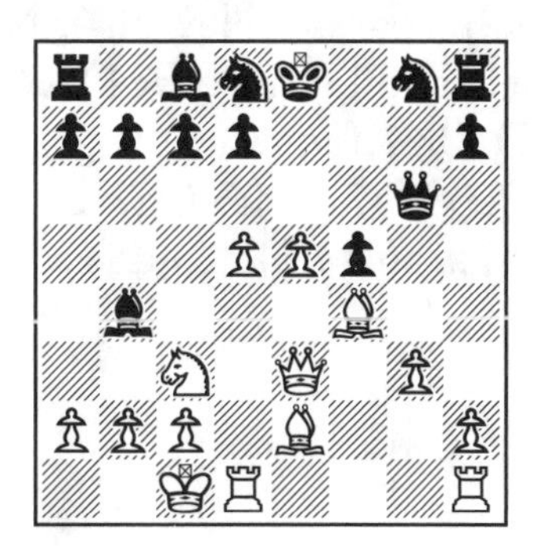

7-2

White has sacrificed his king's knight for a commanding lead in development and potent attacking prospects. Black, on the other hand, urgently needs to rectify his inert Q-side and weakened K-side squares.

Probably only Steinitz would take Black's position! If 13... Bc3 (for 13... h6 see the Illustrative Game), then 14 Qc3 △ Qc7-e6 is strong. Other plans include d6-e6 and Rhe1-Bc4-e6 when a dire fate awaits Black after only slightly indifferent play. Black should probably plan to return his material gain in a proper fashion in order to avoid a quick-kill by his opponent though it is by no means clear how Black can accomplish this.

No better after **4... g5? 5 d4 g4 6 Bf4! gf3 7 Qf3** is **7... h5.** Besides depriving White of the checking maneuver Qh5, this move prepares ...Ne7-Ng6. Nevertheless, following **8 Bc4** (△ Bg8-Qh5) **Qh4** (anyway!) **9 g3 Qg4 10 Qe3 Ne7 11 h3 Qg7 12 Nc3 c6** (12... a6 13 a4) **13 d5±,**

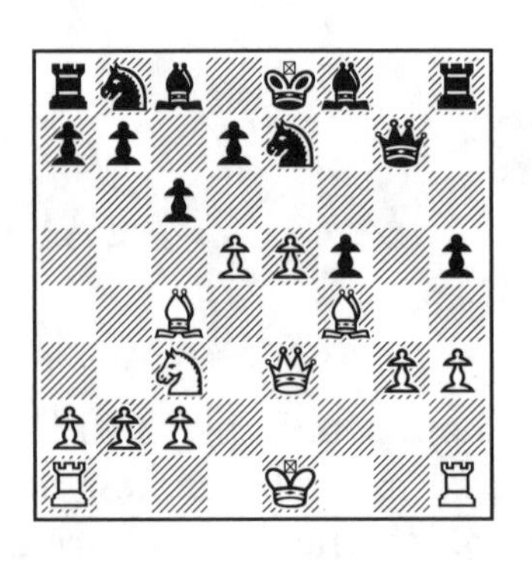

7-3

White's bishop-grip on the board emerges like a vise.

As Black squirms to meet the imminent threats of e6-Be5 and Bg5-Bf6, White might well intend 0–0–0-e6-Rhe1 to bare the center and expose Black's king to attack. For instance, unavailing is 13... Ng6?! due to 14 0–0–0 b6 15 d6 Nf4 16 gf4 Na6 (16... c5? 17 Nd5) 17 e6! de6 (17... Qf6 18 Rhe1 Bg7 19 ed7 △ Qe7) 18 Be6 Be6 19 Qe6 Kd8 20 Rhe1+– when Black can resign in good conscience.

From Diagram 7-1, Black may vary with 4... d6, but 5 Qe2! de5 (5... Be7 6 d4 Nc6 7 Bf4 de5 8 de5 Nd4 9 Qc4 Ne6 [9... Nf3 10 gf3 Bh4 11 Ke2] 10 Bd3) 6 Ne5 Qe7 7 d4 g5 8 Qh5 Kd8 9 Qg5!± [9] still offers him no solace. More sedate lines arise from **4... d5,** since after **5 d4** (h4) **g5 6 h4** (c4)

g4 White should reject 7 Bf4?! gf3 8 Qf3 due to 8... Be6!∓.

Correct here is **7 Ng1,** when an amusing configuration occurs which is somewhat akin to the Fischer Variation (cf. Diagram 4A-3). Once again, no pieces by either side are yet observed to have been moved! Here the burden of proof rests with Black as to whether his pawn structure is a bane or a boon. On **7... f3** (7... Be7? 8 Bf4 Bh4 9 g3) there comes **8 Bg5! fg2 9 Bg2 Be7 10 Nc3! Be6**[3] **11 Nge2 Qd7** (11.... h6 12 Nf4!) **12 Nf4 c6 13 Bf1**± [9].

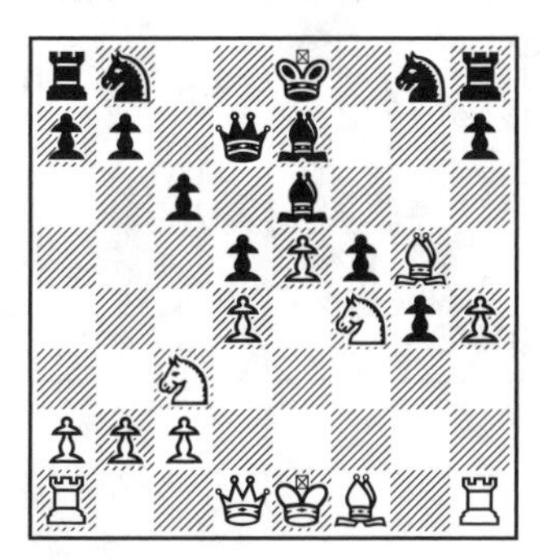

7-4

White's intentions are becoming more lucid. After Bd3 the natural Nce2-Ng3-c3-Qc2-0–0–0 will converge on the P/f5 while tucking away the king. Black can attempt to loosen the center by ...c5, but White is for choice owing to the excellent placement of his pieces.

ILLUSTRATIVE GAME

Schlechter—Teichmann
Wien 1903

1	e4	e5
2	f4	ef4
3	Nf3	f5
4	e5!	g5?
5	d4	g4
6	Bf4!	gf3
7	Qf3	Qh4
8	g3	Qg4
9	Qe3	Nc6
10	Be2	Qg6
11	Nc3	Bb4
12	d5	Nd8
13	0–0–0	h6
14	g4	Ne7
15	d6	Ne6
16	de7	Bc5
17	Qg3	Be7
18	gf5	Qf5
19	Be3	Bg5
20	Nd5	Be3
21	Qe3	Kd8
22	Rhg1	Qf8
23	Rdf1	Qc5
24	Qf3	Rf8
25	Rg8!	1–0

PROBLEMS

1. From Diagram 7-5, examine the alternatives:

a) **5... d5.**
b) **5... Bg7.**

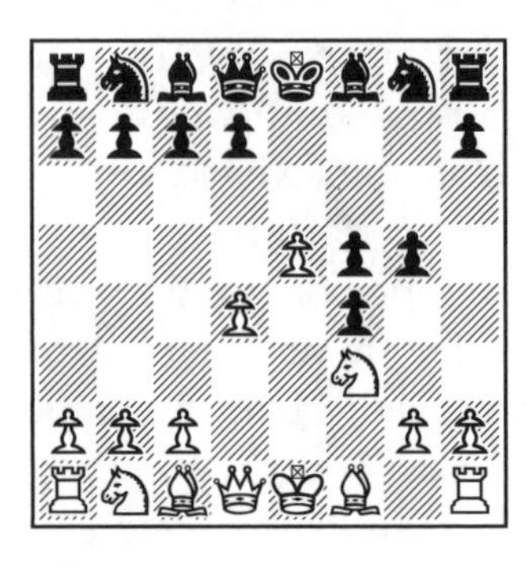

7-5

2. Black has lesser replies which White need not fear either. From Diagram 7-6, demote:

a) **7... d5?**
b) **7... Ne7?!**
c) **7... d6.**
d) **7... Qe7.**

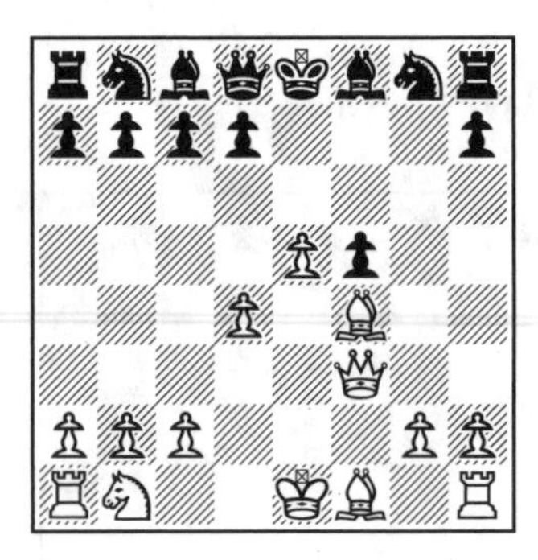

7-6

3. After **10... Bg5** (see Diagram 7-7), how should White proceed?

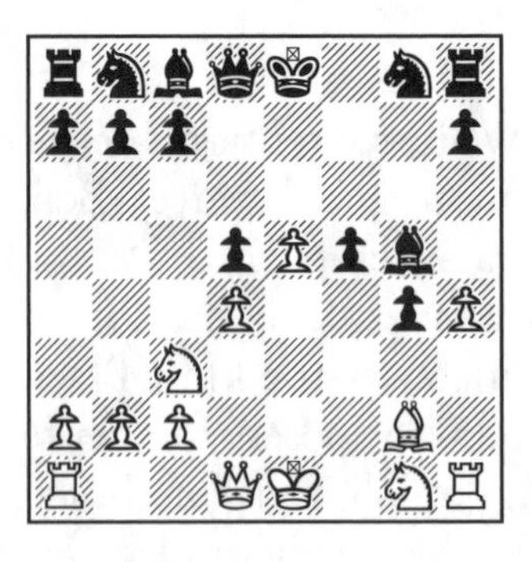

7-7

8: SCHALLOPP VARIATION

In the Schallopp Variation Black develops with attack:

1	**e4**	**e5**
2	**f4**	**ef4**
3	**Nf3**	**Nf6**
4	**Nc3**	

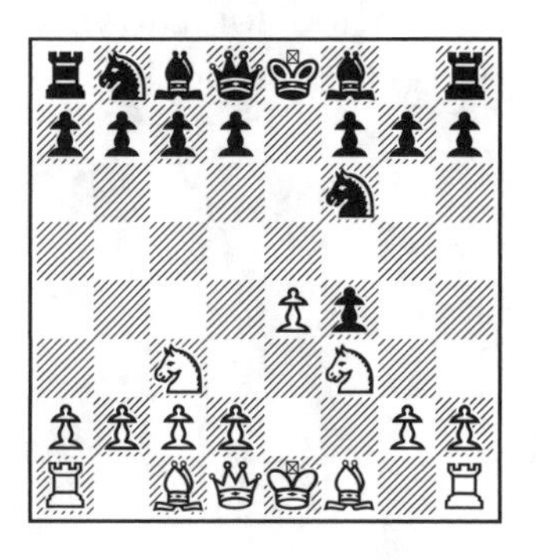

8-1

The alternative, 4 e5, may be overly ambitious (cf. the discussion of Diagram 5C-1). After the natural 4... Nh5, White gets nothing to write home about from 5 Be2 d6! 6 0–0 de5 7 Ne5 Bc5 8 Kh1 Nf6 9 Nd3 (9 c3 g5 [∞] 10 d4 Bd6 11 Nd2! Nbd7 12 Ndf3 h6 13 Bc4 Qe7 14 Qb3± [19] deserves attention) Bd6 10 Nf4 0–0 11 d4 c5! Probably no better, however, is Keres' 5 Qe2. Following 5... Be7 6 d4 0–0, either 7 Nc3 d6 8 Bd2 Nc6 9 0–0–0 Bg4 or 7 g4 fg3 8 Qg2 (8 Nc3 d6) d6 9 hg3 Bg4 10 Nh2 Ng3! 11 Rg1 Bf5! seems fine for Black.

Even on 5 d4, Black can secure a good position with 5... d6 (5... d5 6 c4 g5 7 g4 Ng7 [or 7... Bg4 8 Rg1±] 8 Nc3 Bb4 9 Rg1 h5 10 h3 c6 [19]. Further study of this new line is in order.) 6 Bb5 (6 Qe2 d5 7 c4 dc4! and if 8 Qc4 or 8 Qe4, then 8... Be6!) c6 7 Bc4 (7 Be2? de5 8 Ne5 Qh4, etc.) Bg4 8 0–0 Nd7 9 Qe1 d5 10 Be2 g5 △ ...h6-Be7-0–0-f5. Clearly then, in the 4 e5 continuation, ...d6 provides Black with a pressing challenge to White's intended grip on the center.

Instead, by calmly developing with 4 Nc3 White saves time and takes the bite out of ...d6. As in the Cunningham Variation (cf. Section 5C), Black's best reaction is to strike back in the center. Thus to be expected is **4... d5** (4...

h6 5 d4 g5 6 h4 g4 7 Nh2± — cf. Diagram 6-3) when White can avoid the complications of 5 e5 Ne4 6 Ne2! g5 7 d3 g4 8 Nf4 gf3 9 de4∞ [1] and achieve a promising setup with **5 ed5 Nd5**[1] (5... c6 6 d4 Bd6 leads to Diagrams 11A-4 and 11A-5, whereas 6... Nd5 can be met by 7 Nd5 Qd5 8 c4 Qe4 9 Kf2± [1]) **6 Nd5 Qd5 7 d4 Be7!**[2] **8 Be2!** Even here, care is required since 8 c4 Qe4 9 Be2 (9 Kf2 Bf5 10 Qa4 Nc6 11 Bd2 0–0–0 12 Re1 Qc2) Nc6 10 0–0 Bf5 11 Re1 0–0–0 12 Bf1 Qc2 allows Black to equalize comfortably. By postponing c4, White increases his options and forces his opponent to take time to protect the P/f4. Next, **8... g5 9 0–0 0–0** (9... Nc6 is similar) **10 b3**$\overline{\overline{\infty}}$ reaches Diagram 8-2.

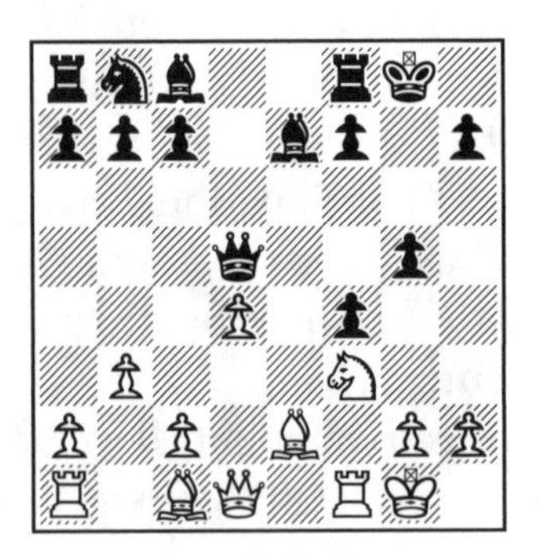

8-2

White has sufficient positional compensation for his sacrificed pawn. He can gain a tempo with Bc4 or c4 and may acquire good play on the a1-h8 diagonal with his dark-squared bishop.

Black, on the other hand, will be restricted in mobility by his inferior center and must stay alert for tactical shots. On 10... Bf5 11 c4 Qd6 12 Bb2 Bf6, White can consider 13 Bd3 Bg6 14 Bg6 hg6 15 Qc2 followed by Rad1-(Ne5) and Q-side expansion. If Black develops his queen knight to c6, then a3-b4-b5 may provide an effective method for carrying out this plan (cf. Diagram 9B-3).

PROBLEMS

1. Other moves are less natural. From Diagram 8-3, explore:

a) **5... Bd6.**
b) **5... Bb4.**

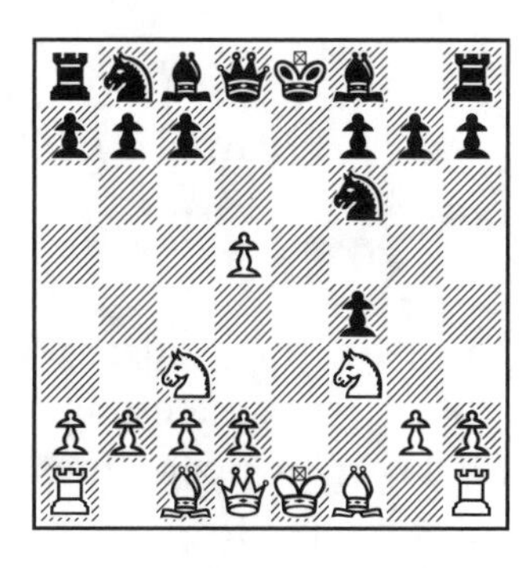

8-3

2. From Diagram 8-4, prove that Black errs with:

a) **7... Bd6.**
b) **7... Bg4.**
c) **7... g5?**

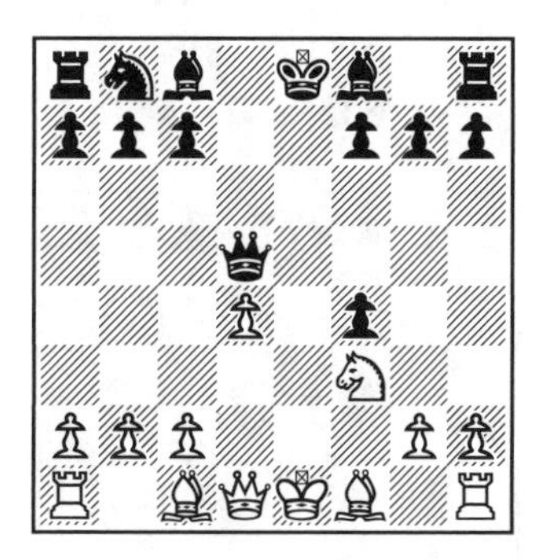

8-4

9: MODERN VARIATION (A)

On 3... d5, the Modern Variation, Black renounces material gain in favor of open lines and rapid development:

1	e4	e5
2	f4	ef4
3	**Nf3**	**d5**
4	**ed5**	

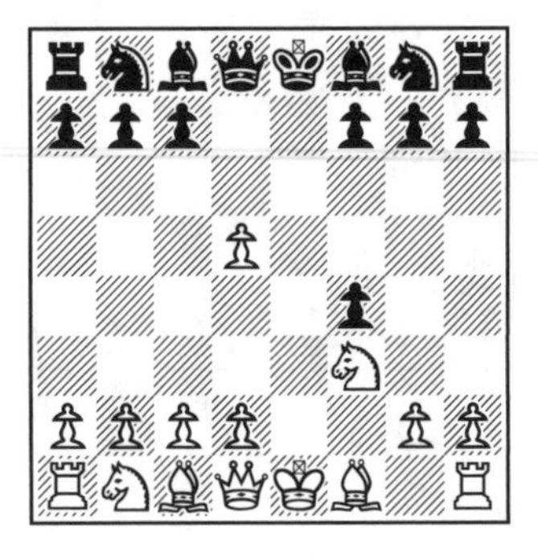

9A-1

With the sole exception of the transpositional line 1 e4 e5 2 f4 d5 3 ed5 ef4 4 Nf3 from the Falkbeer Variation (initiated by 2... d5), Black's counterattack in the center differs greatly from its counterpart in the King's Gambit Declined, (though in either line Black must play accurately). Here both 4... c6?![1] 5 d4 (5 dc6) cd5 (5... Bd6 6 dc6 Nc6 7 Bd3 Nf6 8 Qe2!) 6 Bf4 Nf6 7 Bd3 Bd6 8 Qe2 Be6 9 Bd6 Qd6 10 0–0 0–0 11 Nbd2 Nbd7 12 c3± [13] and 4... Qd5?! 5 Nc3 Qe6[2] (5... Qa5 6 Bb5 c6 7 Qe2!) 6 Kf2 (Be2) Qb6 (6... Nc6 7 Bb5 Ne7 8 d4 Qd6 9 Re1 Bd7 10 Ne4 Qh6 11 d5! Nb8 12 Bd7 Nd7 13 d6 Nc8 14 Nf6 Kd8 15 Re8 mate, Mazzeo–Bandoni, *Corres. 1983)* 7 d4 Nf6 8 Bb5 Δ Re1± [1] fail to do the job. If 4... g5?, then 5 Bc4 (Qe2) g4 (5... Bg7 6 d4 h6 7 Nc3 Ne7 8 0–0 Bf5 9 Ne5 Δ Qh5) 6 Qe2 Qe7 7 Nd4± [1] assures White of a substantial advantage.

More flexible but still inferior is **4... Bd6** Δ ...Ne7-Ng6. Enticing for White in this position is 5 Bb5, but 5... c6! 6 dc6 bc6 (also good is 6... Nc6 7 d4 Ne7!) 7 Bc4 (Be2) Ne7! Δ ...Ng6 leads to complex play for both sides. Therefore, **5 d4!** is in order so that White can contest 5... Ne7 with 6 c4 when 6... Ng6 7 Be2 0–0 8 0–0 b6 9 Nc3 c6 10 dc6 Nc6 11 Nb5 Be7 12 d5 Bc5 13 Kh1 Nce7 14 Nfd4 a6 15 Nc3 Bd6 16 Ne4 Be5 17 Nf3 Bb8 18 b4± [19] or 6... c6 7 Bd3 Bg4 8 0–0 Nd7 9 Nc3± [13] is promising for the first player. Even after **5... Nf6,** simply **6 c4 Bg4** (6... 0–0 7 Be2 Re8 8 0–0 c5 9 Nc3 Bg4 10 Kh1) **7 Bd3 0–0 8 0–0**± [13] leaves Black in discomfort.

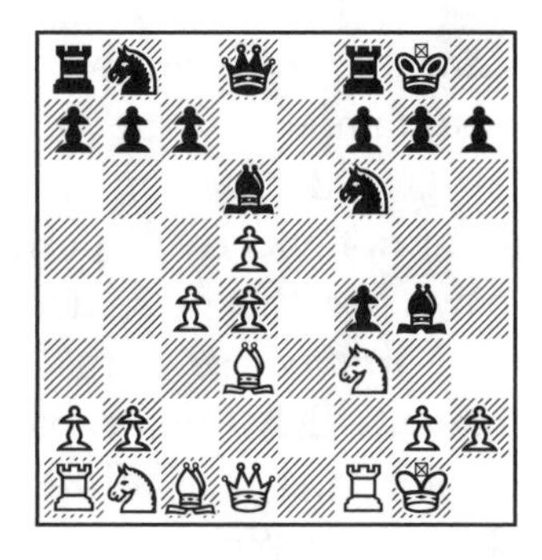

9A-2

White has achieved material parity and a bind with his central pawn mass. Since White controls most of the central squares, Black's pieces cannot easily advance onto enemy terrain. Here 8... b6 fails to 9 Qc2 c5 10 b4!, while 8... Nh5 9 Qc2 △ Ne5 is probably worse yet. Instead, 8... Bf3 9 Qf3 g5 may be necessary, though White retains a variety of attractive plans including Bf5-g3-c5 and g4-Kg2-h4-Rh1.

From Diagram 9A-1, on **4... Nf6, 5 Bb5** (or 5 Bc4!?, or 5 Nc3 which heads for Diagram 8-2) becomes thematic.

Here **5... Bd7 6 Bd7!** (6 Bc4 b5! 7 Qe2 Qe7 8 Qe7 Be7 9 Bb3 c5! 10 dc6 Nc6 11 d4 Bd6 12 Nc3 a6 13 0–0 0–0 is equal because tactically neither Nd5 nor Ne2 seems to generate lasting pressure despite the apparent weakness of the P/f4) **Nbd7** (6... Qd7 7 c4! Bd6 [7... c6 8 Ne5! △ 0–0] 8 0–0 0–0 9 d4 when possible are 9... c6 10 c5 △ d6-Ne5-Bf4, 9... Na6 10 Ne5 △ Bf4, and 9... Nh5 10 c5 Be7 11 Nc3 g6 12 Ne5 Qf5 13 g4! △ (Ne4)-gh5) **7 0–0 Nd5 8 c4± [13].**

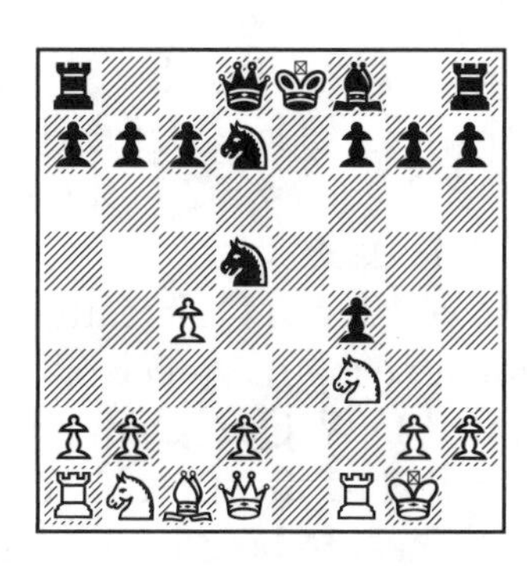

9A-3

Black is hardpressed to castle and develop his pieces efficiently. In particular, if 8... N5f6, then 9 Re1 Be7 10 Qe2 is exceedingly clumsy for Black; 8... N5b6 is similar. If 8... Ne7, then 9 Re1 Nb6 10 d4 △ Ne5/Bf4 offers White a completely fluid and natural attacking position. Note here that 10... Nc4?? loses to 11 Qa4.

After **4... Nf6 5 Bb5** (for 5 Bc4 see Illustrative Game II) Black can also call on **5... Nbd7,** although **6 c4** (for 6 0–0 see Illustrative Game I) guarantees White a plus. Now 6... a6 (6... Bd6 7 d4 0–0 8 0–0) 7 Bd7! Bd7 8 0–0± [9] clarifies the position at once as seein in the subsequent game Tait–Littlewood, *Sheffield 1991*, which went: 8... Be7 9 d4 b5 10 b3 0–0 11 Bf4 Qb8 12 Qd3 Qc8 13 Nbd2 Bf5 14 Qc3 a5 15 Ne5 Bb4 16 Qf3 bc4 17 bc4 Qa6 18 Bg5 Bd2 19 Qf5 Bg5 20 Qg5 Rae8 21 Rae1 Re7 22 Re3 h6 23 Qh4 Qb6 24 Rb3 Qd6 25 c5 Qd5 26 Rf6 Re5 27 de5 gf6 28 Qh6 Qc5 29 Kh1 1–0.

However, **6... Qe7** really does not improve matters much as demonstrated by **7 Qe2 Qe2 8 Ke2 Bd6 9 Re1 0–0 10 Kf1 a6 11 Bd7 Bd7 12 d4 b6 13 Nc3 Rfe8 14 Ne5 Be5 15 de5 Nh5 16 Bd2 Rad8 17 Kf2 g6 18 g3 fg3 19 hg3**± [12].

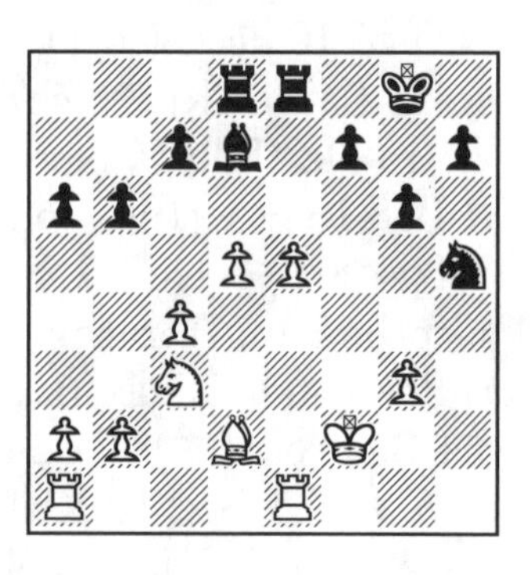

9A-4

White has a discernible pull. Black is cramped by the central duo on *d5* and *e5*, even though White cannot effectively push either pawn for the present. The position warrants an eventual ...c6 to achieve a light-square blockade in the center, but White can discourage this plan with Rad1 and/or Bg5. White might also select Bf4-Rh1-Rh2-Kf3-Rah1-g4 with the ultimate idea Rh7, provided the safety of the central duo is assured. By preparing g4 first, White can retain his dark-squared bishop. Opening a file for the R/a1 is yet another idea. Black might respond by trying to create an isolated pawn as a target, but inadvisable would be 19... Ng7 △ ...Nf5 on account of 20 Bg5.

ILLUSTRATIVE GAME I

Bronstein—Ragozin
Saltsjobaden 1948

1	e4	e5
2	f4	d5
3	ed5	ef4
4	Nf3	Nf6
5	Bb5	Nbd7
6	0–0 (c4)	Nd5
7	c4	N5f6
8	d4	Be7
9	Bf4	0–0
10	Ba4	Nb6
11	Bb3	Bg4
12	Nc3	c6
13	Qd2	a5
14	a3	a4
15	Ba2	Nbd7
16	Rae1	Re8
17	Ng5	Bh5
18	Kh1	Bg6
19	Nf3	Nh5
20	Be3	Qc7
21	Qd1	Qa5
22	Bd2	Qa7
23	c5!	b6
24	Bg5!	Bg5
25	Ng5	Nhf6
26	Re8	Re8
27	Qa4	Qa4
28	Na4	bc5
29	dc5	Re2
30	Bc4	Rc2
31	Bb3	Re2
32	Nf3	Ne4
33	Bd1	Re3
34	Kg1!	Nec5
35	Nc5	Nc5
36	Re1	Re1
37	Ne1	Kf8
38	Kf2	Ke7
39	Ke3	Kd6
40	b4	Na6
41	Be2	Nc7
43	Nf3	Nd5
43	Kd4	Nf4
44	Bf1	f6
45	Nd2	Ne6
46	Kc3	Nc7
47	Nc4	Ke7
48	Nb6	Nb5
49	Kb2	Bf5
50	a4	Na7
51	Kc3	h5
52	Kd4	Kd6
53	Nc4	Kc7
54	Kc5	Bd7
55	Nd6	h4
56	Be2	f5
57	g3	hg3
58	hg3	Nc8
59	Nc8	Bc8
60	Bf3	Bb7
61	a5	g5
62	Be2	f4
63	gf4	gf4
64	Bf3	Ba6
65	Bc6	Be2
66	b5	f3
67	a6	1–0

ILLUSTRATIVE GAME II

Gallagher—Balashov
Lenk 1991

1	e4	e5
2	f4	d5
3	ed5	ef4
4	Nf3	Nf6
5	Bc4	Nd5

6	0–0	Be7
7	d4	0–0
8	Bd5	Qd5
9	Bf4	c5
10	Nc3	Qc4
11	Qe1	Bf6
12	Bd6	Bd4
13	Kh1	Rd8
14	Ne4	f5
15	Qh4	Nc6
16	Ne5	Be5
17	Nf6	Bf6
18	Qc4	Kh8
19	Bc5	Ne5
20	Qe2	b6
21	Be7	Be7
22	Qe5	Bf6
23	Qc7	h6
24	Rae1	Ba6
25	Rf5	Bb2
26	h3	Rdc8
27	Qe7	Bc4
28	Qb4	Bd4
29	Re4	a5
30	Qd2	Bb2
31	Rh5	Rc6
32	Rc4	Rc4
33	Rh6	gh6
34	Qh6	Kg8
35	Qe6	1–0

PROBLEMS

1. Dispense with **4... Be7** (see Diagram 9A-5).

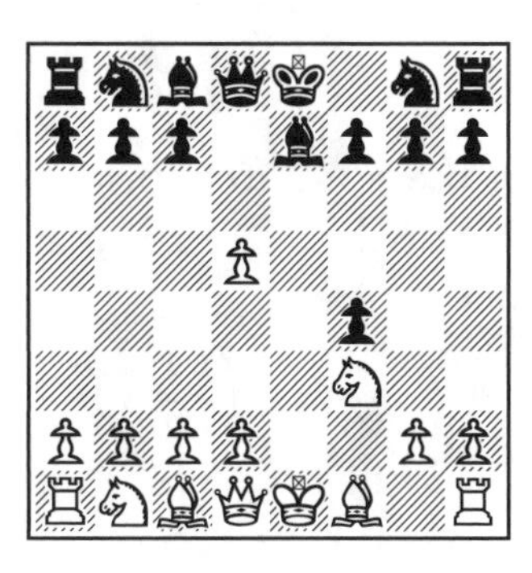

9A-5

2. Equally inadequate is **5... Qh5.** After **6 Be2** (see Diagram 9A-6), dismiss:

a) **6... Bd6.**
b) **6... Bg4.**

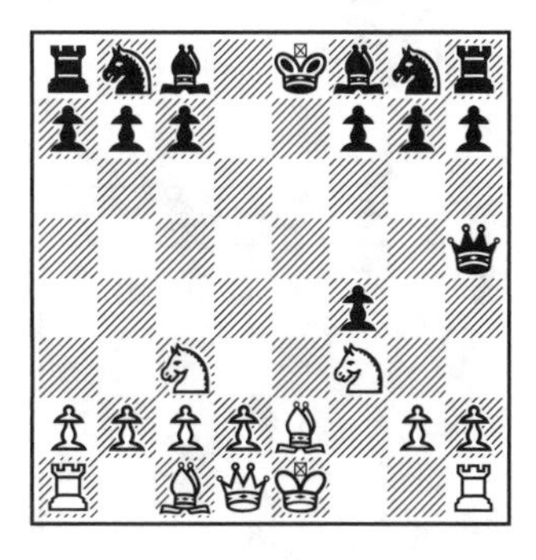

9A-6

Modern Variation (B)

In the 4... Nf6 continuation, Black also has 5... c6, a rather popular choice:

1	**e4**	**e5**
2	**f4**	**ef4**
3	**Nf3**	**d5**
4	**ed5**	**Nf6**
5	**Bb5**	**c6**
6	**dc6**	**bc6**[1]
7	**Bc4** (Be2)	

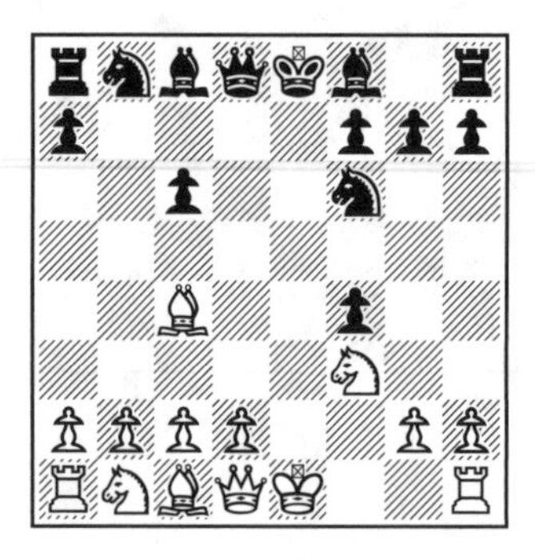

9B-1

Now both 7... Bg4? 8 Bf7! △ Ne5-Ng4 and 7... c5?! 8 Ng5± are bad for Black. **7... Nd5**[2] **8 Nc3!** (0–0) leaves him stymied for an adequate reply. One try, **8... Be6**[3], leads to **9 Bb3** (Qe2) **Bd6 10 Ne4 Bc7 11 Nc5** (see Diagram 9B-2).

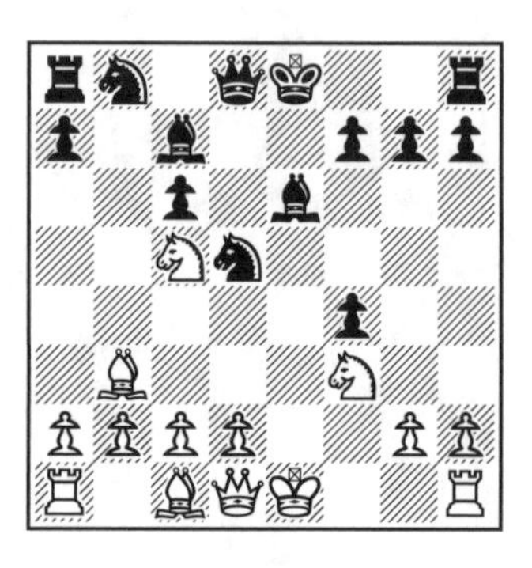

9B-2

Here neither 11... 0–0 12 Ne6 Re8 (12... fe6 13 d4) 13 0–0 Re6 14 c4± nor 11... Bg4 12 Qe2± [9], preparing to meet 12... Ne7? with 13 Bf7!, gives Black equality. Black's P/f4 stands in a firing range, and White will soon evict Black's knight from *d5*.

Another attempt after **7... Nd5 8 Nc3!** involves **8... Be7.** There follows **9 0–0** (d4) **0–0 10 d4 Nb6** (10... g5 transposes, and 10... Nc3 11 bc3 g5 12 h4 h6 — 12... g4 13 Ng5! — 13 hg5 hg5 14 Ne5 △ Ng6/Nf7-Qh5) **11 Bd3 g5 12 Ne2 Be6 13 b3 N8d7 14 c4 Bf6 15 Qc2** (Bc2!? △ Qd3) **h6 16 Bb2 Re8±** [9].

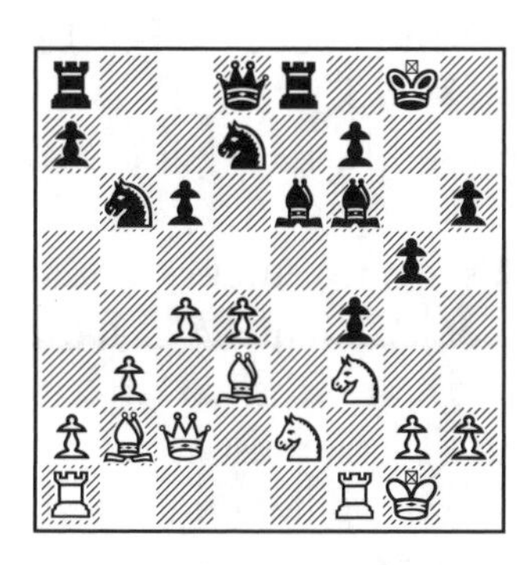

9B-3

White has a distinct positional superiority. In the long run, he has good chances to create a connected pair of passed pawns since the imminent a4-b4, along with Be4, should induce Black to further compromise his Q-side pawn structure. To draw off Black's P/c6, White also can break on *d5* and, when expedient, temporarily sacrifice a pawn on that square.

More directly, however, Black must handle an annoying invasion of White's pieces. After 17 Nd2, both 17... a5 18 Ne4 Bg7 19 Nd6 △ Ba3-Nf5 and 17... Bg7 18 Ne4 Qe7 (18... Qc7 19 Ba3 △ Bd6/Nd6) 19 a4 △ Ba3-Nd6 force Black to muster all his defensive faculties to avoid a lethal cramp.

From Diagram 9B-1, Black can vary with **7... Bd6.** The reply 8 **Qe2** leaves Black with two main alternatives, **8... Qe7** (8... Be7 9 d4) and 8... Kf8. The first results in **9 Qe7 Ke7 10 0–0.**

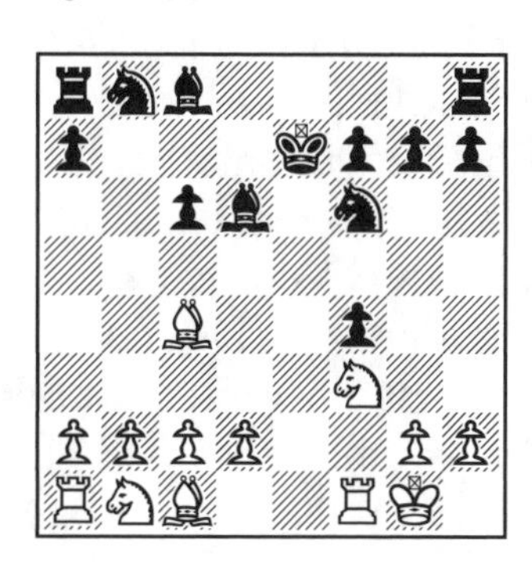

9B-4

Here, nothing comes of 10... Rd8 (10... Nh5 11 d4 Be6 12 Ne5, and for 10... Re8 11 Nc3 see Illustrative Game II which transposes), a move played to worry White on the d-file. A plausible sequel is 11 Nc3 Nbd7 12 d4 h6 13 Bd2 g5 14 Rae1 Kf8 15 Bc1± [12], whereupon White, having taken his queen bishop out of the reach of Black's R/d8, can consider h4-(Ne5). If Black tries 15... Nb6 △ Bb7-Nbd5, then 16 Bd3 △ Ne4-h4 still offers White active play against Black's extended K-side pawns and also heralds the onset of a Q-side pawnstorm.

In contrast, Black might prefer 10... Be6 (from Diagram 9B-4) to exchange off White's well-placed B/c4 without losing time. The drawback of this strategy is that Black must accept a weak pawn on *e6*. Thus, if 11 Re1 Nbd7 12 d4 Rhe8 13 Be6 fe6 14 Nbd2 h6 15 Nc4± [9], White can plan b3-Bb2-Ne5 to smother Black's ...e5 break before thematically advancing the Q-side pawns.

Returning to Diagram 9B-1, Black's best move after **7... Bd6 8 Qe2** may well be **8... Kf8.** There can follow **9 d4** (Ne5!?) **Bg4 10 0–0 Nbd7** (10... c5 11 dc5 Bc5 12 Kh1 g5 13 Qe5±) **11 Nc3** (also note 11 Bb3 Qc7 12 Na3 Re8 13 Qd3 △ c3-Bd2-Rae1 [1]) **Qc7**⩲ [9]

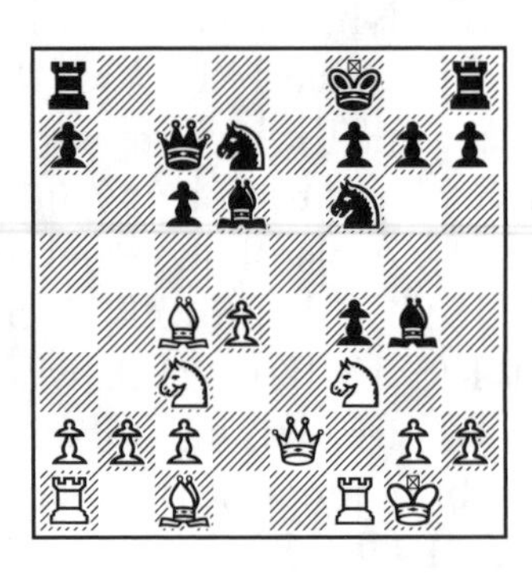

9B-5

when both ...Re8 and ...g5-Rg8 are in the air.

White, of course, is not impotent. With 12 Qf2! he can quietly build pressure against Black's P/f4 while removing his queen from its uncomfortable post on the e-file. Now both 12... Re8 13 Ng5± and 12... Nb6 13 Bb3 Nbd5 14 Ne5± favor White; but 12... Bf3 13 Qf3 Qb6 (13... g5 14 Ne4!) 14 Kh1!± also misses the mark, since on 14... Qd4? 15 Qc6 △ Qa8-Nb5+– Black's game quickly collapses. Steadier is 12... h6 (△ g5), though 13 Ne5 can lead to an ending wherein Black must cope with his lag in development and the peculiar position of his king.

ILLUSTRATIVE GAME I

Spassky—Sakharov
USSR Ch, Leningrad 1960

1	e4	e5
2	f4	ef4
3	Nf3	d5
4	ed5	Nf6
5	Bb5	c6
6	dc6	bc6
7	Bc4	Nd5
8	0–0 (Nc3)	Bd6
9	Nc3	Be6
10	Ne4	Be7
11	Bb3	0–0
12	d4	Nd7
13	Qe2	g5
14	c4	N5b6
15	h4!	h6
16	hg5	hg5
17	Nfg5	Bg5
18	Bf4 (Qh5!)	Bf6
19	Rad1	Bf5
20	Be5!	Be4

21	Qe4	Be5
22	de5	Qg5
23	Rf5	Qg7
24	Qf4	Rfe8
25	Rg5	Ne5
26	Rg7	Kg7
27	Rd6	Ng6
28	Qf6	Kg8
29	Bc2	Nc4
30	Rd7	1–0

ILLUSTRATIVE GAME II

Tripolsky—Tsayek
Dnyepropetrovsk 1987

1	e4	e5
2	f4	ef4
3	Nf3	d5
4	ed5	Nf6
5	Bb5	c6
6	dc6	bc6
7	Bc4	Bd6
8	Qe2	Qe7
9	Qe7	Ke7
10	Nc3	Re8
11	0–0	Kf8
12	d4	h6
13	Ne5!	Be5
14	de5	Ng4
15	Bf4	Be6
16	Be6	Re6
17	Rad1	g5
18	h3	Ne5
19	Be5	Re5
20	Rd6	h5
21	Rd8	Re8
22	Re8	Ke8
23	Ne4	g4
24	Nf6	Ke7
25	h4	Na6
26	Nh5	Rb8
27	b3	Rd8
28	Re1	Kf8
29	Re2	Rd5
30	Nf6	Rd4
31	c3	Rf4
32	Rf2	1–0

ILLUSTRATIVE GAME III

Dahl—Chance
Golden Knights, 1988

1	e4	e5
2	f4	d5
3	ed5	ef4
4	Nf3	Nf6
5	Bb5	c6
6	dc6	Nc6
7	d4	Bd6
8	0–0	0–0
9	Nbd2	Bg4
10	c3	Rc8
11	Nc4	Bb8
12	Qd3	Qd5
13	Bc6	bc6
14	Nfe5	g5
15	Bf4	gf4
16	Rf4	1–0

PROBLEMS

1. **6... Nc6** (Black's best recapture) **7 d4** (see Diagram 9B-6) leaves Black to try to blunt White's growing initiative. Combat:

   a) **7... Qa5.**
   b) The important **7... Bd6.**

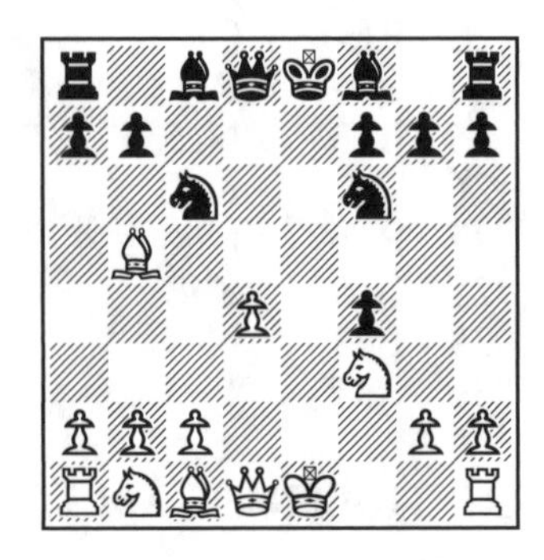

9B-6

2. Following **7... Qe7 8 Be2** (see Diagram 9B-7), answer:

   a) **8... g6.**
   b) **8... Bg4.**

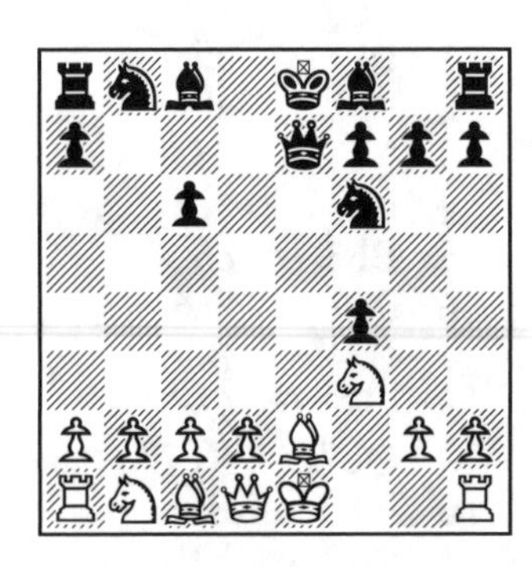

9B-7

3. **8... Nc3 9 dc3!** (see Diagram 9B-8) does not enhance Black's prospects. Investigate:

   a) **9... Qd1.**
   b) **9... Bd6.**

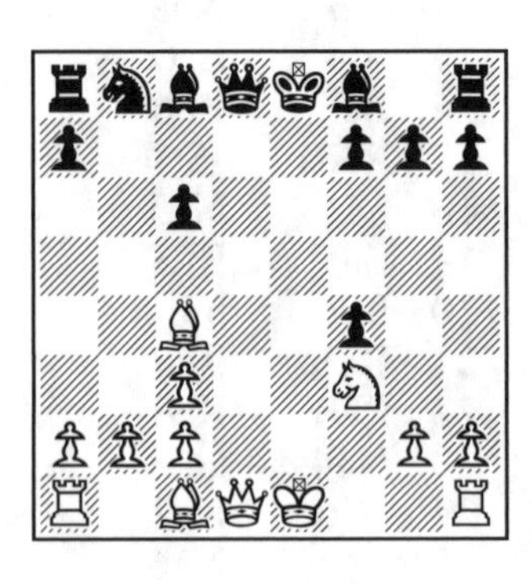

9B-8

10: LESSER ACCEPTED VARIATIONS

On his third move, Black can avoid conventional setups by entering one of the Lesser Accepted Variations:

1	**e4**	**e5**
2	**f4**	**ef4**
3	**Nf3**	

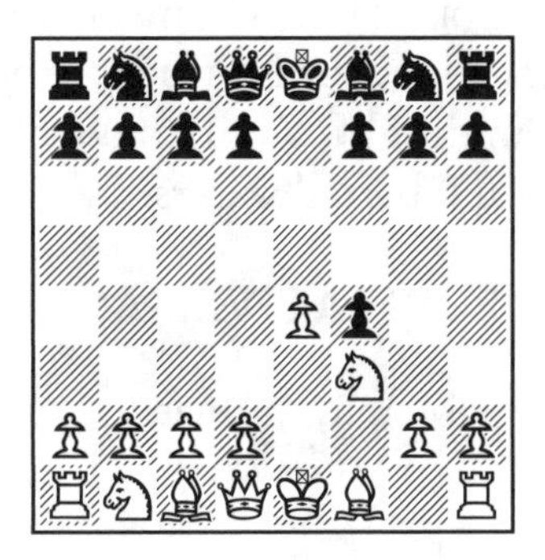

10-1

If 3... b6 then 4 d4. Iowa City master Kevin Burnett has tested out the Sicilian-like line 3... c5 4 Bc4 (4 d4) Nc6 5 d4 cd4 6 Bf4 Qf6 7 Bg5 Qg6 8 0–0 Be7 9 Be7 Nge7 10 Nd4 0–0 when 11 Nf5!?± (Nc3) can be essayed. The jury is still out on Burnett's idea.

The only other offbeat moves worth serious attention are 3... c6[1] and 3... Ne7. Against the former, Morphy once chose 4 Nc3 and speedily dismantled an amateur at a simultaneous blindfold exhibition (see Illustrative Game I). More forcing, however, is 4 d4 when on 4... d5 (else the P/f4 falls) White can head for Diagram 11A-3 or 11A-4 of the Falkbeer Variation with 5 ed5, or select quieter lines with 5 Nc3.

Less demanding of White is **3... Ne7,** since Black remains worse after the logical **4 d4.** Faulty next is 4... Ng6 due to 5 Bc4[2] (clearer than 5 h4!? h5 6 Nc3 Be7 7 Bc4 Nh4 8 0–0∞̄), but even **4... d5 5 Nc3** (e5) **de4 6 Ne4 Nd5**[3] (6... Bg4 7 Be2 Nd5 8 0–0 Nc6 9 c4 Ne3 10 Be3 fe3 11 d5 Nb4 [11... Bf3 12 Rf3 Ne5 13 Re3] 12 a3 Na6 13 Ne5 Be2 14 Qe2 f6 [14... Qh4 15 Qe3 △ Nf7] 15 Qh5 g6 16 Ng6 hg6 17 Qg6 Kd7 18 Nf6+–) **7 Qe2 Be7 8 c4 Ne3 9 Be3 fe3 10 Qe3 0–0 11 0–0–0!±**

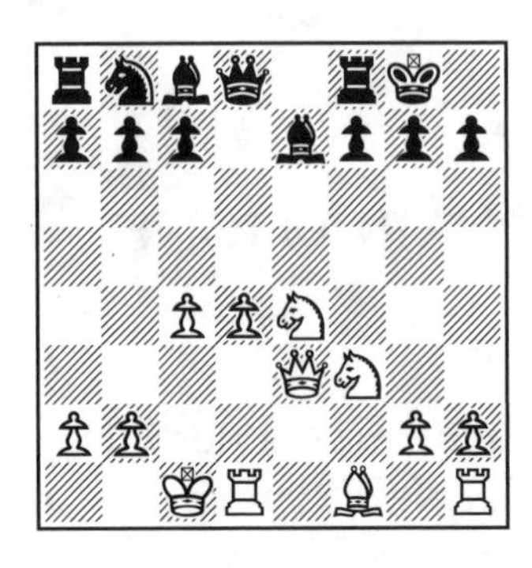

10-2

leaves White with a considerable advantage in space. After 11... Nc6, the natural 12 Bd3 △ Rhe1 can be played to complete the centralization of White's forces while preparing shots like d5 and Neg5.

Finally, near to press-time a new line—the Diemer Variation—has been unearthed by Tim Sawyer, having apparently been played by E.J. Diemer of Blackmar-Diemer fame. In the Diemer Variation, Black plays 3... Qe7 with the view to pressuring White's e4-pawn from the get-go. This Queen junket is also seen, it might be noted, in the Keene Variation (cf. Ch. 15). As in the Keene Variation, here too Black's concept appears non-trivial.

White's best fourth move answer from among 4 e5 d6, 4 Qe2 b6 △ Ba6, 4 d3 d5, 4 d4 Qe4, and 4 Nc3 is unquestionably 4 Nc3. Black, the reader should verify for himself, blithely appears to equalize in the other lines. After 4 Nc3 Nf6 5 e5 d6 6 d4 de5 7 de5 Ng4 8 Bf4 Nbd7 9 Qe2 △ 0–0–0 White must be judged the better owing to superior development. Another idea for Black is 4... d5 when 5 e5 c6 (5... Be6 6 d4 g5 7 h4 g4 8 Ng5 or 5... Bg4 6 d4 Bf3 7 Qf3 Qh4 8 Qf2 Qf2 9 Kf2 Nc6 10 Bb5 Nge7 11 Bf4 0–0–0 12 Rad1 a6 13 Ba4 f6 14 ef6 gf6 15 Rf1 △ Kg1) 6 d4 g5 7 h4 g4 8 Ng1 Bh6 9 Nge2 is reminiscent of the Fischer Variation of Ch. 4. This survey is intended to spur the reader to burn the midnight oil in navigating these uncharted waters.

ILLUSTRATIVE GAME I

Morphy—Amateur
1858

1	e4	e5
2	f4	ef4
3	Nf3	c6?
4	Nc3 (d4)	Bb4
5	Bc4	Bc3
6	dc3	Ne7
7	Qd6	0–0
8	Bf4	Ng6
9	Bg5	Qe8
10	0–0	Kh8
11	Rae1	f6
12	e5	f5
13	Nd4	f4

14	e6	de6
15	Ne6	Be6
16	Re6	Qc8
17	Rg6	hg6
18	Qg6	Qf5
19	Rf4!	Qg6
20	Rf8	Kh7
21	Bg8	Kh8
22	Bf7	Kh7
23	Bg6	1–0

ILLUSTRATIVE GAME II

Spassky—Seirawan
1985

1	e4	e5
2	f4	ef4
3	Nf3	Ne7
4	d4	d5
5	Nc3	de4
5	Ne4	Ng6
7	h4	Qe7
8	Kf2	Bg4
9	h5	Nh4
10	Bf4	Nc6
11	Bb5	0–0–0
12	Bc6	bc6
13	Qd3	Nf3
14	gf3	Bf5
15	Qa6	Kb8
16	Nc5	Bc8
17	Qc6	Rd4
18	Rae1	Rf4
19	Qb5	Ka8
20	Qc6	Kb8
21	Re7	Be7
22	Rd1	Rf6
23	Nd7	Bd7
24	Qd7	Rd8
25	Qb5	Kc8
26	Rd8	Bd8
27	Qa4	g5
28	Qa7	Rf4
29	Qa6	Kb8
30	Qd3	Be7
31	Qh7	g4
32	Kg3	1–0

ILLUSTRATIVE GAME III

Glazkov—Soloviev
Moscow 1971

1	e4	e5
2	f4	ef4
3	Nf3	Nc6
4	Nc3	g5
5	h4	g4
6	Ng5	h6
7	Nf7	Kf7
8	d4	d5
9	Bf4	Bb4
10	Be2	Bc3
11	bc3	Nf6
12	0–0	Kg7
13	c4!	de4
14	d5	Ne7
15	Be5	Rf8
16	Qd4	Ng6
17	Bf6	Rg6
18	h5	Nf8
19	Rf4	Nh7
20	Raf1	Bd7
21	Bg4	Bg4
22	Rg4	Kf7
23	Qe4	Rf1
24	Kf1	Ng5
25	Qg6	Ke7
26	Qg7	Nf7
27	Re4	Kd6
28	Qg3	Kc5
29	Qf2	1–0

PROBLEMS

1. The "waiting move" **3... Nc6** (see Diagram 10-3) is interesting. If White responds with 4 Nc3, reaching a Vienna Game (see Illustrative Game III), then a favorable version of the Hamppe-Allgaier Gambit occurs. What other move works here for White?

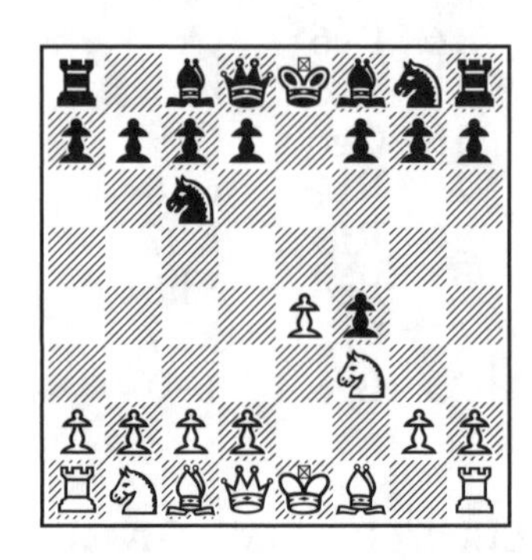

10-3

2. Following **5... Be7 6 0–0** (see Diagram 10-4) White can snare Black's P/f4. Take a look at:

a) **6... 0–0.**
b) **6... d6.**

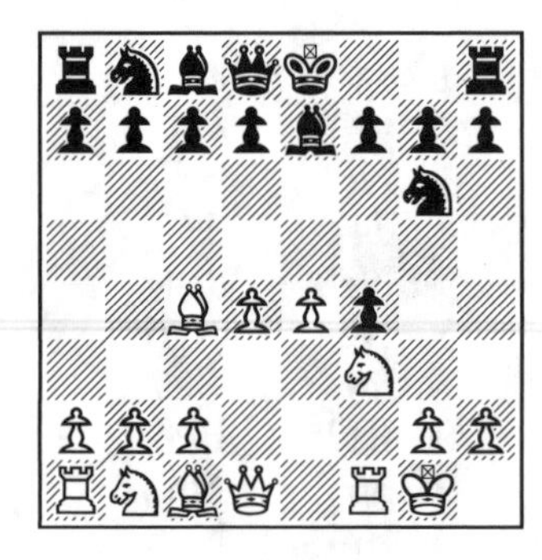

10-4

3. If instead **6... Ng6,** then **7 h4!** (see Diagram 10-5) applies strong pressure:

a) Prove that Black cannot afford **7... h5?!**
b) After **7... Be7** (for 7... Qe7 see Illustrative Game II preceding), what nettlesome riposte keeps Black off balance?

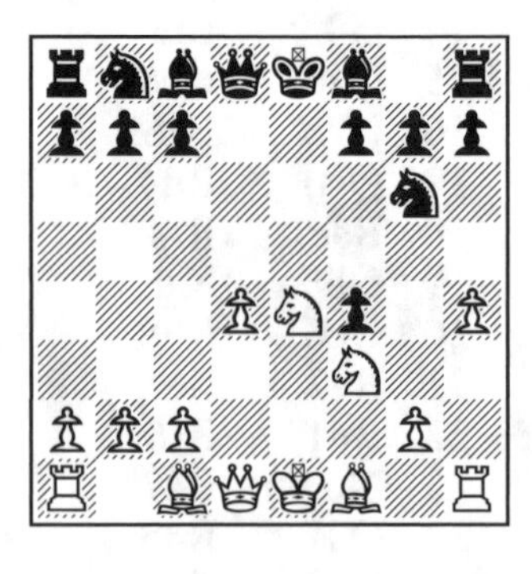

10-5

Part II

THE KING'S GAMBIT DECLINED

11: FALKBEER VARIATION (A)

One of Black's most violent attempts to wrest the initiative in the King's Gambit is 2... d5 — the Falkbeer Variation:

1	**e4**	**e5**
2	**f4**	**d5**
3	**ed5**	
	(Nf3!?)	

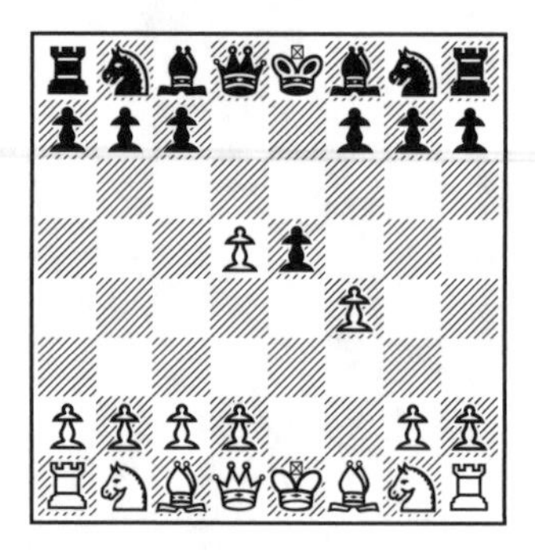

11A-1

The position is double-edged, and a fierce struggle can already be predicted. Black has disrupted the center to attain open diagonals for both of his bishops with a view toward easy development. In some lines Black even elects to remain a pawn down to disorganize White's forces. Still, White can expect the better chances by carefully wending his way through the tactical maze of this countergambit.

First of all, 3... ef4 (on 3... Bc5 the retort 4 Nc3!± deters ...e4, as in 4... Bg1 5 Rg1 Qh4 6 g3 Qh2 7 Rg2 Qh1 8 fe5 Bh3 9 Rf2 △ Qf3. Note that 4... Nh6 was tried in Illustrative Game II.) 4 Nf3 transposes to the Modern Variation (cf. Ch. 9). Alternatively, Black can grab a center pawn with 3... Qd5. After 4 Nc3 Qd8[1] 5 Nf3 (fe5!?) Bc5 6 Bb5[2]±, however, White threatens both fe5-d4 and Qe2.

Quite different lines arise from **3... c6,** the Nimzovich Continuation. One accurate response, **4 Nc3** (better than 4 dc6 Nc6 or 4 Qf3 ef4 5 dc6 Nc6 6 Bb5 Qb6!, although 4 d3 Qd5 5 Qe2! [13] warrants consideration), allows Black several roads from which to choose. Unrecommendable next is 4... Bb4 due to 5 Nf3 Bc3 6 dc3 e4 7 Ne5 cd5? 8 Bb5±, e.g., 8... Nd7? 9 Qd5+– [9].

Somewhat steadier is **4... cd5.** Nevertheless, **5 Bb5!±,**

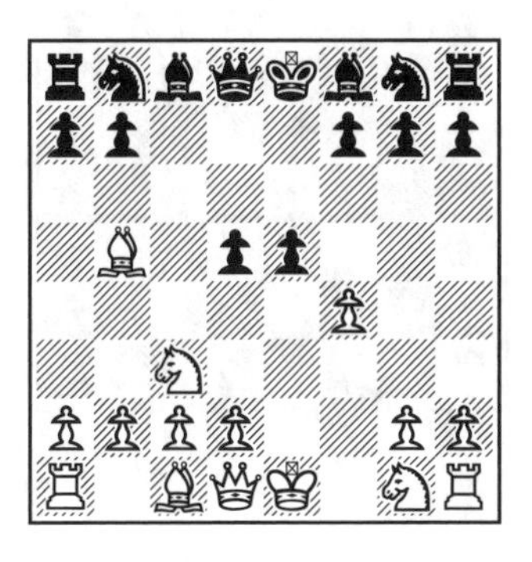

11A-2

intending 6 Qe2, appears to improve over Estrin's 5 fe5 d4 6 Ne4 Qd5 7 Bd3 (7 d3!? or 7 Qe2 Nc6 8 Nf3 Bg4 9 c4 dc3 10 dc3 0–0–0 11 Bf4 Ne5 12 Be5 Bf3 13 Qf3 Qe5 14 Be2 f5!) Nc6 8 Qe2, since 8... Ne5 9 Bb5 Bd7 10 Bd7 Kd7! △ ...Re8 would permit Black to become too active.

Here 5... Nc6 (5... Bd7 6 Qe2) 6 Qe2 e4 7 d3 Bb4 8 de4! cuts across Black's plans. As 8... Bc3 9 bc3 △ Ba3 offers White a pair of mighty bishops, Black must turn to 8... d4.

However, with 9 Qc4! White remains in command. For instance, if 9... Bd7, then 10 Bc6 Bc3 11 bc3 Bc6 12 Nf3! is hard to meet. A sample line is: 12... dc3 13 Ne5 Qc7 14 Ba3 Nh6 15 Qc3 0–0–0 16 Nc6 Qc6 17 Qc6 bc6 18 0–0 Rd2 19 Rf2 Rhd8 20 Bc5 Rf2 21 Bf2 Kb7 22 h3 Rd2 23 Rc1 △ Kf1-Be3. Or, 12... Be4 13 Ne5 Nh6 14 Qa4 Kf8 15 Ba3 Kg8 16 0–0 △ cd4/Rad1.

Going back to Diagram 11A-1, following **3... c6 4 Nc3** Black might prefer **4... ef4** △ ...Qh4. Then **5 Nf3** leaves Black with two main possibilities: 5... Bd6 and 5... Nf6. In the first place, quite commonly seen is **5... Nf6** (5... cd5 6 d4 transposes) when **6 d4 Bd6**[3] **7 Qe2** presents Black with yet another decision. On one try, the radical **7... Kf8!?,** White has **8 Ne5 cd5 9 Bf4! Nc6** (9... Qb6 10 0–0–0) **10 0–0–0 Be5** (for 10... a6 cf. Illustrative Game I, whereas 10... Bf5 can be met by 11 Qe3± [9]) **11 de5 Bg4 12 Qd2 Ne4**[4] **13 Ne4 Bd1** (13... de4 14 Qd6±) **14 Nd6**$\overline{\overline{\infty}}$

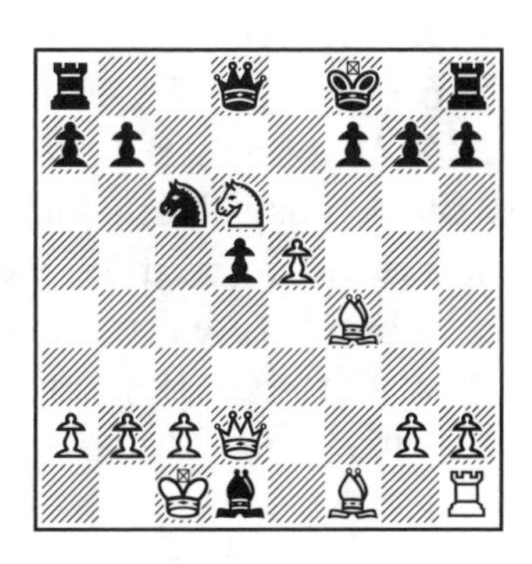

11A-3

with comfortable compensation

for the exchange.

As Black must retreat his B/d1, he cannot hold his pawn on *d5*. Clearly 14... Bh5 15 Qd5± △ Bc4-Rf1-e6 gives White excellent attacking prospects, but even after 14... Bg4 Black stays on the defensive. A typical sequel is 15 Qd5 Be6 16 Qc5 Qe7 (16... Qb6 17 Qb6 ab6 18 a3 Ra4 19 Bg3 Bd5 20 Rg1 △ Bb5-c4-Nb7) 17 Nb7 Qc5 (17... Rc8 18 Nd6 Rc7 19 Bb5±) 18 Nc5$\overline{\overline{\infty}}$ with two pawns for the exchange and a promising ending for White. Examples include 18... Ke7 19 Bg5 f6 20 ef6 gf6 21 Ne6! Ke6 22 Bc4 △ Bd2/Bh4 and 18... Bf5 (18... Ba2? 19 b3+-) 19 c3 Rd8 (19... Rc8 20 Ba6 Rc7? 21 e6+-) 20 Bc4 h6 (20... Ke7? 21 Bg5! △ Re1+-) 21 e6! with strong pressure.

Returning (from Diagram 11A-1) to **3... c6 4 Nc3! ef4 5 Nf3 Nf6 6 d4 Bd6 7 Qe2,** safer is **7... Qe7,** though **8 Qe7** still keeps Black busy. Necessary, of course, is **8.. Ke7** (8... Be7? 9 dc6 △ Bf4±) when White can improve on 9 Ne5 Bf5 10 Bf4 cd5! △ ...Nc6= with **9 Bc4±.**

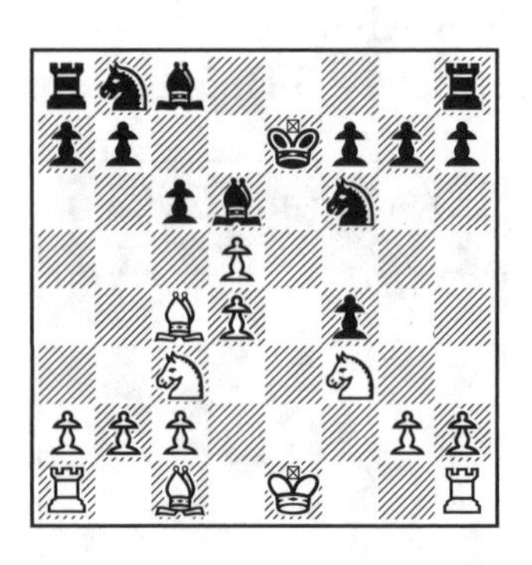

11A-4

Now on 9... Bf5[5] 10 Ne5 (0–0) the reply 10... cd5 (also weak are 10... Bc2 11 dc6! Nc6 12 Nf7 Rhe8 13 0–0 and 10... Be5 11 de5 Nh5 12 d6 △ 0–0) loses its punch due to 11 Bd5! Nd5 12 Nd5 Ke8 (12... Kf6 13 Nf4) 13 Bf4±. An interesting option is 9... b5; however, after 10 Bb3 (Bd3!?) b4 11 Ne2 Nd5 (11... cd5 12 Bf4 Re8 — 12... a5 13 Bg5 or 12... Nc6 13 a3 — 13 0–0 Nc6 14 Rae1±) 12 Bd5 (Ne5) cd5 13 Bf4 Bf4 14 Nf4 Be6 15 a3± [13], White's potential for piling up on Black's a-pawn or d-pawn maintains the edge.

Finally (from Diagram 11A-1), on **3... c6 4 Nc3 ef4 5 Nf3,** Black does best with **5... Bd6,** intending to meet 6 Qe2?! by 6... Ne7. So, White should favor **6 Bc4** (6 d4 Ne7 is presently all the rage as 7 Bc4 [see Illustrative Game IV], 7 Bd3, and 7 dc6 have of late been under the microscope with some success for White), since he cannot meet ...Ne7 with c4 as in the Modern Variation (contrast Diagram 9A-2). The line **6... Ne7 7 0–0 0–0 8 dc6 Nbc6 9 Ne4 Bb8** (9... Bc7 10 d4 Bg4 11 c3 Nd5 12 Nc5 Rb8 13 Qd3) **10 d4**± results

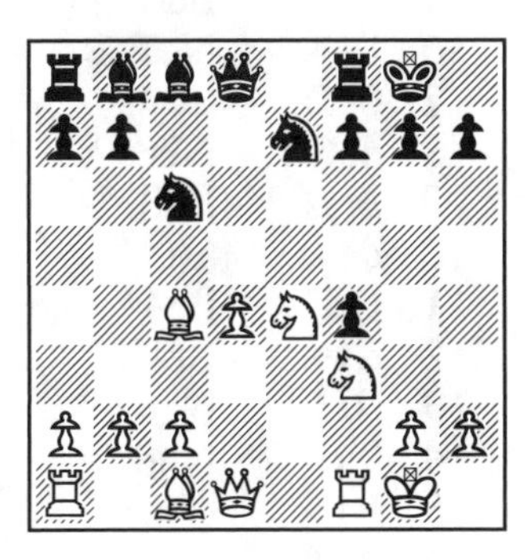

11A-5

in a complex game in which White's center and 4-2 queenside pawn majority seems a bit better than Black's 4-2 kingside pawn majority.

White's primary task here is to continue developing as quickly as possible while avoiding tactical tricks on the P/d4. One logical plan would incorporate c3-Qd3-Bd2-Rae1-(Nc5)-(Kh1) with queenside expansion and, perhaps, a relocation of White's king bishop to c2. Whenever Black selects ...h6-g5, White might also be on the lookout for a favorable piece sacrifice, especially on Black's P/f4. Sharpest may be 10... Bg4 11 c3 h6 12 Qd3 with complicated play ahead.

ILLUSTRATIVE GAME I

Green—Sahr
Golden Knights 1978

1	e4	e5
2	f4	d5
3	ed5	c6
4	Nc3	ef4
5	Nf3	Nf6
6	d4	Bd6
7	Qe2	Kf8!?
8	Ne5	cd5
9	Bf4!	Nc6
10	0–0–0	a6 (Be5)
11	Qe3	Be6
12	Be2	Qc7
13	Rhf1	b5
14	Bb5	Be5
15	de5	d4
16	Rd4	Ng4
17	Qe4	ab5
18	Rd6	Rc8
19	h3	Nge5
20	Be5	Ne5
21	Qe5	b4
22	Qe6	bc3
23	Rf7	1–0

ILLUSTRATIVE GAME II

Hebden—Miles
Kettering 1981

1	e4	e5
2	f4	d5
3	ed5	Bc5
4	Nc3!	Nh6
5	Nf3	Bg4
6	fe5	Nf5
7	Be2	Bf3
8	Bf3	Qh4
9	g3	Ng3
10	hg3	Qg3
11	Ke2	Qf2
12	Kd3	Nc6
13	Nb5	0-0-0
14	Rf1	Qh4
15	c3	Ne5
16	Kc2	Nf3
17	d4	Qe4
18	Qd3	Ne1
19	Re1	Qe1
20	dc5	Rhe8? (Qf2)
21	Qf5	Kb8
22	Nc7	Re5
23	Qf7	Qe4
24	Kb3	Rf5
25	Qg7	Rc8
26	d6	Rc5
27	Qd4	Qf5
28	Bf4	Rd8
29	Re1	Qf7
30	c4	Rf5
31	Ne6	Kc8
32	Qa7	Rf4
33	Qa8	Kd7
34	Qd8	Kc6
35	Nf4	1-0

ILLUSTRATIVE GAME III

Haag—Jacobi
1984

1	e4	e5
2	f4	d5
3	ed5	c6
4	Nc3	ef4
5	Nf3	Bd6
6	Bc4	Ne7
7	0-0	0-0
8	dc6	Nbc6
9	Ne4	Bb8
10	d4	h6
11	Qd3	Bg4
12	c3	Bf3?!
13	Rf3	Ng6
14	Nc5	Nh4
15	Rf2	b6
16	Na6	Na5
17	Nb8	Rb8
18	Bf4	Rb7
19	Ba6	Re7
20	b4	Nb7
21	Raf1	Nd6
22	Bg3	Ng6
23	Qg6!	1-0

ILLUSTRATIVE GAME IV

Westerinen-Motwani
London 1988

1	e4	e5
2	f4	d5
3	ed5	c6
4	Nc3	ef4
5	Nf3	Bd6
6	d4	Ne7

Westerinin–Motwani continued

7	Bc4	cd5 (0–0)
8	Bd5	0–0
9	0–0	Nbc6
10	Bb3	Bg4
11	Ne4	Bc7
12	c3	Ng6
13	h3	Bf5
14	Nfg5	h6
15	Qh5	hg5
16	Ng5	Nh8
17	Nf7	Nf7
18	Qf5	Qf6
19	Qf6	gf6
20	Bf4	Bf4
21	Rf4	Kg7
22	Rg4	Kh6
23	Rf1	Ng5
24	h4	Nh7
25	Bc2	Ne7
26	Re1	Rf7
27	Bb3	Raf8
28	Bf7	Rf7
29	Rge4	Ng6
30	g3	f5
31	Re6	Nf6
32	c4	Kh5
33	Rf1	Ng4
34	d5	f4
35	d6	f3
36	c5	N6e5
37	Re7	Rf8
38	d7	f2
39	Rf2	Nf2
40	Re5	Kg4
41	Rg5	Kh3
42	d8=Q	1–0

PROBLEMS

1. If Black varies with **4... Qe6** (see Diagram 11A-6), what is required of White?

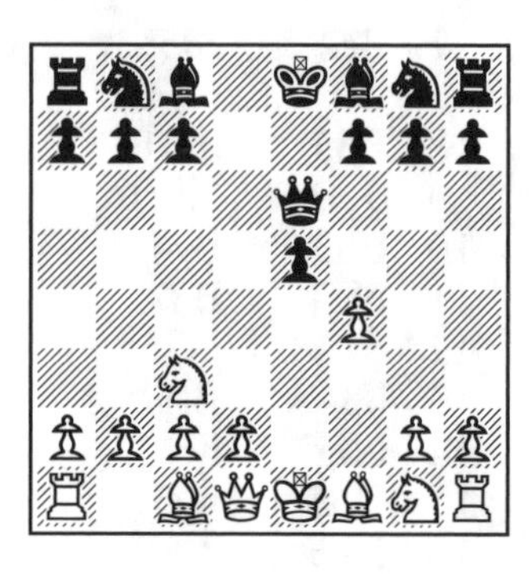

11A-6

2. Here Black must rely on **6... c6,** but **7 Bc4** (see Diagram 11A-7) keeps up the pressure. Countermine:

a) **7... ef4.**
b) **7... Qe7.**

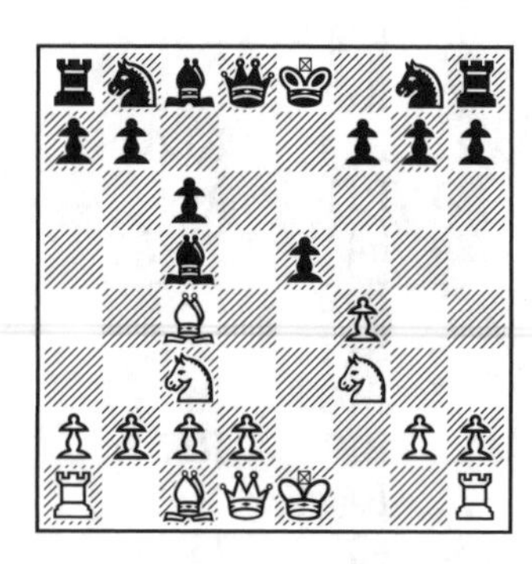

11A-7

3. From Diagram 11A-8, generate plans to deal with:

a) **6... Bg4.**
b) **6... Nd5.**
c) **6... Bb4.**
d) **6... cd5.**

11A-8

4. Show appropriate contempt for **12... Bd1?** (see Diagram 11A-9).

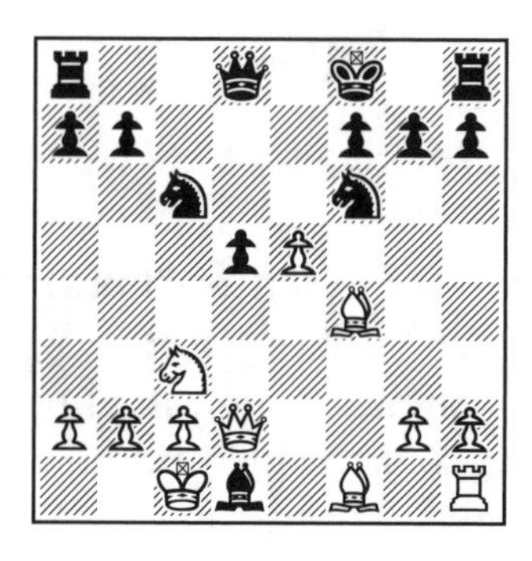

11A-9

5. **9... Re8 10 Ne5 Be5 11 de5** (see Diagram 11A-10) leaves Black in the same boat. Scuttle:

a) **11... Nh5?**
b) **11... Kf8.**

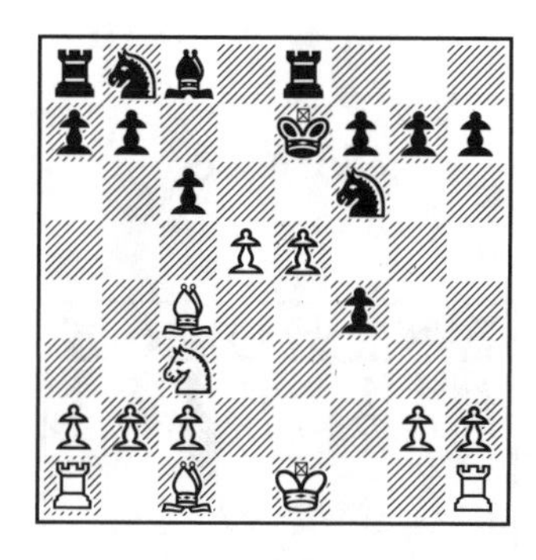

11A-10

Falkbeer Variation (B)

Most of the critical lines in the Falkbeer Variation entail 3... e4. Black offers a pawn, rending the center apart and hindering the natural Nf3 in the process. White is compelled to challenge the control of *e4*, and d3 is the best method to that end:

1	**e4**	**e5**
2	**f4**	**d5**
3	**ed5**	**e4**
4	**d3**	

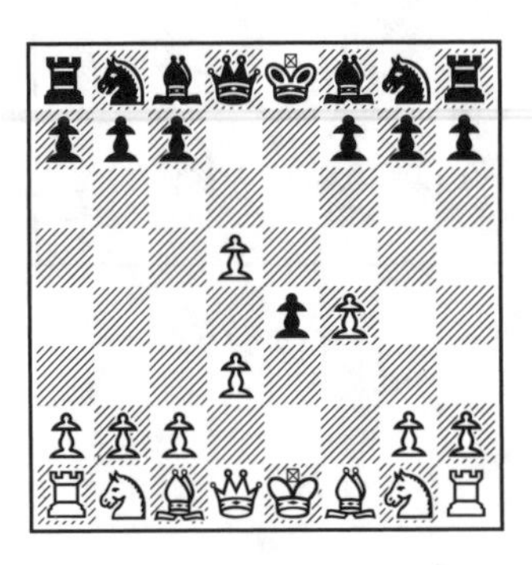

11B-1

Nevertheless, **4... ed3?!** only helps White develop comfortably via **5 Bd3** (Qd3) **Nf6** (5... Qd5 6 Nc3 Qe6[1] 7 Nge2[2] or 5... Bc5 6 Qe2 Qe7 — 6... Ne7 7 Be3 — 7 Nc3 Nf6 8 Bd2 Bg4 9 Qe7 Ke7 10 h3 Bd7 11 0–0–0 [13]) **6 Nc3 Be7[3] 7 Nf3 0–0 8 0–0 Nbd7 9 Bc4 Nb6 10 Bb3 Bb4** (10... Bg4 11 Qd3 and 10... a5 11 a4 Bc5 12 Kh1 Bf5 13 Ne5 Bb4 14 g4 Bc8 15 Be3 Bc3 [15... Nbd7 16 g5 Bc3 17 bc3 Ne4 18 d6 Ne5 19 fe5, 1–0, Keres–Lilienthal, *USSR 1941]* 16 Bb6 with attack) **11 Ne5 Bc3 12 bc3 Nbd5 13 Ba3 Re8 14 Qd4 c6** (14... Bf5? 15 g4!+–) **15 f5**± [1].

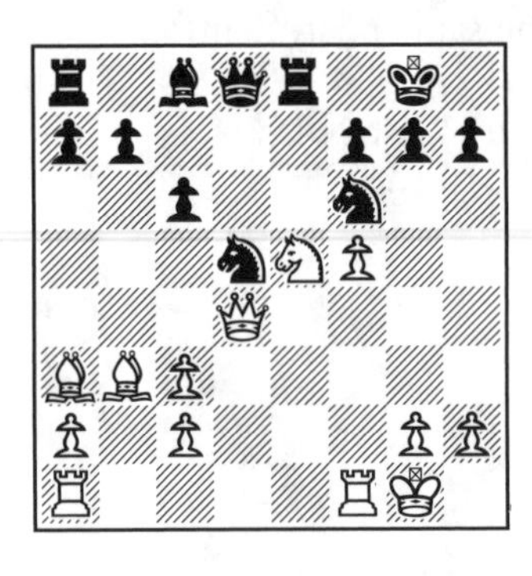

11B-2

White's pieces blanket the board, whereas Black still has back-rank problems due to his inability to connect his rooks. Here both Rad1-c4 and the double-edged Rad1-Rd3-g4-Rg3-g5 may provide good attacking chances. On 15... Qc7, White might also examine Nc4 △ Nd6.

Hardly more promising for Black is **4... Qd5.** After **5 Qe2** Black can choose between 5... Nf6 (5... Bf5 6 g4) and **5... f5.** The latter leads to **6 Nc3 Bb4 7 Bd2 Bc3 8 Bc3 Nf6 9 de4** (0–0–0!?) **Qe4**[4] (9... Ne4 10 Bg7) **10 Qe4 fe4 11 Bc4**± [9].

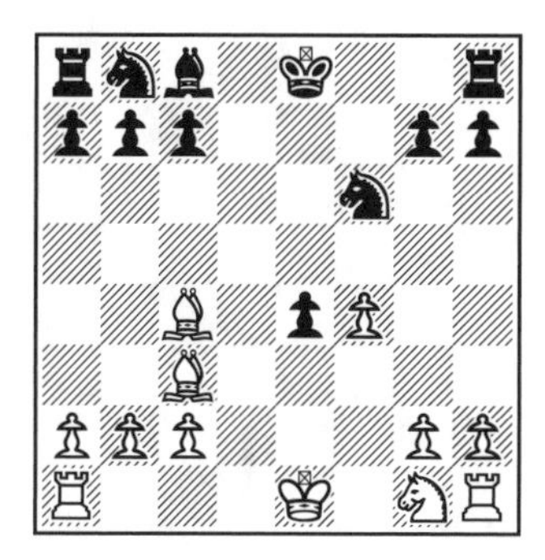

11B-3

Black's isolani on *e4* as well as White's very active bishops assure White a plus. Logical here is 0–0–0, though Ne2-Ng3 makes no attempt to hide White's intentions regarding the P/e4. Another idea is Ne2-Nd4, after which the knight threatens to go to *b5* or *e6*. Finally, White should consider unleashing a kingside pawnroller with h3-g4-(f5)-g5-h4 while watching for the schismatic f5-Bf6-Bd5 to pick off the P/e4, especially when his king blockades on *e3*.

Returning to **4... Qd5 5 Qe2,** Black can also test **5... Nf6** (developing while defending the P/e4). Following **6 Nc3** (or 6 Nd2 Bg4 7 Ngf3 Bf3 [7... Nc6 8 de4 Qh5 9 Qb5 0–0–0 10 Qh5 Nh5 11 Nc4 Nb4 12 Bd3! Nd3 13 cd3 Bf3 14 gf3 Rd3 15 Ne5! Rd4 16 Be3 Rb4 17 Nf7 Rg8 18 0–0–0] 8 gf3 e3 9 Ne4 Be7 10 Be3 [19]±) **Bb4 7 Bd2 Bc3 8 Bc3 0–0**[5] (8... Nbd7 9 de4 Ne4 10 Bg7 Rg8 11 Rd1 Qe6 12 Be5! f5 [12... Ne5 13 Qe4] 13 Qh5 [15]) **9 Bf6 ed3 10 Qd3 Qd3** (10... Re8 11 Be5±) **11 Bd3 gf6 12 0–0–0**±, [15]

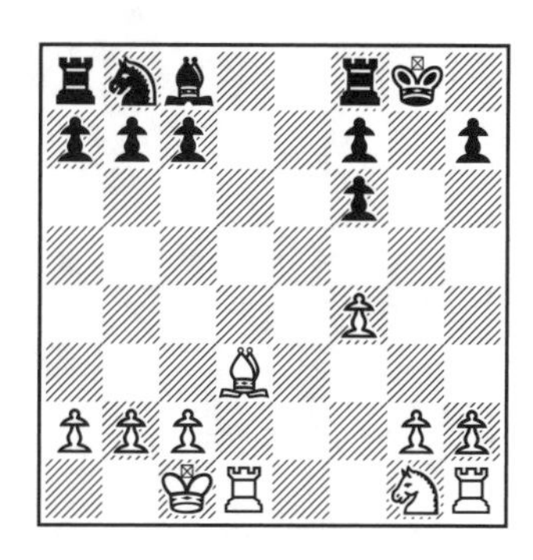

11B-4

we find White ahead in development with chances of attacking Black's weakened kingside. Here 12... Nc6 △ ...Nb4 can be rebuffed by 13 Be4, threatening to demolish Black's queenside pawn formation; yet 12... Bg4 13 Re1 △ h3 also looks uncomfortable for Black. Perhaps Black should assess 12... Be6, though 13 Ne2 △ f5-Nc3 maintains the pressure.

PROBLEMS

1. Other moves are no better. From Diagram 11B-5:

a) Destroy **6... Qg2??**
b) Probe **6... Bb4 7 Bd2 Bc3.**

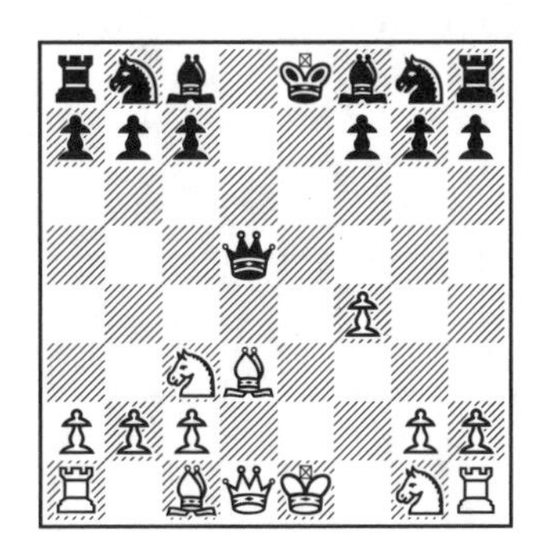

11B-5

2. From Diagram 11B-6, exact a solution to:

a) **7... Nh6.**
b) **7... Nf6.**

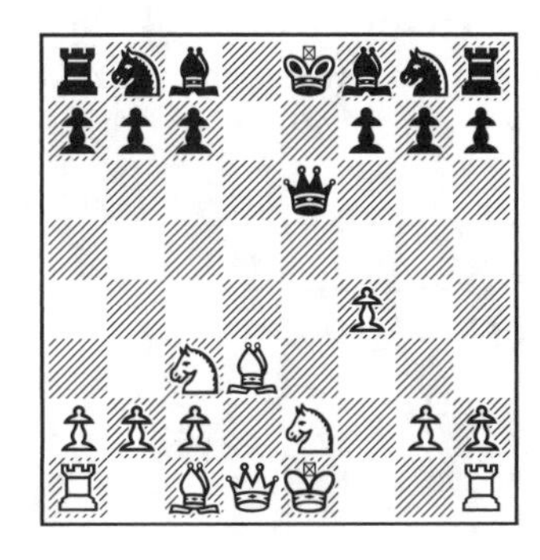

11B-6

3. Review (from Diagram 11B-7):

a) **6... Nd5?**
b) **6...c6.**

11B-7

4. What about **9... fe4** (see Diagram 11B-8)?

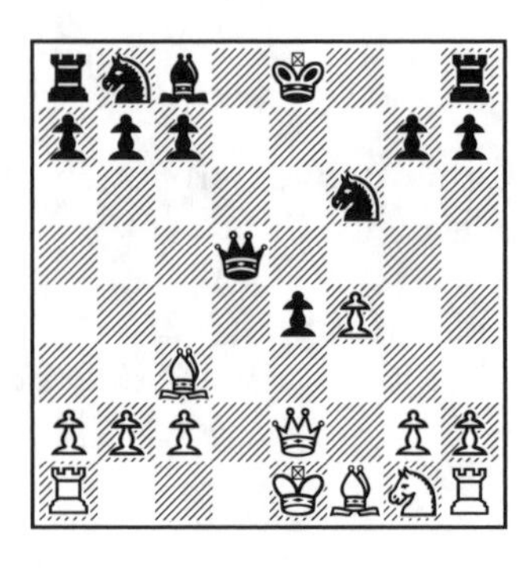

11B-8

5. Interesting is **8... Bg4.** Proceeding with **9 de4** (see Diagram 11B-9), engineer plans for:

a) **9... Qe4.**
b) **9... Be2.**
c) **9... Qe6.**

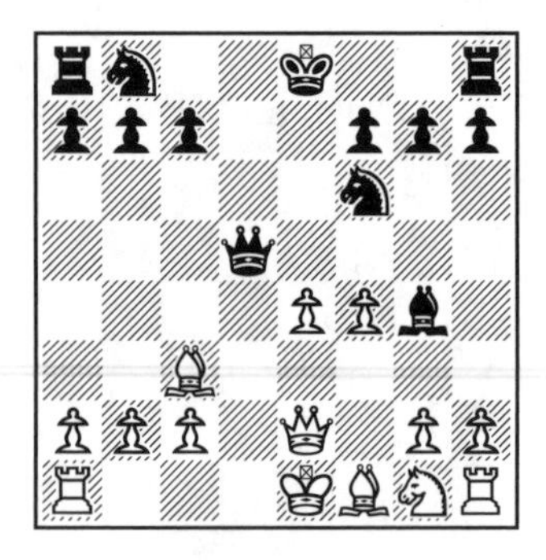

11B-9

Falkbeer Variation (C)

Black's customary fourth move in the Falkbeer Variation is 4... Nf6:

1	**e4**	**e5**
2	**f4**	**d5**
3	**ed5**	**e4**
4	**d3**	**Nf6**
5	**de4**	**Ne4**
6	**Nf3!**	**Bc5**[1]
7	**Qe2** (Bd3!?)	

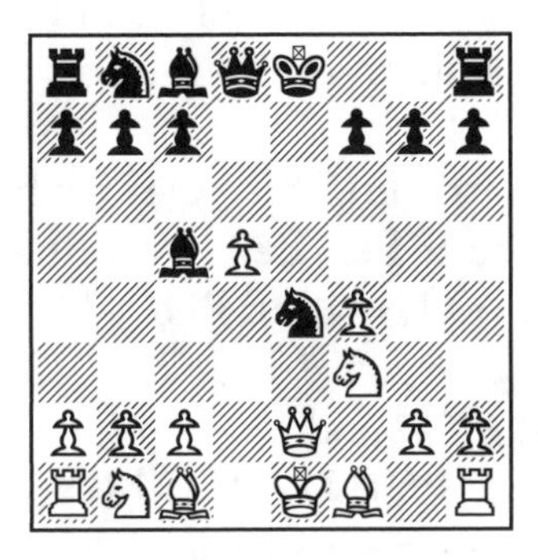

11C-1

Black must adhere to a strict move order in this continuation. On 5... Bc5 △ ...Ne4 White can upset Black's plans with 6 Nc3 0–0 7 Qf3± [8], since 7... Bg4 8 Qg3 just leaves Black two pawns down. Moreover, from Diagram 11C-1 Black still has no leeway. One misstep is **7... 0–0**[2] because following **8 Qe4 Re8** White can shield his queen with **9 Ne5.**

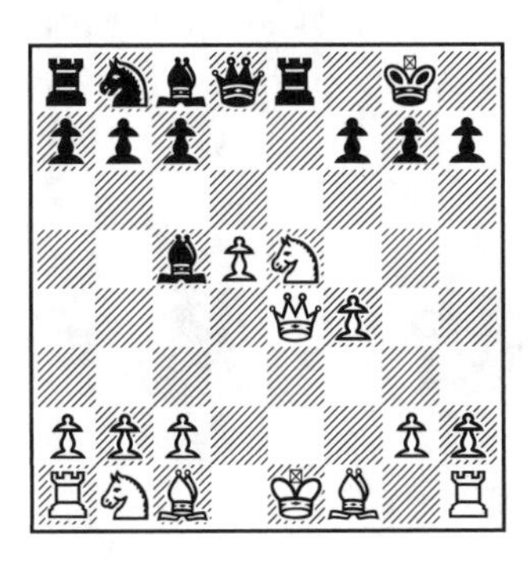

11C-2

Here 9... f6 10 Bd3 (Bb5 or even d6!?) g6 11 Qc4 Na6 (inadequate for Black in this position are 11... Bd6? 12 0–0 fe5 13 f5!, 11... Bb6 12 d6 Be6 13 dc7 Bc7 14 Qa4, and 11... Qd6?! 12 Nc3 △ Ne4 [15]) 12 b4! Bb4 13 Nd2 fe5 (13... b5 14 Qc6) 14 0–0± [13] justifies White's strategy completely. More flexible is 9... Nd7, but 10 Bd3 (Be2) g6 (10... Nf6? 11 Qc4+–) 11 Nc3! f6 12 Bd2 △ 0–0–0 again keeps White in charge. No matter how Black reacts, his prospects look rather forlorn.

Remarkably, **7... Qd5** (from

Diagram 11C-1) also fails tactically, as White has the necessary but effective rejoinder **8 Nfd2(!).** This finesse precedes Nc3 to strip Black of the defensive resource ...Bb4. Suddenly it is White who seizes the initiative by threatening to win Black's N/e4. Probable next is **8... f5** (for 8... Bf2 cf. Problem 11C#3) **9 Nc3 Qd4 10 Nce4 fe4 11 Nb3±** [1]

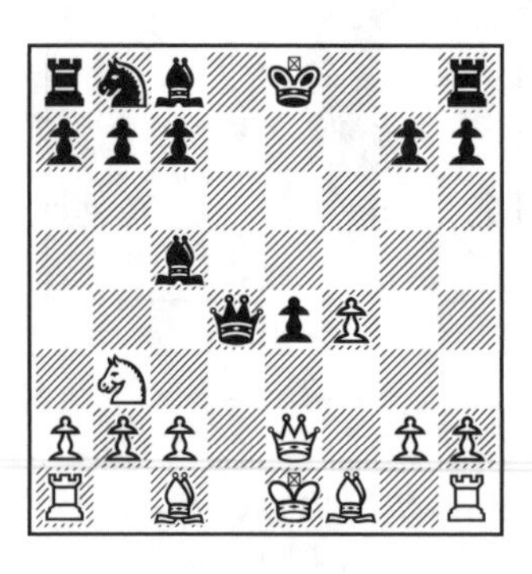

11C-3

whereupon White will exchange Black's actively posted bishop and win the isolani on *e4*. As in so many other lines of the Falkbeer Variation, White gains advantage only after delicately side-stepping early traps.

Black does no better (from Diagram 11C-1) with 7... Bf2 8 Kd1±[3] or 7... Qe7 8 Be3! Na6 (8... Be3 9 Qe3 Nd7 10 Nbd2 Ndf6 11 Ne4 Ne4 12 0–0–0 0–0 13 Bd3± [14] and 8... Bd6 9 Nbd2 Bg4 10 0–0–0 0–0 11 Re1 Nf6 12 Qd3 Qd7 13 Nh4 Qa4 14 Qc4 Qa5 15 Bd3± [14]) 9 Bc5 Nac5 10 Nbd2 0–0 11 0–0–0 Bf5 12 Nd4 Qf6 13 Nf5 Qf5 14 Ne4 Ne4 15 Qf3 Nd6 16 Bd3 Qd7 17 g4!± [13]. Instead, he should protect his N/e4 with his light-squared bishop.

Following **7... Bf5 8 Nc3** (avoiding 8 Nbd2? Qe7 9 Ne4 Be4 10 c4 c6!∓), Black can try 8... 0–0!? (not 8... Bb4?? 9 Qb5+–); however, 9 Ne4 Be4 (9... Re8 10 Ne5 Be4 11 Qe4 f6 is refuted by 12 d6! Qd6 — 12... cd6 13 Bc4 Kf8 14 Qd5 — 13 Be3! Be3? 14 Qc4+– [13]) 10 Qe4 Re8 11 Ne5± [12] again favors White (cf. Diagram 11C-2).

Correct is **8... Qe7,** which leads to **9 Be3 Be3**[4] (9... Bb4 10 Bd4 0–0 11 0–0–0 Re8 [11... Bc3 12 Bc3 Qc5 13 Bg7! Kg7 14 Nh4!± [14] and 11... Nd7 12 Ne4 Be4 13 Be5 (Ne5) Ne5 14 fe5 Bf3 15 gf3 Qg5 16 Kb1 Rfe8 17 Qc4 Ba5 18 f4±] 12 Qb5 Bc3 13 bc3 Nd6 14 Qb3 Nd7 15 c4 b6 16 Ne5 Ne5 17 fe5 Bg4 18 Re1 Qg5 19 Kb1 b5 20 cb5 a6 21 a4 ab5 22 ab5 Bf5 23 Be3 Qg6 24 Bd4 Ne4 25 Qb4 Reb8 26 Bd3 Nf2 27 Bf5 Qf5 28 Rhf1 Qd7 29 Bb2 Rb5 30 e6 fe6 31 de6 Qc6 32 Qd4 R5b8? 33 Qg7 mate, Leisebein—Weiz, *East German Postal 1986)* **10 Qe3**

Nc3 (for 10... 0–0 see Illustrative Game III) **11 Qe7 Ke7 12 bc3⩲.**

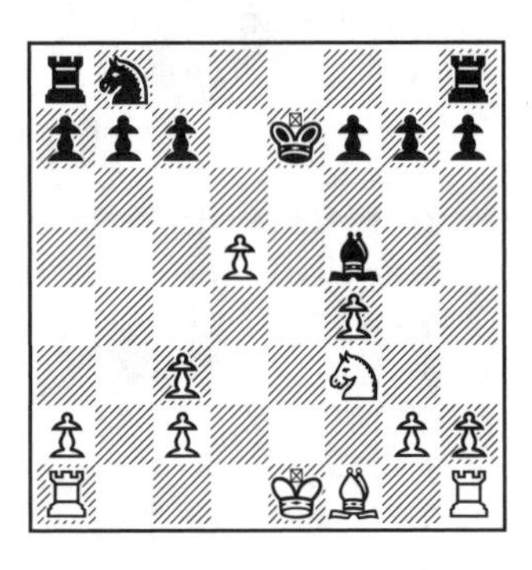

11C-4

White has played just twelve moves, yet an endgame has effectively been reached! Now on 12... Bc2 13 Kd2 Ba4 (13... Bg6 14 Re1 Kd8 [or 14… Kd6 15 Nd4 Kd5 16 f5 Bh5 17 g4 △ Bg2-Bb7. Note that 15… Nd7 16 Nb5 and 15… h5 16 f5 Bh7 17 Rb1! make Black's life difficult. {19}]15 Nd4 and 13... Bf5 14 Re1 Kf6 15 Nd4 Bd7 16 h3 g6 17 g4 Re8 18 Bd3 Re1 19 Re1 a6 20 g5 Kg7 21 f5 Kf8 22 f6 are even worse for Black) 14 Re1 Kd8[5] (for 14... Kf6 see Illustrative Game II) 15 Re4 Be8 16 Bc4 b5 17 Bb3 Na6 18 Rhe1± [1], White obtains a definite pull.

More prudent is **12... Be4,** though with **13 Ng5!** White still maintains some pressure. One example is 13... Bc2 14 Kd2 Bg6 15 Re1 Kf8 (15... Kf6? 16 g4! Rd8 17 c4 c6 18 Nh3! △ g5+– and 15... Kd7 16 Bd3 f6 17 Ne6 Bd3 18 Kd3 Na6 19 Ng7 Rhg8 20 Nh5± [14]) 16 Bb5 c6 17 f5 Bh5 (17... Bf5 18 Rhf1 g6 19 g4±) 18 dc6 Nc6 19 Bc6 bc6 20 c4!? g6 21 f6 h6 22 Ne4 Bg4 23 Kc3 Kg8 24 Nc5 g5 25 Re7 Kh7 26 Rf7 Kg6 27 Rg7 Kf6 28 Rc7 Rhc8 29 Rf1 Ke5 30 Nd3 Kd6 31 Rh7 Rf8 32 c5 Kd5 33 Re7 Rae8 34 Rfe1 Re7 35 Re7 Be6 36 Nb4 Ke5 37 Nc6 Kf6 38 Ra7 Bd5 39 Ra6 Bg2 40 Nd4 Ke7 41 Rh6 Ra8 42 Rg6 Ra2 43 Rg5 Bh3 44 Nc2 Kf6 45 Rh5 Bf5 46 Nb4 1–0, Bangiev—Gutgarch, *USSR Postal 1986-87*.

Predictable next is **13... Bd5 14 0–0–0 c6**[6] (14… Ba2 15 c4 b5 16 cb5 a6 17 Kb2±; 14… Be6 15 Ne6 fe6 16 Bc4 Rf8 [16… Nd7 17 Be6] 17 Rhe1 Rf6 18 f5±; and 14…Rd8 15 c4 Be6 16 Rd8 Kd8 17 Ne6 fe6 18 Bd3 h6 19 Re1 Kd7 20 Re3 Nc6 21 Rg3+– [19])**15 Bd3** (c4)⩲ [13].

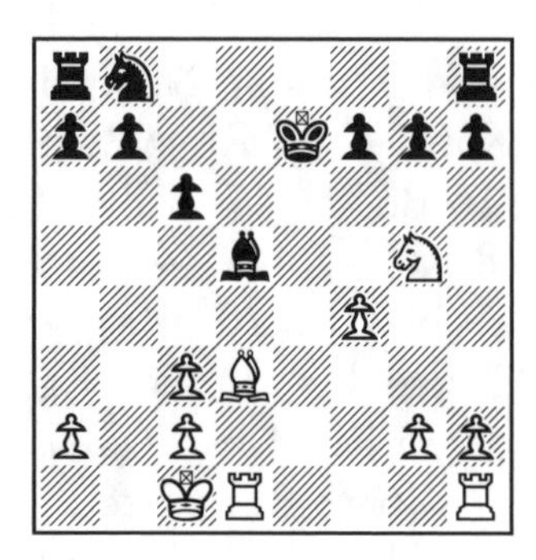

11C-5

In this position Black must not falter with 15... h6? (15... Bg2? 16 Rhe1 △ Nh7), since 16 Rhe1 Kd6 17 Nf7!+− leaves him defenseless against the double-threat Nh8/Ba6 as shown by 17... Bf7 18 Ba6! Kc7 19 Re7 Kb6 20 Bb7 1−0, Szymanski—Petrik, *Warsaw 1971*. Also inaccurate is 15... Nd7?! due to 16 Rhe1 Kf8 (16... Kf6? 17 Nh7+−) 17 c4±, e.g., 17... Bg2? 18 Rd2 h6 19 Nh7 Kg8 20 Rg2 △ Re7+−. Likely, therefore, is 15... g6, when 16 Rhe1 Kf6 17 g4 △ Re3-Rde1-(Ne4/c4) augurs well for White in the tactical fray to come.

ILLUSTRATIVE GAME I

Bronstein—Tal
USSR Team Ch, Riga 1968

1	e4	e5
2	f4	d5
3	ed5	e4
4	d3	Nf6
5	de4	Ne4
6	Nf3!	Bc5
7	Qe2	Bf5
8	Nc3	Qe7
9	Be3	Nc3?!
10	Bc5	Ne2
11	Be7	Nf4
12	Ba3!	Nd7
13	0−0−0	Be4
14	Ng5	Bd5
15	g3! (or Re1)	Bh1
16	gf4	c5
17	Bc4	Bc6
18	Nf7	b5
19	Nd6	Ke7
20	Nb5	Rhf8?
21	Nd4!	Bb7
22	Ne6	Rf5
23	Rg1	Be4
24	Nc7 (Re1!)	Rd8
25	Rg7	Kf6
26	Rf7	Kg6
27	Re7	Nf6
28	Ne6	Rc8
29	b3	Rh5
30	Ng5	Bd5
31	Bd3	Kh6
32	Bb2	c4
33	Bf5	c3
34	Bc8	cb2

35	Kb2	Rh2
36	Ra7	Rf2
37	Ra4	Kg6
38	Rd4	h5
39	a4	h4
40	a5	Bg2
41	a6	Nh5
42	Bb7	Nf4
43	Rf4	1–0

ILLUSTRATIVE GAME II

Anderson—Phillips
1976

1	e4	e5
2	f4	d5
3	ed5	e4
4	d3	Nf6
5	de4	Ne4
6	Nf3!	Bc5
7	Qe2	Bf5
8	Nc3	Qe7
9	Be3	Be3
10	Qe3	Nc3
11	Qe7	Ke7
12	bc3	Bc2
13	Kd2	Ba4
14	Re1	Kf6
15	Bd3 (Re4)	Nd7
16	g4	g6
17	g5	Kg7
18	f5	gf5
19	Bf5	Rhe8
20	c4	b6
21	h4	Nf8
22	h5	Bd7
23	Nd4	Re1
24	Re1	Re8
25	Rf1	Re5
26	Bd7	Nd7
27	Nf5	Kh8
28	Nh6	Re7
29	Nf7	Kg7
30	Nh6	Kh8
31	Kc3	Rg7
32	Rf5	Re7
33	Kd4	a6
34	Nf7	Kg7
35	Nd8	Nc5
36	Re5	Rd7
37	Ne6	Ne6
38	Re6	Kf7
39	Ke5	a5
40	a4	Kg7
41	Kf5	Rf7
42	Rf6	Re7
43	h6	Kg8
44	g6	hg6
45	Kg6	Rd7
46	Re6	Rd8
47	h7	Kh8
48	Kh6	Rf8
49	d6	cd6
50	Rd6	b5
51	ab5	1–0

ILLUSTRATIVE GAME III

S. Polgar—Hirsch
New York Open, 1985

1	e4	e5
2	f4	d5
3	ed5	e4
4	d3	Nf6
5	de4	Ne4
6	Nf3	Bc5
7	Qe2	Bf5
8	Nc3	Qe7
9	Be3	Be3
10	Qe3	0–0
11	Nd4	Bc8
12	0–0–0	Re8
13	Re1	f5

14	g4	Qf6
15	gf5	Nd6
16	Ne6	Nf5
17	Qf2	Be6
18	de6	Ne7
19	Rg1	Nbc6
20	Bc4	Rad8
21	f5	Rd4
22	Ne4	Qh6
23	Kb1	Kh8
24	Bd3	Rf8
25	Ng5	Qf6
26	Qg3	h6
27	Ne4	Nf5
28	Nf6	Ng3
29	Nh7	Rfd8
30	Rg3	Rd3
31	Rd3	Rd3
32	cd3	Ne7
33	Nf8	Kg8
34	Ng6	Nc8
35	e7	Nd6
36	e8=Q	Ne8
37	Re8	Kf7
38	Re7	Kg6
39	Rc7	Kf6
40	Rb7	a5
41	Ra7	g5
42	Ra5	1–0

PROBLEMS

1. From Diagram 11C-6, foil:

a) **6... Bg4?**
b) **6... Bf5?**
c) **6... c6.**
d) **6... Bb4.**
e) **6... Be7.**

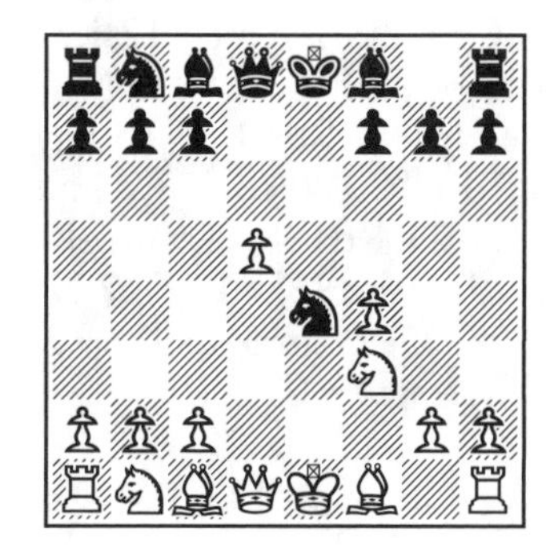

11C-6

2. In this sharp position, Black has no time for **7... f5.** Proceeding with **8 Be3** (see Diagram 11C-7), dissect:

a) **8... 0–0.**
b) **8... Qd5.**
c) **8... Be3.**
d) **8... Na6.**

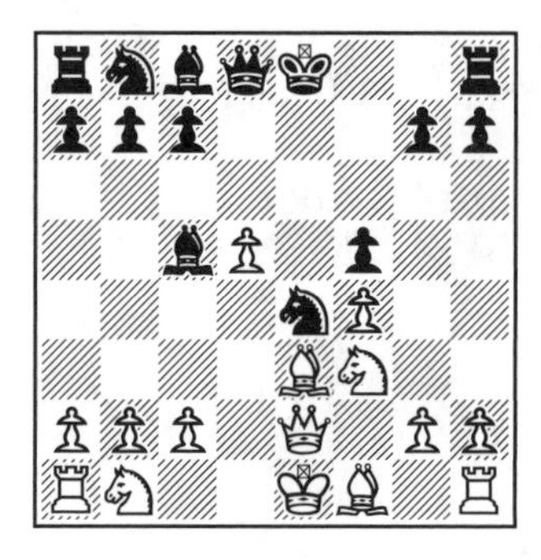

11C-7

3. Find the thematic remedy (from Diagram 11C-8) that turns back Black's offensive after:

a) **8... Qd5.**
b) **8... f5.**

11C-8

4. **9... Nc3?!** may appear promising at first glance, but **10 Bc5 Ne2** (10... Qe2 11 Be2 Ne2 12 Ke2 Bc2 13 Kd2 Be4 14 Rhe1 f5 15 Ng5 Nd7 16 Ne4 fe4 17 Re4 Kd8 18 Be7 Kc8 19 Rc1 Re8 20 d6 c6 21 Rd4 Nb6 22 g4 Nd5 23 Rd5 1–0, Zindel—Etemadi, *Geneva 1987*) **11 Be7 Nf4 12 Ba3!** (see Diagram 11C-9) bankrupts Black's strategy. Check:

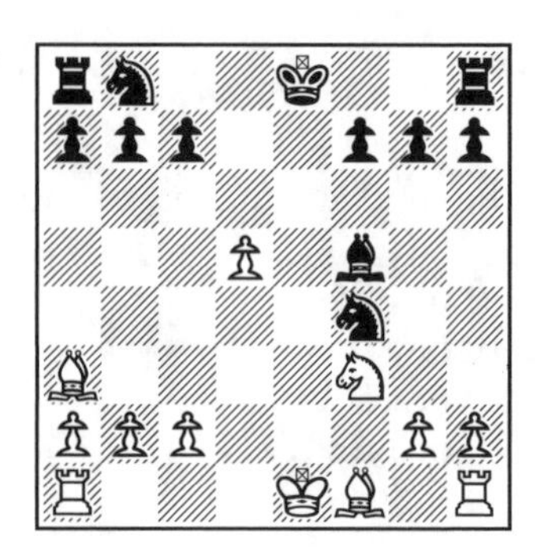

11C-9

a) **12... Nd7 13 0–0–0 0–0–0.**
b) **12... Nd5.**
c) **12... Be4.**

5. Keep Black on the hook (from Diagram 11C-10) if he goes in for:

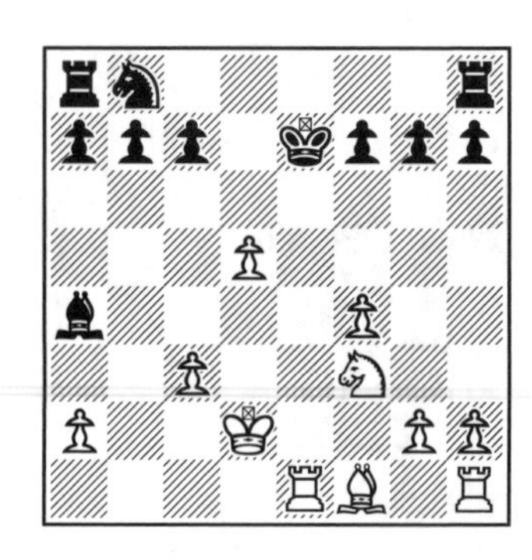

11C-10

a) **14... Kd6.**
b) **14... Kf8.**

6. From Diagram 11C-11 Black has a broad choice of fourteenth moves. Analyze:

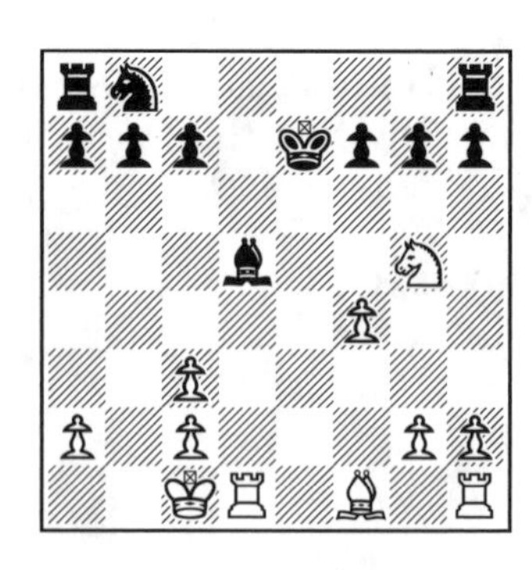

11C-11

a) **14... Ba2.**
b) **14... Be6?!**
c) **14... Rd8.**
d) **14... Bc6.**

12: CLASSICAL DECLINED VARIATION (A)

One of Black's most popular ways to decline the gambit is 2... Bc5, the Classical Declined Variation:

1	e4	e5
2	f4	Bc5
3	Nf3	

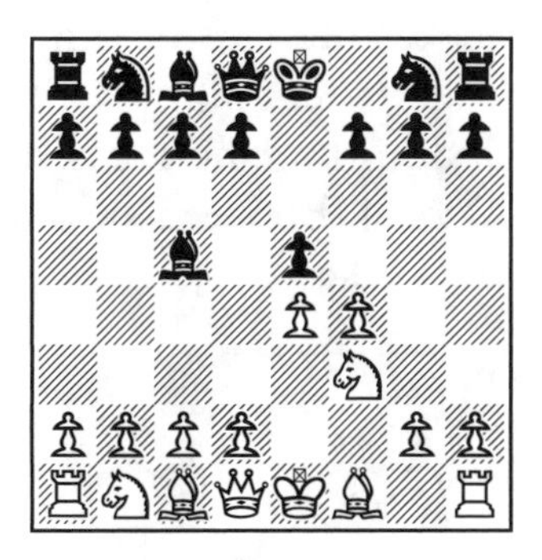

12A-1

Each line, it seems, has an interesting twist. For instance, after 3... Nc6?![1], the enterprising 4 Ne5![2], or even 4 fe5 d6 5 ed6 Qd6 6 c3!, immediately places Black in a quandary. Necessary, therefore, is **3... d6** when White should again postpone the development of his king bishop by **4 Nc3**[3] so that he can answer **4... Nc6**[4] (for 4... Nf6 see Sections 12B through 12D) with **5 Bb5**,

12A-2

though 5 Na4 is also serviceable. This thematic pin defuses a subsequent ...Bg4-Nd4 and undermines Black's P/e5.

In the 4... Nc6 continuation, White often strives for an appropriately timed Bc6-fe5 to break up Black's Q-side pawn structure. Alternatively, if Black plays ...Bg4, Bc6-h3 can be contemplated so long as Black must reply by trading his light-squared bishop for White's king knight. This exchange, by bringing White's queen to *f3*, would keep an enemy knight from intruding on *g3* and thereby minimize the weakness created by h3. (Cf. Illustrative Game I)

Thus if 5... Bg4[5], logical is 6 fe5 de5 7 Bc6 bc6 8 Qe2 (8 h3 allows 8... Be6, since 9 Ne5?? loses to 9... Qh4) Ne7 9 h3, forcing 9... Bf3 (±) as in Illustrative Game II — but not 6 d3 Ne7 7 h3 Bf3 8 Qf3 0–0∓ (Alapin—Rubinstein), giving Black free rein over *d4*.

Going back to Diagram 12A-2, not much new applies to **5... Nf6.** White plays **6 d3,** when Black's response will determine White's best plan. One choice, **6... 0–0,** leads to **7 Bc6 bc6 8 fe5 de5 9 Qe2**± [1].

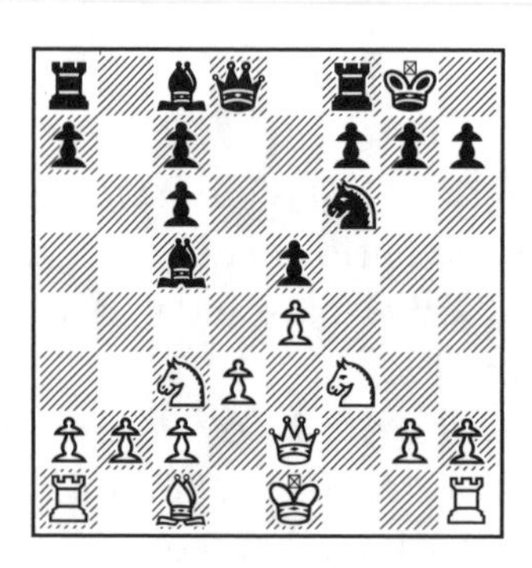

12A-3

As White's queen now defends *f2*, Black must protect his P/e5. Next, 9... Bg4 10 h3 would just force Black to exchange on *f3*; so more likely is 9... Re8, leaving White the pleasant choice of Be3-0–0 or Bd2-0–0–0. If White castles long, he should proceed with a K-side minority attack via h3-g4-g5-h4-h5, since Black's scattered Q-side pawns will retard any offensive on the opposite wing. These isolated pawns may cause the second player more than a little concern should an endgame be reached.

Again, on **5... Nf6 6 d3** Black can also try **6... Bg4.** Less enticing here is 7 Bc6 bc6 8 fe5 de5 due to 9 Qe2 Nh5 or to 9 h3 Be6!? Instead, White can obtain a secure edge by eliminating Black's B/c5 and castling short. There follows **7 Na4 Bb6 8 Nb6 ab6 9 0–0 0–0 10 c3**± [1].

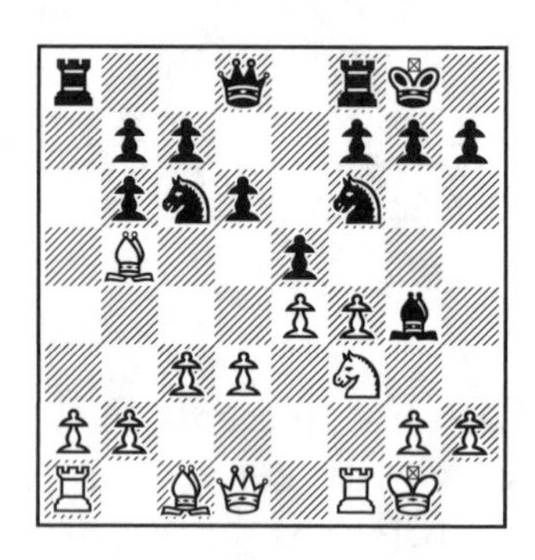

12A-4

White's N/f3 can be quickly unpinned by Be3-Qd2 or Qe1 △ Qg3/Qh4. Another buildup for White would involve an eventual d4. Note that if Black cooperates, there is the trap Qe1-Be3-Nd2-f5-h3-g4 to win the B/g4. In many lines, White can keep the bishop pair by redeploying his B/b5 to *c2*. Curiously, the resulting position would then gain some affinity with the Ruy Lopez.

Lastly (from Diagram 12A-2), Black's most stalwart retort may be **5... Nge7.** With Black's N/c6 reinforced, White should give the nod to **6 Na4** (6 fe5!? de5 7 Ne5 0–0!∞). There can follow **6... Bb6 7 Nb6 ab6 8 d3** (fe5!?) **0–0 9 0–0 ef4 10 Bf4 d5 11 ed5 Nd5**± [1].

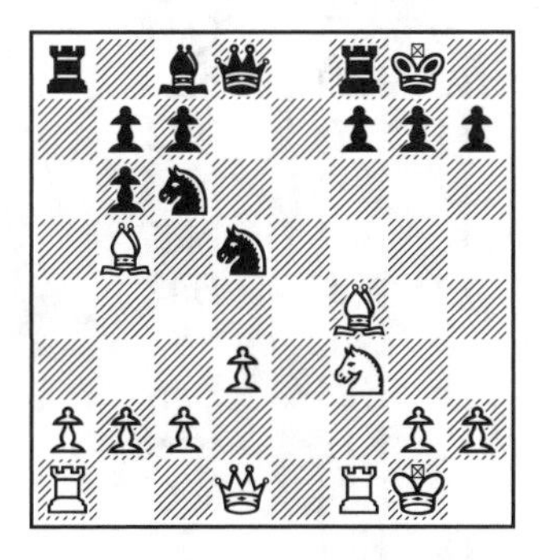

12A-5

White has the bishop pair, a center pawn which yearns to expand to *d4*, and the Q-side majority to go with his typical semi-open f-file play. After 12 Qd2, Black should discard 12... Nf4?! due to 13 Qf4± △ Ng5-(Bc4) with powerful f-file pressure. In order to maintain the balance, Black can try instead to exchange one of his knights for the B/b5 while overseeing his potentially weak *f7* square. In the long run, a minority attack aided by the half-open a-file may offer him some reasonable prospects.

ILLUSTRATIVE GAME I

Vega—Noordhock
Sevilla 1993

1	e4	e5
2	f4	Bc5
3	Nf3	d6
4	Nc3	Nc6
5	Bb5	Bg4
6	Na4	Bb6
7	Nb6	ab6
8	d3	ef4
9	0–0	Nf6
10	h3	Bf3
11	Qf3	g5
12	Bf4!	gf4
13	Qf4	Rg8
14	Qf6	Qf6
15	Rf6	Ke7
16	Raf1	Rg7
17	Bc6	bc6
18	a3	b5
19	R6f5	c5
20	g4	Rb8
21	Kg2	Ke6
22	Kg3	c6
23	Rf6	Ke7
24	e5	de5
25	Rc6	h5

26	Re1	hg4
27	hg4	Rg5
28	Rc5	Kd6
29	d4	f6
30	Rf1	Rg6
31	b4	Rbg8
32	Rf6	1–0

ILLUSTRATIVE GAME II

Gunsberg—Mieses
Hastings 1895

1	e4	e5
2	f4	Bc5
3	Nf3	d6
4	Nc3	Nc6
5	Bb5	Bg4
6	fe5	de5
7	Bc6	bc6
8	Qe2	Ne7
9	h3	Bf3
10	Qf3	0–0
11	g4	Ng6
12	Ne2!	Qe7
13	d3	Nh4
14	Qg3	Rab8
15	b3	Rbd8
16	Bd2	Bb6 (Bb4)
17	0–0–0	a5
18	a4	Qa3
19	Kb1	Ng6
20	Bc1	Qb4
21	h4	Rb8
22	h5	Nf4
23	Bf4	ef4
24	Qf4	Bc5
25	Qe5!	Be7
26	Qd4	Qa3
27	Qb2	Qd6
28	h6!	gh6
29	Nd4	Bf6
30	Nf5	Bb2
31	Nd6	cd6
32	Kb2	Kg7
33	Rh5	

White won in the ending.

ILLUSTRATIVE GAME III

Westerinen—Kaabi
Manila Olympiad 1992

1	e4	e5
2	f4	Bc5
3	Nf3	d6
4	c3	Nf6
5	d4	Bb6
6	fe5	de5
7	Ne5	0–0
8	Bg5	c5
9	dc5	Qd1
10	Kd1	Ne4
11	cb6	Nf2
12	Ke1	Nh1
13	Bc4	Nd7
14	Nd7	Bd7
15	Nd2	h6
16	Be3	Bc6
17	Kf1	Rfe8
18	Bd4	ab6
19	Kg1	b5
20	Bf1	Ra4
21	a3	Rd8
22	Rb1	Re8
23	Kh1	Raa8
24	Kg1	Re6
25	Kf2	g5
26	Nf3	Rae8
27	Re1	Re1
28	Ne1	f6
29	Bd3	Kf7
30	Nc2	h5

31	Nb4	Rd8
32	Nc6	bc6
33	Ke3	Re8
34	Kd2	Rd8
35	Kc2	Ke6
36	Bb6	Rb8
37	Bc5	f5
38	c4	Ke5
39	Kc3	bc4
40	Bc4	f4
41	a4	g4
42	a5	h4
43	a6	1-0

PROBLEMS

1. Transposing to a version of the Falkbeer Variation with **3... d5?!** is as bad for Black as it looks. Proceeding with **4 Ne5** (see Diagram 12A-6):

a) Inspect **4... de4.**
b) Demolish **4... Nf6.**

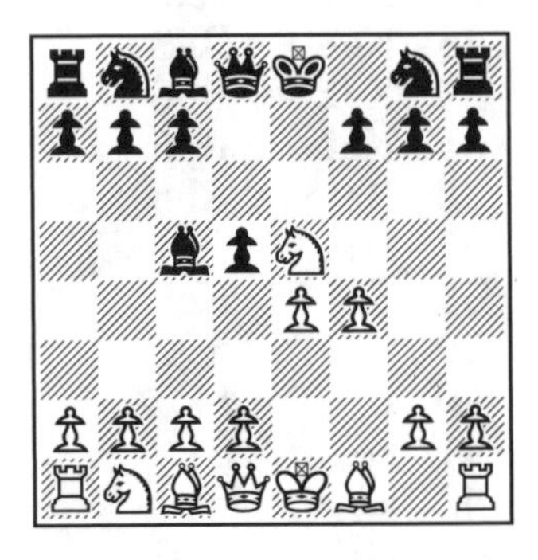

12A-6

2. One option here is 4... Nf6 5 Nc3 0–0 6 Be2 Re8 7 Bf3 which leads to an advantage for White. However, Black may try **4... Ne5** (see Diagram 12A-7), since 5 fe5?? Qh4–+ is crushing. What amusing zwischenzug crosses him up?

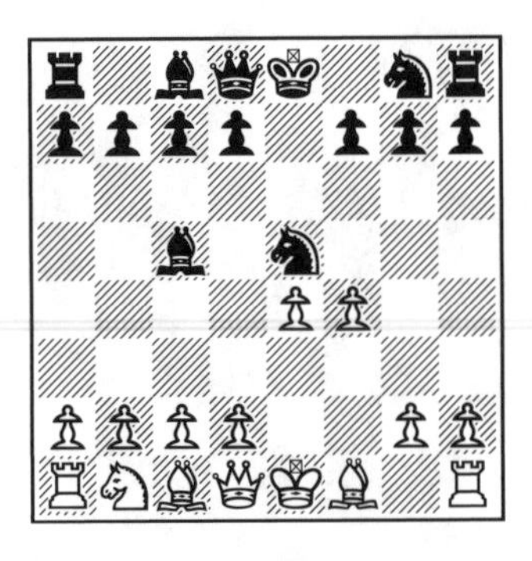

12A-7

3. Not totally resolved is **4 c3.** The principal line involves **4... Nf6** (4... Bg4 5 h3 and 4... f5!? 5 fe5 de5 6 d4 ed4 7 Bc4 fe4 8 Nd4 [19]) **5 fe5!** (for 5 d4 see Illustrative Game III) **de5 6 Ne5** (d4) reaching Diagram 12A-8. Delve into the intricacies of:

a) **6... 0–0.**
b) **6... Qe7.**

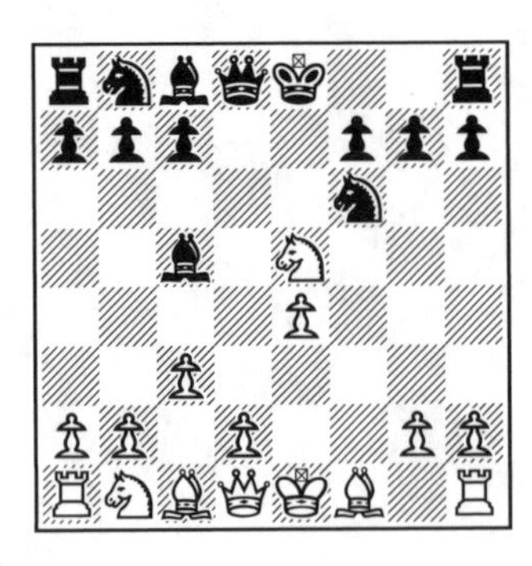

12A-8

4. From Diagram 12A-9, dress down:

a) **4... Bg4.**
b) **4... a6.**

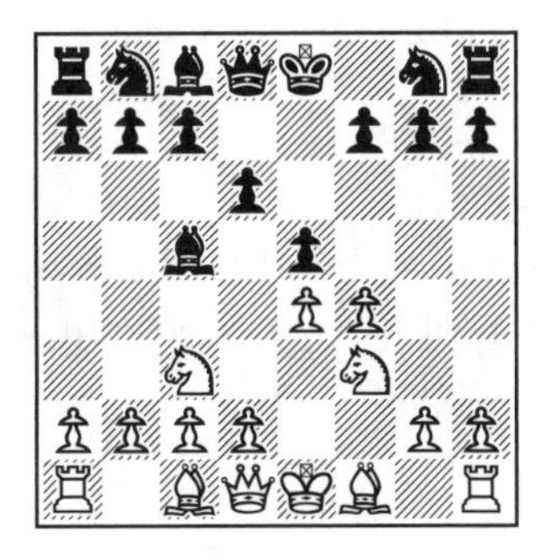

12A-9

5. Why is **5... Bd7** (see Diagram 12A-10) amiss?

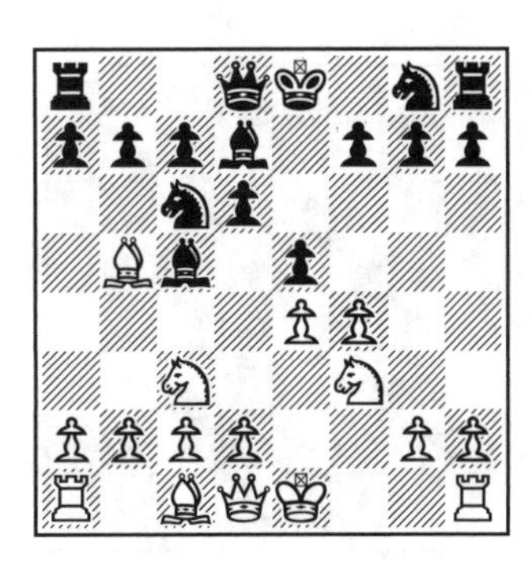

12A-10

Classical Declined Variation (B)

After 4 Nc3, Black can avoid the pin of his queen knight with the flexible 4... Nf6:

1	**e4**	**e5**
2	**f4**	**Bc5**
3	**Nf3**	**d6**
4	**Nc3**	**Nf6**
5	**Bc4**	

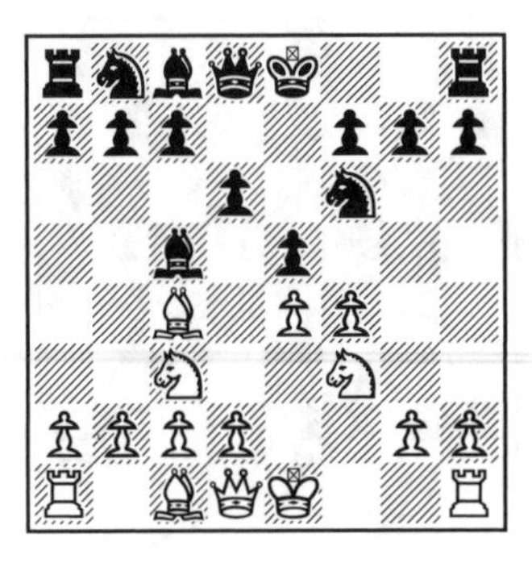

12B-1

White wisely resists 5 fe5 de5 6 Ne5, winning a pawn, as after 6... Qd4 7 Nd3 Bb6 △ ...0–0-Re8 the half-open e-file would give Black too much counterplay (contrast Problem 12A#4b).

Now (after 5 Bc4), however, if Black challenges White's powerfully posted light-squared bishop with 5... Be6[1] (for 5... Ng4 see the Illustrative Game, whereas for 5... Nc6 see Sections 12C and 12D), White comes out on top by utilizing the e-file himself!

Another possibility from Diagram 12B-1 is 5... 0–0, though after 6 d3 White appears to obtain the better chances in all lines. For instance, both 6... Be6 (premature is 6... Ng4 due to 7 Rf1 Nh2 8 Rh1 Ng4 9 Qe2 Bf2 10 Kf1 Nc6 11 f5 Bc5 12 Ng5 Nh6 13 Qh5 Qe8 14 Nh7!+– Neumann—Defresne, *1864*) 7 Be6 (thematic whenever White can safely win the P/e5) fe6 8 Na4 Bb6 (8... ef4 9 Nc5 dc5 10 Bf4 Ne4 11 Be3!) 9 Nb6 ab6 10 fe5 de5 11 Ne5 Ne4 12 Nf3!± and 6... Bg4 7 h3 Bf3 8 Qf3 c6 9 f5 Nbd7 10 g4 Nb6 11 Bb3 a5 12 a4 Bb4 13 Bd2 d5 14 g5± [13] are in White's favor. Consequently, here Black should consider 6... Nc6, heading for Diagram 12C-3, or 6... Nbd7 (6... c6 is similar) leading to Diagram 12B-2.

Returning to Diagram 12B-1, Black's major alternative to 5... Nc6 is 5**... c6** (5... Nbd7 transposes), after which **6 d3** (fe5) **Nbd7**[2] (6... Qe7 7 Qe2 Bg4 8 fe5 de5 9 Be3 Nbd7 10 Nd1±) **7 Qe2**

0–0 8 fe5 (f5) **de5 9 Rf1**±

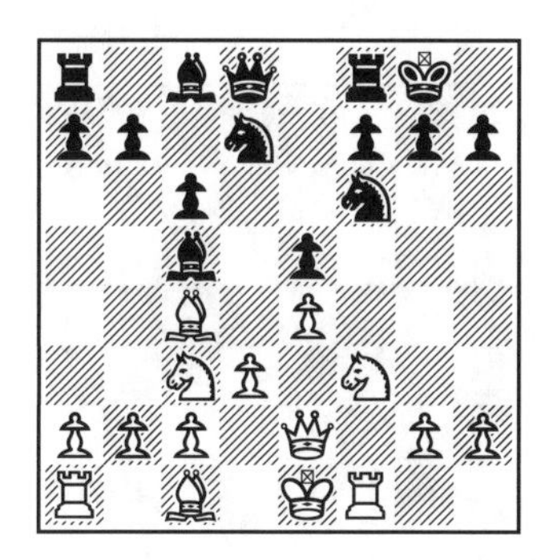

12B-2

enters little-explored territory.

Here White can plan to increase pressure by Bg5-(Nh4). There is no need to worry about 9... b5 10 Bb3 a5 11 a4 b4 due to 12 Nd1. White's queen knight would become very active on *e3* by threatening, among other possibilities, to reach the focal-square, *f5*. On 9... Qe7 10 Bg5 h6, White can go in for 11 Be3 Be3 12 Qe3 Ng4 13 Qe2 Qc5 14 Kd2 or, of course, for 11 Bh4 △ 0–0–0, with a rich middlegame ahead in both cases.

ILLUSTRATIVE GAME

Westmoreland—Kestler
Postal 1985

1	**e4**	**e5**
2	**f4**	**Bc5**
3	**Nf3**	**d6**
4	**Nc3**	**Nf6**
5	**Bc4**	**Ng4**
6	**Ng5**	**0–0**
7	**d3**	**h6**
8	**f5**	**Nf2**
9	**Qh5**	**hg5**
10	**Bg5**	**Qd7**
11	**f6**	**Qg4**
12	**Qg6**	**1–0**

PROBLEMS

1. Simply **6 Be6 fe6 7 fe5** (or 7 d3) **de5 8 Ne5 Qd4 9 Nd3** (see Diagram 12B-3) puts White a safe pawn up, since the e-file is now closed. Examine:

   a) **9... Ne4?!**
   b) **9... Bb6.**

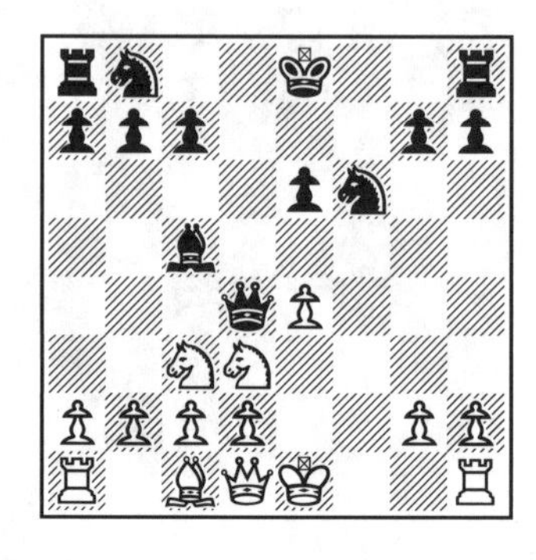

12B-3

2. Why is **6... b5 7 Bb3 a5** (7... Qe7 8 Qe2 Nbd7 9 Rf1 Bb4 10 fe5 [19]± was reached in Short–Speelman, 1991 Candidates' Match, Game 2) **8 a4 b4** (see Diagram 12B-4) positionally inaccurate for Black?

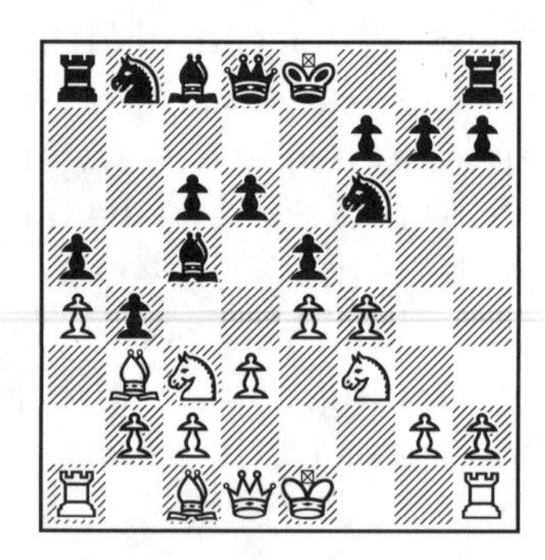

12B-4

Classical Declined Variation (C)

In the main line of the Classical Declined Variation, Black's best fifth move is to bring his queen knight to **c6:**

1	**e4**	**e5**
2	**f4**	**Bc5**
3	**Nf3**	**d6**
4	**Nc3**	**Nf6**
5	**Bc4**	**Nc6**
6	**d3**	
	(fe5!?)	

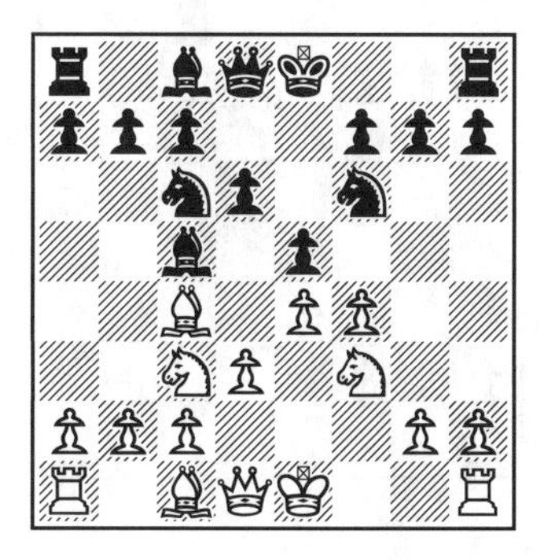

12C-1

Unwarranted here are 6... Nd4[1] and 6... Ng4.[2] Also unimpressive is 6... Qe7 because of 7 f5 Nd4 (7... h6 8 Na4) 8 Bg5± [8] when Black is not well-placed to organize the counterstroke ...d5.

An interesting "pass move" is 6... h6, restraining White's dark squared bishop from reaching g5. Together with the ubiquitous exchange fe5-... de5 it was seen by transposition in Gurevich–Kamsky, *US Ch 1991*, drawn, 41 moves: 7 fe5 de5 8 Na4 Bd6 when 9 Be3 Ng4 10 Bg1 △ h3-Qd2-0–0–0± would leave White successfully challenging key central dark squares.

Although Black does have a variety of more dependable replies, **6... Be6,** strangely enough, is not one of them. It is true that on 7 Be6 fe6 8 fe5 de5 White's deposed king bishop would bequeath Black a useful (though doubled) center pawn (contrast the ...Be6 lines stemming from Diagram 12B-1), but White can simply deliberate in favor of **7 Bb5.** Then **7... a6**[3] **8 Bc6 bc6 9 fe5! de5 10 Qe2**± (avoiding 10 Ne5?? Qd4 △ ...Qf2 or Qe5–+) [9] reaches Diagram 12C-2.

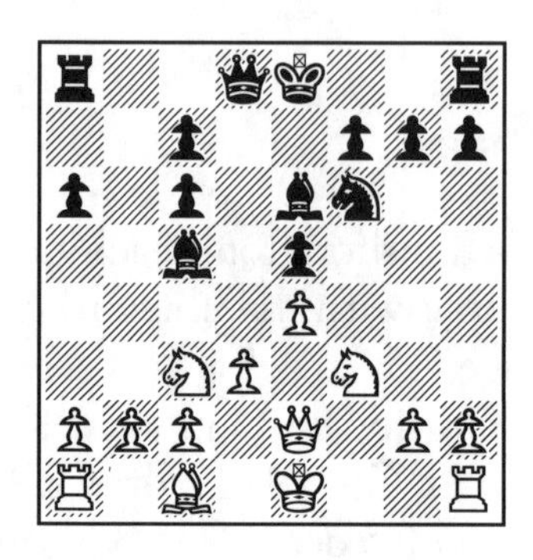

12C-2

Black's P/e5 must now be defended and his shattered Q-side pawns are targets. In partial compensation, Black has two active bishops and decent squares for his pieces. Logical is 10... Qd6 (in White's favor are 10... Ng4 11 h3 and 10... Nh5 11 Ng5), although White can count on 11 Be3 (unrewarding is 11 Na4?! Ba7) to maintain his advantage.

For instance, after 11... Bb6 White can close the lines on the Q-side with 12 Bb6 (contrast Diagram 12A-3 where ...ab6 would be possible), castle long, and proceed with a K-side minority attack. Alternatively, against 11... Be3 White might prefer to castle short and plan to work on Black's Q-side debilities.

Returning to Diagram 12C-1, a little more promising for Black are 6... 0–0, 6... Na5, and 6... a6 (for 6... Bg4 see Section 12D). The routine **6... 0–0** should be met by **7 fe5** (or 7 f5 with a subsequent K-side attack in mind) **de5 8 Bg5**⩲ [5], establishing an annoying pin on Black's N/f6, though 7 Na4 Bb6 8 Nb6 ab6 9 fe5 (not 9 c3?! d5!∓) de5 10 a3 (c3) △ 0–0= [13] is also interesting.

Next (after 8 Bg5), both 8... Qd6? (8... Na5 9 Nd5) 9 Nb5± △ Bf6-Nc7 and 8... h6 9 Bf6 Qf6 10 Nd5 △ Qd2-0–0–0-Rdf1 do not help Black, so probable is **8... Be6.**

Nonetheless, **9 Bb3!**⩲

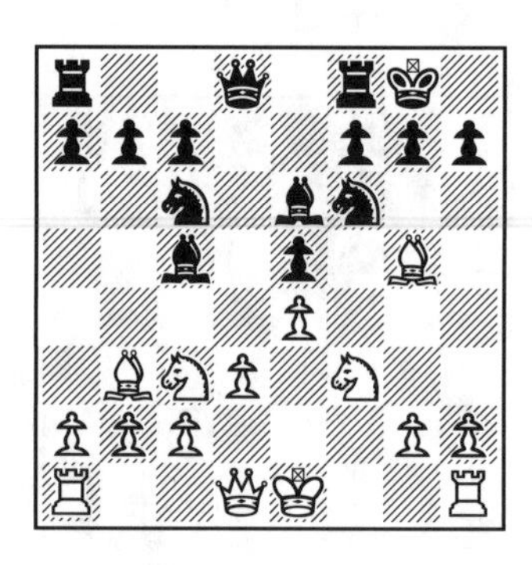

12C-3

postpones Nd5 for a more propitious moment and invites 9... Bb3 10 ab3 (threatening 11 Nd5) Nb4 (10... Qd6? 11 Nb5) 11 Na4 Bd6 12 0–0! △ Nh4, etc. If instead 9... Na5, White may proceed methodically with 10 Qe2, keeping Nd1-Ne3-0–0 or Rf1-(Be3)-0–0–0 in reserve. Black, meanwhile, could well have to face an unremitting search for an effective plan.

Optionally (from Diagram 12C-1), with **6... Na5** Black plays to remove White's king bishop. Here **7 Bb3** (Qe2) can lead to 7... a6 (not 7... Be6? due to 8 Be6 fe6 9 fe5 de5 10 Ne5 Qd4 11 Ng4! Ng4 12 Qg4 Qf2 13 Kd1 0–0 14 Qe2!±) 8 Qe2 (always plausible when Black cannot reinforce ...Bg4 with ...Nd4) Nb3 9 ab3. However, with White's queen guarding the *f2* square, Black would then be hard-pressed to find a comfortable way to meet the threat of fe5-Ne5. More common, therefore, is **7... Nb3 8 ab3 Bg4** (Highly instructive play follows 8... a6 9 h3! h6 10 Ne2 Qe7 — 10... d5 11 Ne5! de4 12 d4 Ba7 13 c4 — 11 fe5 de5 12 Bd2! Bd7 13 Bc3 Bd6 14 0–0 as in Spielmann—Fleischmann, *Barmen 1905.)*. There may occur **9 h3** (Na4) **Bf3 10 Qf3**⩲,

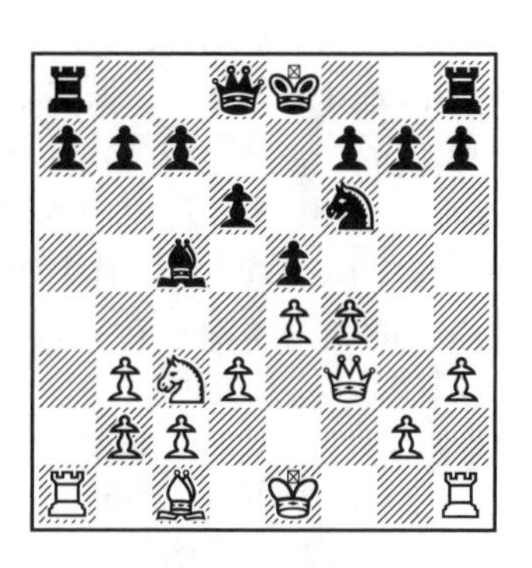

12C-4

wherein Black remains unable to lay claim to full equality.

White's position is very elastic. The semi-open a-file discourages ...0–0–0, and on 10... 0–0 White can saddle Black with an unpleasant pin via 11 fe5 △ Bg5-Nd5, though 11 f5 △ 0–0–0 is worth consideration as well. If Black prevents Bg5 with 10... h6, White can continue with Be3-(f5)-Ne2-c3-d4 to prepare K-side castling while mobilizing the center pawns.

Finally (from Diagram 12C-1), Black may first attend to the safety of his dark-squared bishop by selecting the well-trafficked **6... a6.** This move intends to preserve Black's dark-squared bishop while preventing K-side castling by White. Once again, **7 fe5** (playable also are 7 Rf1!?, 7 Ng5!?, and 7 f5!?) **de5 8 Bg5,** restricting the activity of Black's N/f6, is White's preferred course. Here, 8... Bg4 9 h3 just improves White's position, so usual next is **8... Qd6** (8... h6 looks transpositional although Glazkov gives 9 Bf6 Qf6 10 Nd5 Qd6 11 Qd2 Be6=), leaving White several testable choices. One of them, 9 Rf1, can lead to wild complications after 9... Na5 10 Qe2!? Nc4 11 dc4 Bb4 12 Rd1! Bc3 13 bc3∞ when Black's attackable position might offset White's tripled pawns.

Easier to recommend, however, is **9 Qd2,** a flexible move which improves slightly on 9 Bf6 as played in Spielmann—Maroczy, *1905*. Because White is then prepared to answer 9... 0–0 with 10 a3 (both 10... Be6 11 Bf6 and 10... Bg4 11 Rf1 are good for him), Black does better to eradicate White's light-squared bishop with **9... Na5 10 Bb3 Nb3 11 ab3.** Next, Black can sidestep the buildup Rf1-Nh4 with **11... h6** (11... 0–0 12 Nb5! or 11... Nh5 12 Nd5 f6 13 Be3 Be3 14 Ne3 △ 0–0-b4), triggering **12 Bh4 Be6** (for 12... Nh5 △ ...g5 see Illustrative Game II) **13 Rf1 0–0–0 14 0–0–0±** [5].

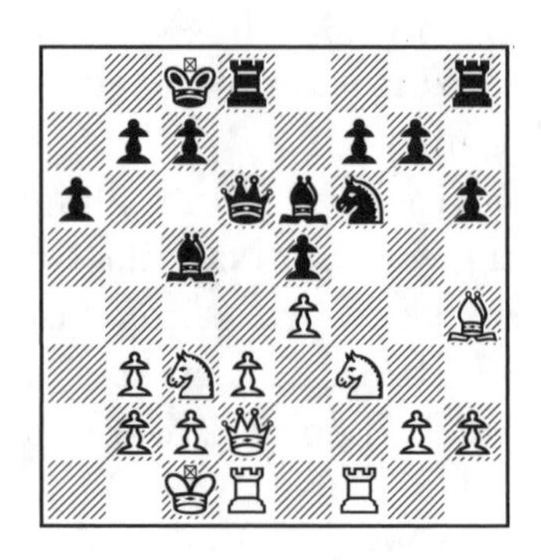

12C-5

To make use of the half-open f-file, White should eye Bf6-Nh4-Nf5 as well as Ne2-Bf2-Ng3-Nf5. Another plan is Ne2-d4 with the intention of incorporating Bg3 at the right moment. Black, by contrast, has wrought doubled pawns in the vicinity of White's king. He has the bishop pair and good development. Throughout the middlegame, both sides will need to monitor the central outpost squares *d4* and *d5*.

In particular, on 14... Ng4 (△ Be3) White has 15 Rde1 g5 16 Bg3 Qb6 17 Na4±. The immediate 14... g5 15 Bg3 Ng4 (15... Nh5? 16 Be5+−) transposes.

ILLUSTRATIVE GAME I

Raingruber—Fritzinger
Berkeley 1978

1	e4	d5
2	f4	Bc5
3	Nf3	d6
4	Bc4	Nc6
5	d3	Nf6
6	Nc3	Na5
7	Bb3	a6
8	fe5 (Qe2)	de5
9	Bg5	c6
10	Qe2	Qc7
11	Rf1	Nb3
12	ab3	Nd7
13	Nd1	Nf8
14	Bd2	f6
15	Ne3	Be6
16	Nf5	0–0–0
17	Ba5	b6
18	Bd2	g6
19	Ne3	a5
20	Nc4	Bc4
21	bc4	Ne6
22	g3	Rhe8
23	Be3	f5
24	0–0–0	Be3
25	Qe3	f4
26	Qg1	c5
27	gf4	ef4
28	Qg4	Kb7
29	h4	Rd7
30	Ng5	Nd4
31	Rde1	Qc6
32	Kb1	a4
33	Qf4	a3
34	ba3	b5
35	Qf6	Rd6
36	Qf7	Ka8
37	e5	bc4
38	Qc4	Nb5
39	Qa4	Kb8
40	Kc1	Rd7
41	Rf6	Qb7
42	Qa5	Rd3
43	Rb6	Nd4
44	Rb7	Kb7
45	Qc5	Rc8
46	Qc8	1–0

ILLUSTRATIVE GAME II

Hay—Bisguier
Lone Pine 1972

1	e4	e5
2	f4	Bc5
3	Nf3	d6
4	Nc3	Nf6
5	Bc4	Nc6
6	d3	a6
7	fe5	de5
8	Bg5	h6
9	Bh4	Qd6
10	Qd2	Na5
11	Bb3	Nb3
12	ab3	Nh5
13	Nd5	g5
14	Bf2	Bf2
15	Qf2	Be6
16	Ne3	0–0–0
17	g3	c6
18	0–0–0	Qc5
19	Kb1	Rhf8
20	Rd2!	f5
21	ef5	Bf5
22	Nf5	Qf2
23	Ne7	Kd7
24	Rf2	Ke7
25	Rhf1? (Re1!)	Rd5!

26	**Nd2**	**Rf2**
27	**Rf2**	**Nf6**
28	**Kc1**	**Ke6**
	½–½	

PROBLEMS

1. Continuing with **7 fe5 Ng4 8 Nd4 Bd4 9 e6** (see Diagram 12C-6), neutralize:

a) **9... Qh4.**
b) **9... Nf2.**
c) **9... Bf2.**

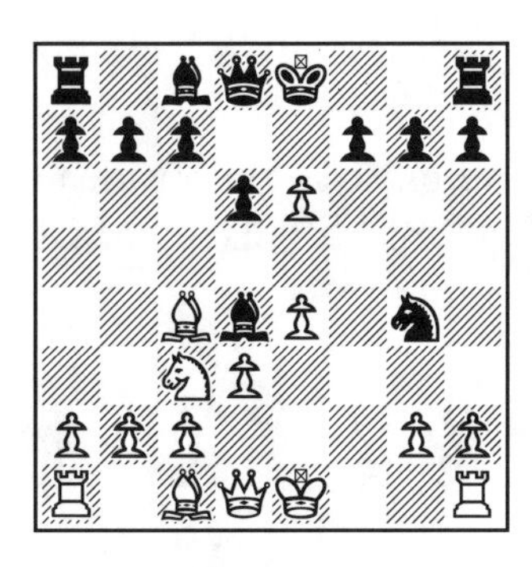

12C-6

2. The salvo **7 Ng5!** (see Diagram 12C-7) begins a potent counterattack. Tackle:

a) **7... Nf2.**
b) **7... h6?**
c) **7... 0–0 8 f5 Bf2 9 Kf1 Ne3.**

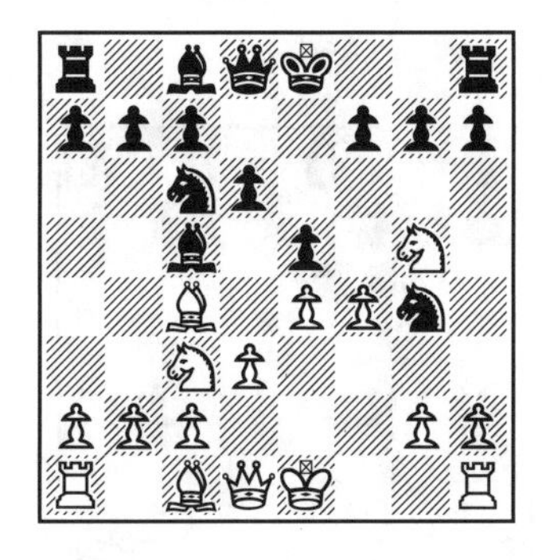

12C-7

3. Amazingly, Black has no better move! From Diagram 12C-8, banish:

a) **7... 0–0.**
b) **7... Bd7.**

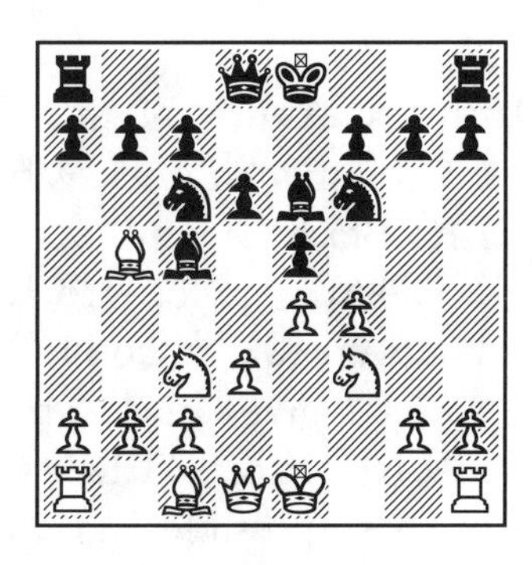

12C-8

Classical Declined Variation (D)

The most common idea over time on Black's sixth move has been to pin the N/f3:

1	**e4**	**e5**
2	**f4**	**Bc5**
3	**Nf3**	**d6**
4	**Nc3**	**Nf6**
5	**Bc4**	**Nc6**
6	**d3**	**Bg4**
7	**Na4!**	

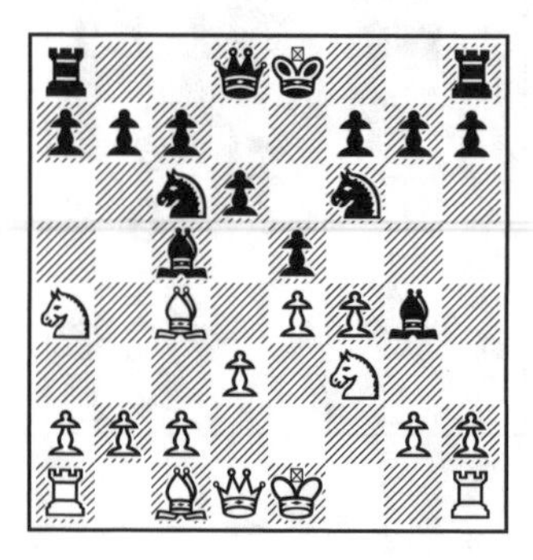

12D-1

With his seventh move (Alekhine's recommendation), White skirts 7 h3 Bf3 8 Qf3 ef4! 9 Bb5! (9 Bf4? Nd4 10 Qg3 loses to 10... Nh5!, but even 10 Qd1 c6 11 Qd2 d5! △ ...0–0∓ gives Black an attack) 0–0 10 Bc6 bc6 11 Bf4 with equality. Also possible is 7 Bb5, though 7... 0–0 8 Bc6 bc6 9 fe5 de5 10 Qe2 Nh5 or even 10... Rb8 can lead to good counterchances for Black (contrast Diagram 12A-3 where Black must stop to defend his e-pawn). Instead, by taking off Black's powerful king bishop, White achieves good prospects for an edge because castling Kingside becomes a quick option.

Black has a considerable number of replies after 7 Na4!, though good ones are not so easy to find. For instance, both 7... Qe7 8 Nc5 dc5 9 Bb5! ef4 10 Bc6 bc6 11 Bf4 c4 12 0–0 0–0 13 Qe2± [13] and 7... Na5?! 8 Nc5 Nc4 9 Nb7 Qb8 10 Nd6! cd6 (10... Nd6 11 fe5) 11 dc4 Qb4 12 c3 (or 12 Qd2 △ Qd3) Qc4 13 Qd6! Qe4 14 Kf2 Bf3 15 Qe5± are unpleasant for him. Clearly, 7... 0–0 8 Nc5 dc5 9 0–0![1] (h3) and 7... ef4 8 Nc5 dc5 9 Bf4[2] are convenient for White, whereas 7... a6 8 Nc5 dc5 9 a4 (0–0) Nh5 10 f5 Nf4 11 0–0 Nd4 12 Bf7 Kf8 13 Bf4 ef4 14 Ba2± does little to improve matters.

Provocative is 7... Nh5!? 8 Nc5 dc5 9 f5 0–0 (for 9... Nf6 see Illustrative Game IV) 10 Be3 Qd6 (10... b6 11 Bd5 and 10... Nf4 11 Bf4 ef4 12 c3 △ 0–0-Qd2) 11 h3

Bf3 12 Qf3 Nf6 13 c3 △ Qf2-0–0–0 or 0–0-g4-g5, etc. Note that 13... Na5 is answered by 14 Bb5 c6 15 Ba4 b5 16 Bc2 when White's plans remain in force. Black should seek another avenue in an effort to equalize.

Robust retaliation with **7... Nd4,** however, still concedes White a pull after **8 Nc5 dc5 9 c3! Nf3 10 gf3.** Next, both 10... Bh3 11 fe5± and 10... Ne4? 11 0–0!+– [1] (not 11 Qe2? Qh4!∓) are insufficient, but **10... Bh5** is more dependable. There follows **11 Qe2** (defending against ...Ne4 and threatening fe5) **Qd6** (11... Nd7 12 Rg1 Qf6 13 f5±, e.g., 13... g6?! 14 Bg5!) **12 fe5 Qe5 13 f4 Qe7 14 Qg2 0–0–0 15 0–0**⩲ [1].

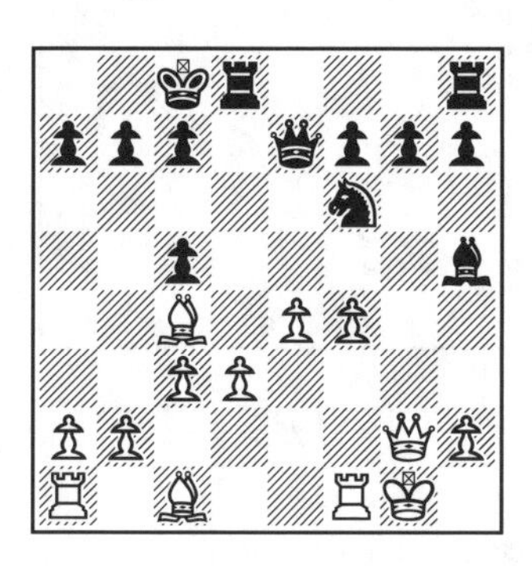

12D-2

White's preponderance of center pawns should not rush to the advance, since an immediate d4 would liquidate Black's main liability — his P/c5. Logical then is a4-a5, after which an appropriately timed e5 might threaten, along with Qh3 △ Qh5, to open the long h1-a8 diagonal with devastating effect. If necessary, White can incorporate Kh1, a useful defensive move which anticipates Black's g-file counterplay and even makes e5-Qg7 possible in some lines. Interestingly, the g-file might later serve as a base for endgame operations by White's rooks.

A reasonable option (from Diagram 12D-1) is the more sedate **7... Bb6,** whereupon **8 Nb6** (h3) **ab6 9 c3** (prohibiting ...Nd4) **ef4!**[3] (9... Na5 10 Bb5 c6 11 Ba4, and if 11... b5, then 12 Bc2, and White is prepared for the thematic pawn thrust d4; 9... 0–0 10 0–0 [fe5] when possible are: a) 10... Na5 [10... Bf3 is similar] 11 Bb5 Bf3 12 gf3 [Rf3]⩲, yielding a good version of Diagram 12A-4. White's bishops [versus Black's knights] and central pawn majority combined with Black's offside queen knight give White the nod. b) 10... ef4 11 Bf4 Ne5 12 Be5 de5 13 Qe1 △ Qg3- Ne5/a3-Rad1. c) 10... d5 transposes to Problem 12D#3 after both sides castle.) **10 Bf4 Nh5 11 Be3 Ne5 12 Bb3 Nf3** (12... Bf3 13 gf3 Qh4 14 Kd2!± [13]) **13 gf3 Be6**⩲ [5] delivers White a bishop pair to go with his vanguard of central pawns.

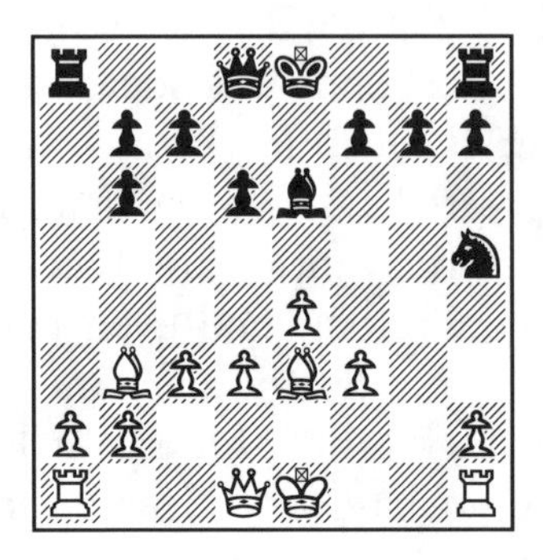

12D-3

Here White might try Kd2-Kc2 to hide away his king, especially if Black checks on *h4*, while Be6-a3 would envisage castling long. In either event White can then mobilize his rooks on the half-open g-file or relocate them in the center to support a future pawnstorm.

From Diagram 12D-1, Black could also undertake the volatile 7... Bf3 8 Qf3 Nd4, but 9 Qg3! ef4[4] 10 Qg7! quickly reveals that White has aggressive intentions, too! Here the obligatory 10... Rf8 (both 10... Nc2? 11 Kd1 △ Qf7/Kc2 and 10... Kd7? 11 Nc5 △ Qf7-Bb3 win for White) still leaves Black to cope with 11 Nc5[5].

More prudent, therefore, is **7... Nd7,** releasing the Black queen for more active duty. After **8 Nc5 dc5[6],** Spielmann—Maroczy continued 9 0–0 ef4 10 Bf4 Nce5 11 Ne5, when 11... Ne5! 12 Bf7 (or 12 Be5 Bd1 13 Bg7 [1]) Kf8 13 Be5 Bd1 14 Rad1∞ would have led to wild complications. Less explosive, however, is **9 h3.** This move limits the scope of ensuing exchanges and avoids the flashy queen sacrifice employed by Spielmann. Now **9... Bf3** (ceding White the two bishops, but on 9... Be6 10 Bb5!± △ f5 or Bc6 Black's position deteriorates) **10 Qf3 Na5** (10... Nd4 11 Qf2) **11 Bb3 Nb3 12 ab3±**

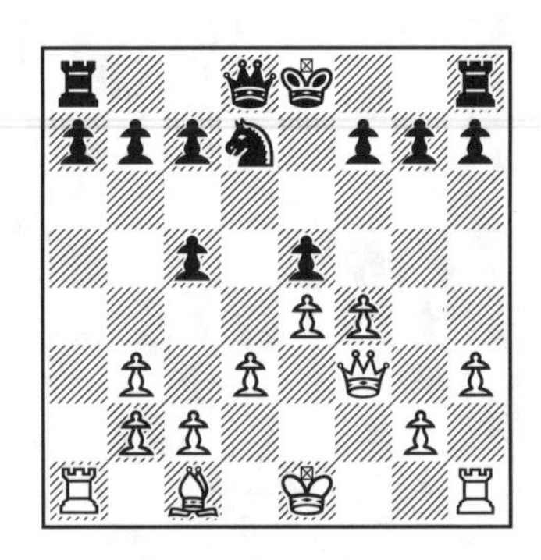

12D-4

yields White, by a natural sequence of moves, a preferable setup at little risk.

Here White can boast of latent f-file pressure, a superior center, and a good bishop. Sample play might go: 12... 0–0 (12...

Qh4 13 Qf2) 13 0–0 f6 when White could elect to storm Black's king by 14 f5 △ Be3-g4-Kh2-Rg1-Rg3!-Rag1-h4-g5.

ILLUSTRATIVE GAME I

Balashov—Matanovich
Skopje 1970

1	e4	e5
2	Nc3	Nf6
3	Bc4	Nc6
4	d3	Bc5
5	f4	d6
6	Nf3	Bg4
7	Na4!	Bf3
8	Qf3	Nd4
9	Qd1 (Qg3)	b5
10	Bf7	Kf7
11	Nc5	dc5
12	fe5	Nd7
13	c3	Ne6
14	0–0	Ke8
15	d4	cd4
16	cd4	Qe7
17	Be3	Rf8
18	d5	Rf1
19	Qf1	Nd8
20	e6	Nf6
21	Rc1	Ne4
22	Qb5	c6
23	Rc6	Kf8
24	Rc1	Kg8
25	Rc7	Qd6
26	Qe8	Qf8
27	Rg7	1–0

ILLUSTRATIVE GAME II

Alekhine—Teichmann
Berlin 1921

1	e4	e5
2	Nc3	Nc6
3	Bc4	Nf6
4	d3	Bc5
5	f4	d6
6	Nf3	Bg4
7	Na4!	a6
8	Nc5	dc5
9	0–0	Qe7
10	h3	Bf3
11	Qf3	0–0
12	Be3	ef4
13	Qf4	Ne5
14	Bb3	Rae8
15	Qf2	Nfd7
16	Rad1	b6
17	c3	Ng6
18	Qf5	Kh8
19	Bf2	Rd8
20	Bg3	Nde5
21	d4	cd4
22	cd4	Nc6
23	d5	Nce5
24	h4	Qc5
25	Kh2	f6
26	Rc1	Qd6
27	Rc6	Qe7
28	Re6	Qd7
29	h5	Ne7
30	Qh3	Nf7
31	Bf4	h6
32	Qc3	Nd6
33	Bh6	Ne4
34	Re4	Nd5
35	Qc1!	1–0

ILLUSTRATIVE GAME III

Dahl—Ryan
Golden Knights 1988/89

1	e4	e5
2	f4	Bc5
3	Nf3	d6
4	Nc3	Nc6
5	Bc4	Nf6
6	d3	Bg4
7	Na4!	Nd4
8	Nc5	Bf3
9	gf3	dc5
10	0–0	b5
11	Bb3	Nh5
12	fe5	Qh4
13	f4	Rd8
14	c3	Ne6
15	Qf3	0–0
16	f5	Ng5
17	Bg5	Qg5
18	Kh1	c4
19	Bd1	g6
20	Rg1	Qf4
21	d4	Qf3
22	Bf3	Ng7
23	d5	Kh8
24	f6	Ne8
25	Rgd1	Rd7
26	b3	h5
27	bc4	bc4
28	Be2	Kh7
29	Bc4	Kh6
30	Rab1	1–0

ILLUSTRATIVE GAME IV

Kristiansen—Nielsen
Aarhus 1992

1	e4	e5
2	Bc4	Nf6
3	d3	Nc6
4	Nc3	Bc5
5	f4	d6
6	Nf3	Bg4
7	Na4	Nh5
8	Nc5	dc5
9	f5	Nf6
10	Be3	Qd6
11	h3	Bf3
12	Qf3	Na5
13	Bb5	c6
14	Ba4	b5
15	Bd2	Nb7
16	Bb3	a5
17	a4	0–0
18	c4	b4
19	0–0–0	Rad8
20	Be3	Kh8
21	g4	Ng8
22	Rd2	f6
23	h4	Qe7
24	g5	Rd7
25	Bc2	Rfd8
26	b3	Qf8
27	Rg1	Rc7
28	Bd1	Rdd7
29	Kc2	Re7
30	Qg3	Red7
31	Bh5	Re7
32	Qg4	Red7
33	Bg6	Nd8
34	Bh7	Kh7
35	Qh5	Nh6
36	gh6	gh6
37	Bc5	Qc5
38	Qg6	Kh8
39	Qg8#	

PROBLEMS

1. By castling before playing c3, prove (from Diagram 12D-5) that White becomes well-equipped for:

a) **9... Nd4.**
b) **9... Na5.**

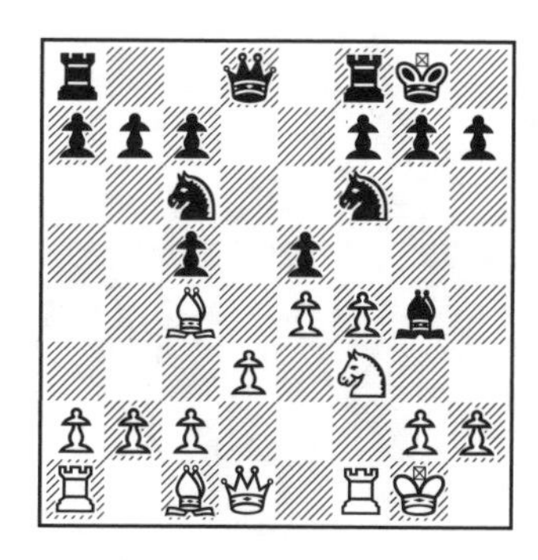

12D-5

2. Allowing the decentralization of his d-pawn does not offer Black good results. From Diagram 12D-6, answer:

a) **9... Na5?**
b) **9... Nh5.**
c) **9... 0–0.**

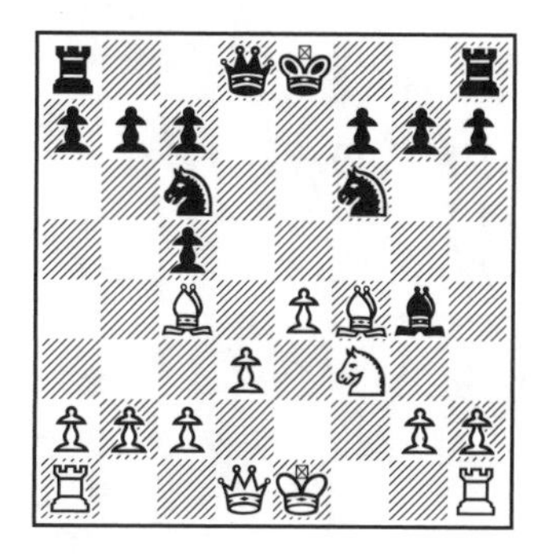

12D-6

3. Though ...d5 is potentially an effective counter before White castles, why does **9... d5** (see Diagram 12D-7) fail here?

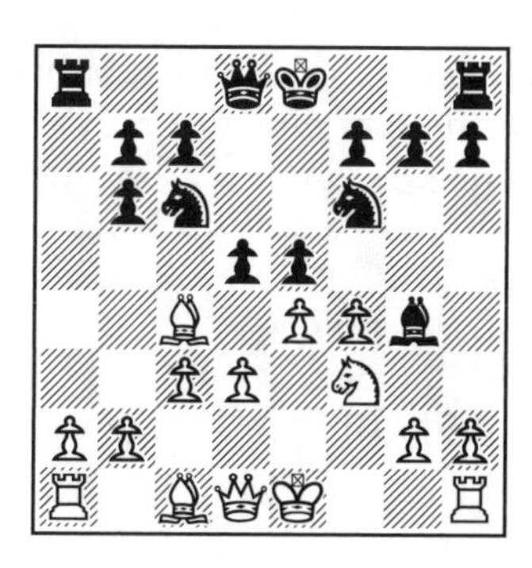

12D-7

4. From Diagram 12D-8, dissuade Black from:

a) **9... 0–0.**
b) **9... Nc2.**

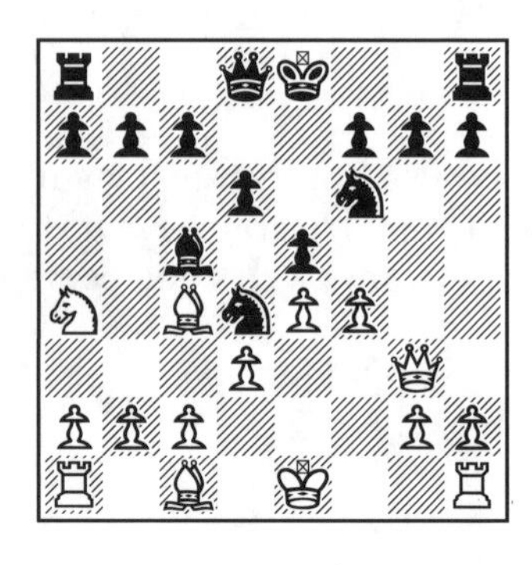

12D-8

5. Black is in trouble here. From Diagram 12D-9, foil:

a) **11... Qe7.**
b) **11... dc5.**
c) **11... Nc2.**

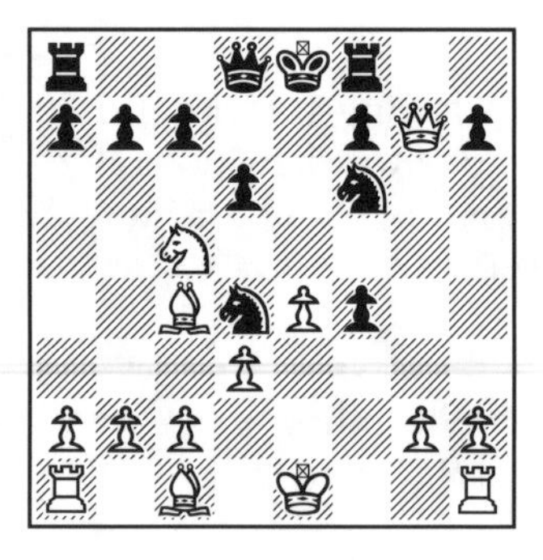

12D-9

6. Though **8... Nc5** keeps Black's pawn structure intact, **9 h3** (Bb5!?), reaching Diagram 12D-10, puts the question to Black. Brush off:

a) **9... Bd7.**
b) **9... Be6.**
c) **9... Bf3.**

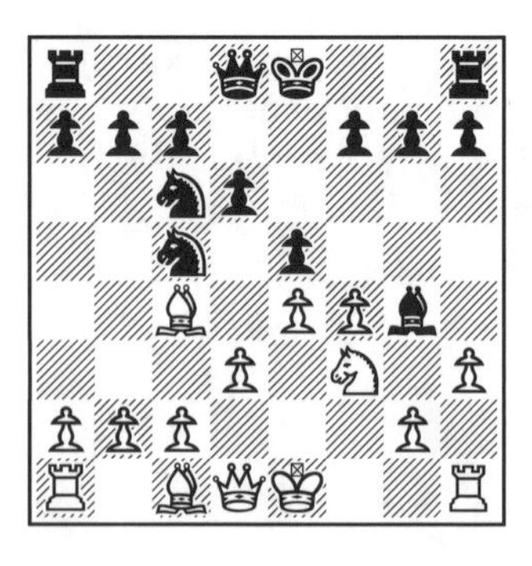

12D-10

13: SOLID VARIATION

With the passive 2... d6 Black introduces the Solid Variation:

1	**e4**	**e5**
2	**f4**	**d6**
3	**Nf3** (d4!?)	

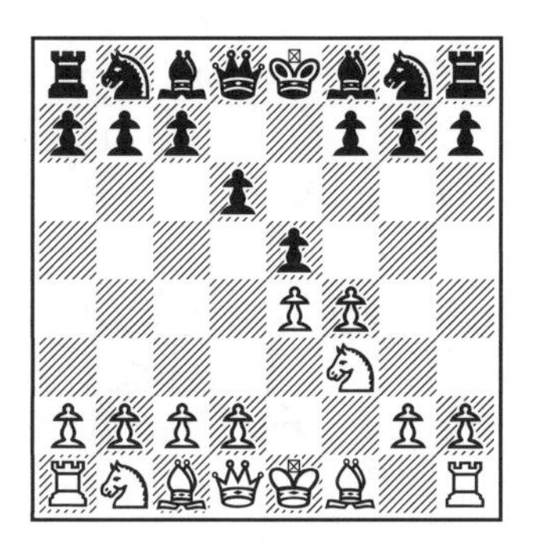

13-1

Experimenting with 3 Nc3 can lead to 3... ef4 4 Bc4 (4 Nf3 g5 is good for Black, since White has not yet played d4) Qh4, a double-edged offshoot of what is known as the Keres Attack. The text (3 Nf3) avoids such complications at the cost of allowing Black to transpose into the Fischer Variation with 3... ef4 (cf. Ch. 4).

Instead, Black can try **3... Nf6**[1] (3... Nc6 4 Bb5 Nge7 5 fe5 de5 6 d3 a6 7 Bc4± or 4... Bd7 5 0–0 Nd4 6 Nd4 ed4 7 Bc4 g6 8 d3 Bg7 9 f5 Nf6 10 Bg5 △ Qf3± [1] or 3... Nd7 4 d4 Ngf6 5 fe5 Ne4 6 Bd3 d5 7 Nc3 Nc3 8 bc3 Be7 9 0–0 0–0 10 Qe1 Re8 11 Qg3 Nf8 12 Ng5 f6 13 ef6 Bf6 14 Bd2 when 14... c5?! allows a double exchange sacrifice by White on 15 Rf6! Qf6 16 Rf1 Qe7 17 Rf8! Kf8 18 Qf3 Kg8 19 Bh7 Kh8 20 Qh5 Bg4 21 Qh4 Qf6 22 Bg6 Kg8 23 Bf7 Kf8 24 Qg4 Re4 25 Nh7 Kf7 26 Nf6 Rg4 27 Ng4± [14]). Then **4 Nc3 Nc6** (4... Nbd7 5 Bc4) **5 Bb5** (thematic pin) **Bd7 6 d3** (0–0!?) reaches a version of Diagram 12A-2 even more favorable to White because Black's king bishop remains at home. One plausible sequel is **6... ef4**[2] **7 Bf4 Be7 8 0–0 0–0 9 d4 Be8**[3] **10 Qd2 Nd7 11 Rae1 Bf6**± [1].

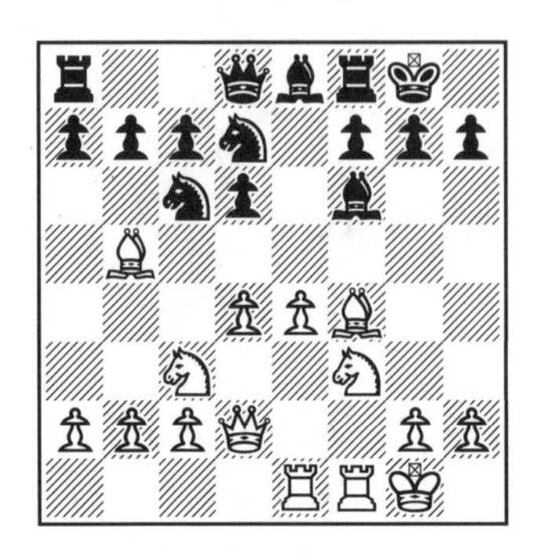

13-2

Black is cramped and his options for obtaining play are limited. White, by contrast, has a mobile pawn center, greater space, and the more effective development. Here Nd5 (△ Nf6 or Ne3), Ne2-c3-Ng3-Nf5, and Bc4-Rf2-Ref1-Bg5 clearly reveal the rich assortment of plans at White's disposal.

Returning to Diagram 13-1, the daring alternative **3... f5** triggers assertive play incorporating **4 Bc4.** Next 4... ef4[4] 5 d3 Nf6 (5... fe4 6 de4 g5 7 h4! △ Ng5) 6 Nc3 Nh5 7 0–0 fe4 (7... g5 8 Ne5!) 8 de4 c6 9 Nd4±[5] already foretells the Black king's trials in this line. More to the point is **4... fe4,** apparently winning a vital center pawn; but following **5 Ne5 de5** (5... d5 6 Qh5 g6 7 Ng6 Nf6 8 Qe5 △ Nh8+–) **6 Qh5 Kd7** (6... Ke7 7 Qe5+–) **7 Qf5** (Bg8!?) **Kc6 8 Qe4 Kb6,** even the natural **9 Nc3±** △ Na4 takes on menacing proportions.

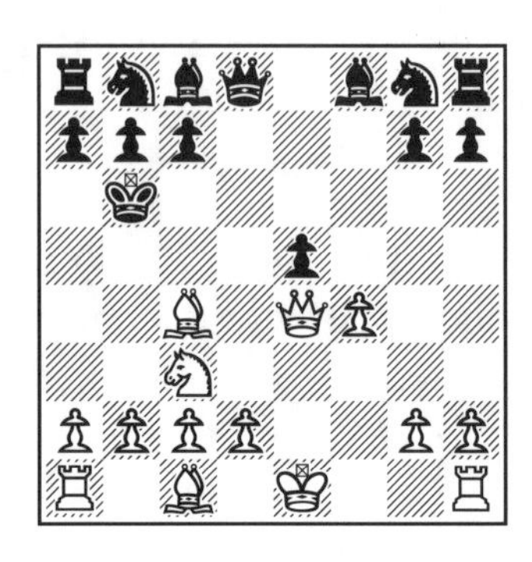

13-3

Black's development is nonexistent — not to mention the plight of his wayward monarch! Despite material superiority, it is hard to see how Black can neutralize White's growing threats. Thus on 9... c6 (what else?) 10 fe5, both 10... Kc7 11 d4 b6 (11... Bb4 12 Bf4 b6 is similar. Black's king needs a haven.) 12 Bf4 △ 0–0–0-d5 and 10... a6 11 d4 Ka7 12 Be3 Nd7 13 d5 △ 0–0–0-d6-e6 saddle Black with an entangled position demanding precise defense.

PROBLEMS

1. On 3... **Bg4** (see Diagram 13-4), can White insist that Black's queen bishop has joined the fray too soon?

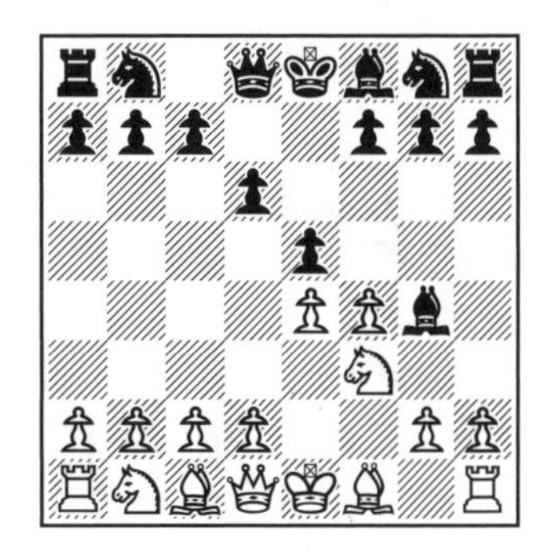

13-4

2. **6... Be7?** (see Diagram 13-5) seems reasonable, but just courts defeat. Why?

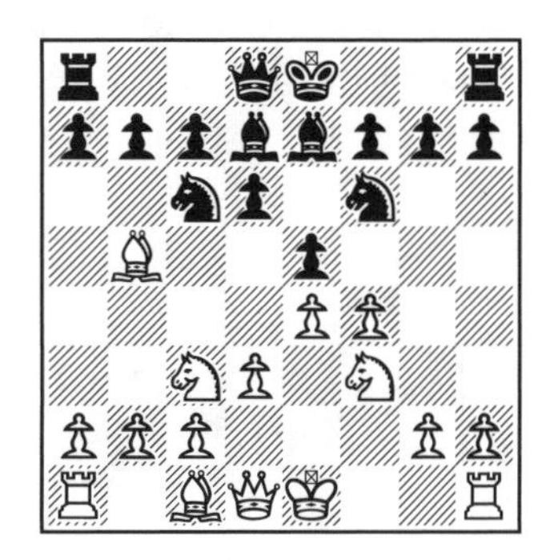

13-5

3. With **9... a6** (see Diagram 13-6), Black hopes to disperse the B/b5 with tempo or win the "minor exchange." Does White have an effective rejoinder?

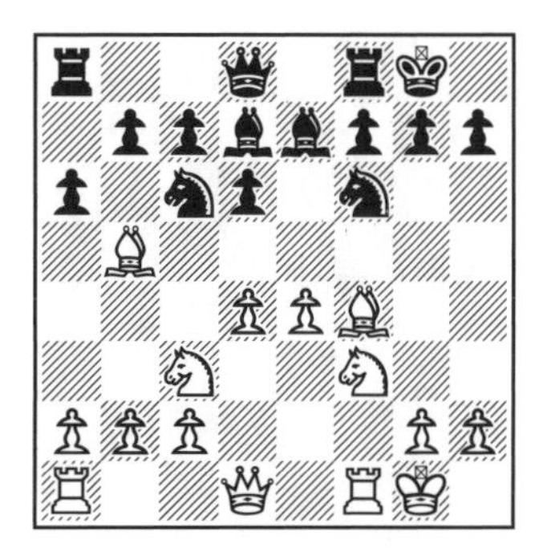

13-6

4. From Diagram 13-7, what simple move solidifies White's position after the unassuming:

a) **4... Nf6.**
b) **4... Nc6.**

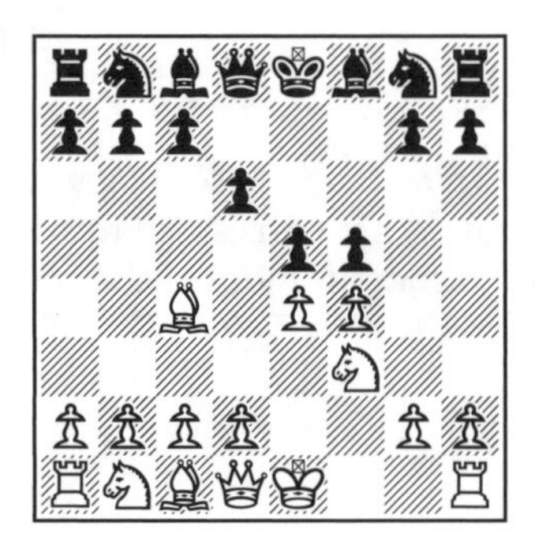

13-7

5. Turn back the futile **9... Qh4?** (see Diagram 13-8).

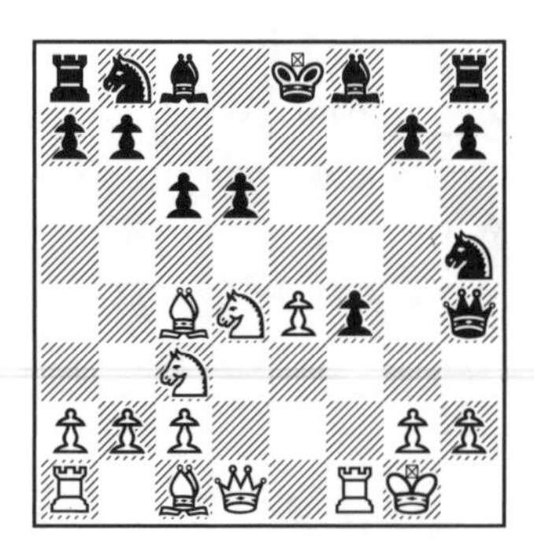

13-8

14: KING KNIGHT DECLINED VARIATION

Black counterattacks the P/e4 in the King Knight Declined Variation:

1	**e4**	**e5**
2	**f4**	**Nf6**
3	**Nf3**	

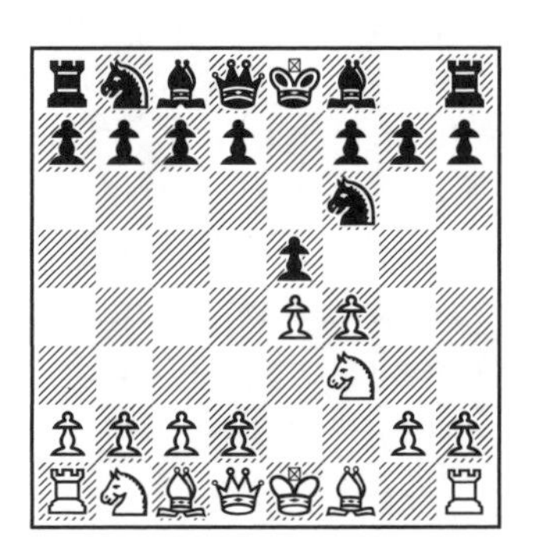

14-1

The alternative 3 fe5 allows 3... Ne4 4 Nf3 Ng5 when 5 d4 (5 Bb5 Bc5! is fine for Black) Nf3 6 Qf3 Qh4 7 Qf2 Qf2 8 Kf2 d6 would produce a hard ending for White to win. The text (i.e., 3 Nf3) offers White good chances for advantage because he can answer 3... Ne4 with 4 d3 (Qe2!?). This finesse forbids early exchanges by driving Black's king knight to c5 before relinquishing control of g5. Now 4... Nc5 5 fe5 leaves Black nothing better than to steer for the position of Diagram 14-3 via 5... d5, since 5... d6 6 d4 Ncd7 7 ed6 △ c4± just puts White firmly in command.

Getting back to Diagram 14-1, 3... ef4 (probably best) 4 Nc3 and 3... d6 4 Nc3 transpose to Chapters 8 and 13, respectively. The only other main counter is **3... d5** (3... Nc6? 4 fe5 Ne4 5 d3 Nc5 6 d4 △ d5), after which **4 fe5** requires Black to choose between **4... de4?** and 4... Ne4. The former foreordains a peculiar exchange of knights; thus, **5 ef6 ef3 6 Qf3 Nc6 7 Bb5! Qf6 8 Qf6 gf6 9 d4!±** [9].

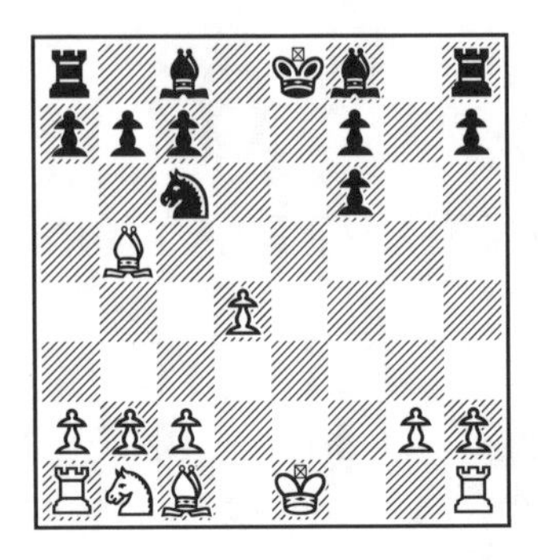

14-2

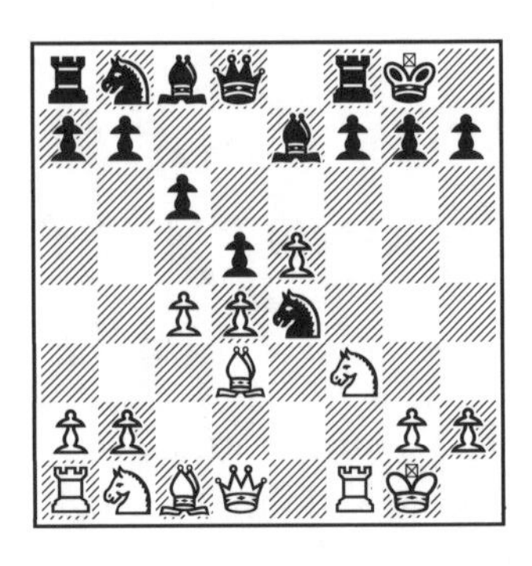

14-3

White's thematic pin on the N/c6 presents Black with ticklish problems. Following 9... Bd7 10 c3, how does Black coordinate castling with the defense of his doubled pawns? White can attack them simply by castling short. Coupling that with White's Q-side majority and its attendant central pressure, it becomes hard to understand why Black would go in for this line.

Consequently, on **3... d5 4 fe5,** necessary is **4... Ne4** inviting **5 d3** (thematic whenever White controls g5) **Nc5 6 d4 Ne4**[1] **7 Bd3 Be7**[2] (7... Bg4 8 0–0) **8 0–0 0–0 9 c4 c6**[3]± [9].

Here 10 Qc2 f5 11 ef6 Nf6 12 Ng5 (weakening the g6 square) h6 13 Nf3 gives White a pedestrian but effective kingside attacking orientation. After Nc3, White can appropriate action against *f7* or *h7* while reserving cd5 until Black develops his queen knight. To sum up, the scales tip in White's favor because of his central superiority.

ILLUSTRATIVE GAME I

Rohde—Martz
1975

1	e4	e5
2	f4	Nf6
3	fe5	Ne4
4	Nf3	d5
5	d3	Nc5
6	d4	Ne4
7	Bd3	Be7
8	0–0	0–0
9	Nbd2 (c4)	Nd2
10	Bd2	c5
11	dc5	Bc5
12	Kh1	Bg4
13	Qe1	Nc6
14	Bh7	Kh7
15	Ng5	Kg6
16	Qh4	Bh5
17	Qh3	f5
18	ef6	Qf6
19	Qd3	Qf5
20	Rf5	Rf5
21	Ne6	Bd6
22	Ng7	Raf8
23	Nf5	Rf5
24	Rf1	Bg4
25	Rf5	1–0

ILLUSTRATIVE GAME II

Bronstein—Yusupov
1981

1	e4	e5
2	f4	Nf6
3	Nf3	Ne4
4	d3	Nc5
5	fe5	d5
6	d4	Ne6
7	c4	Bb4
8	Bd2	Bd2
9	Qd2	c6
10	Nc3	0–0
11	Rc1	Nc7
12	cd5	cd5
13	Bd3	Bg4
14	Ng5!	f5
15	h3	Bh5
16	0–0	Bg6
17	Nb5	Nba6
18	Nd6	h6
19	Nf3	Ne6
20	Kh1	Rb8
21	Ng1	Qg5
22	Qf2	Nb4
23	Bb5	f4
24	Nf3	Qe7
25	Qd2	Na6
26	Bd3	Bh5
27	Bc2	Nac7
28	Qd3	g6
29	Bb3	Kh8
30	Ba4	Rg8
41	Qd2	Rg7
32	Qf2	Rf8
33	Rc3	g5
34	Rfc1	Bg6
35	Bc2	Ne8
36	Bg6	Rg6
37	Qc2	Rgg8
38	Nc8	Qf7
39	Qb3	N6c7
40	Nd6	Nd6
41	ed6	1–0

PROBLEMS

1. **6... Ne6** (see Diagram 14-4) is rebuked by what energetic retort?

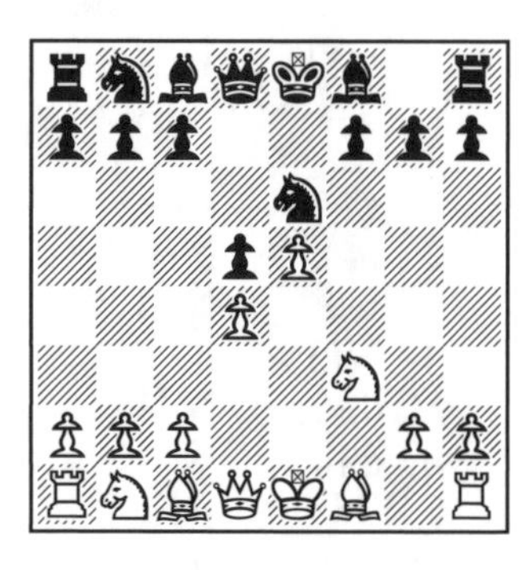

14-4

2. On the impetuous **7... c5** White can exploit Black's overextended king knight with **8 c4** (see Diagram 14-5). Handle:

a) **8... Qa5.**
b) **8... Bf5.**
c) **8... cd4.**

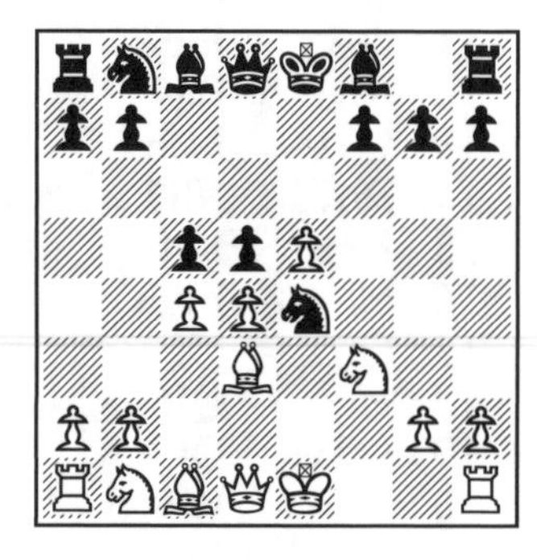

14-5

3. **9... Be6** (see Diagram 14-6) can lead to trouble for Black. Why?

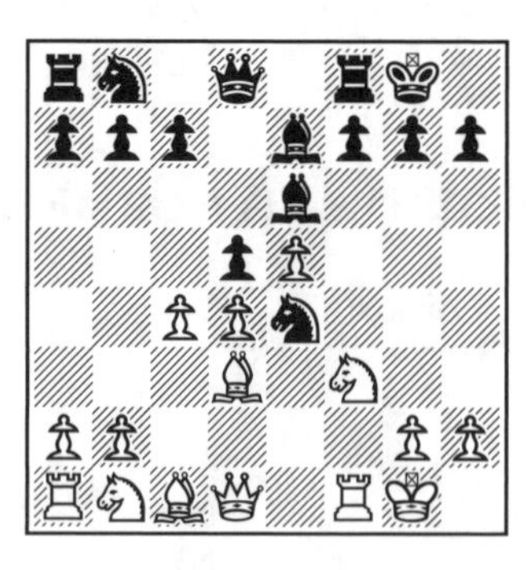

14-6

15: KEENE VARIATION

Not to be taken lightly is the early queen sortie 2... Qh4, hallmark of the Keene Variation:

1	e4	e5
2	f4	**Qh4**
3	g3	**Qe7**
4	d3	

(For 4 Nc3!? see the Illustrative Game.)

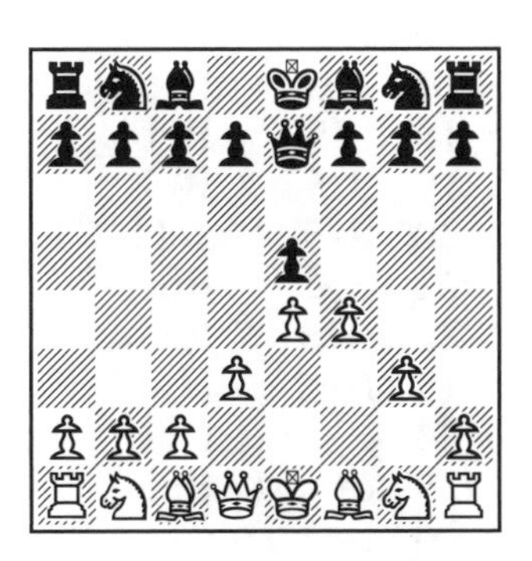

15-1

It is worth noting that White thus passes up 4 fe5 d6 5 ed6 Qe4 6 Qe2 Qe2 7 Ne2 Bd6 8 Nbc3 c6± (even better may be the equalizing try here 8... a6 △ ...Nc6 [19]) because queens come off a bit early.

The adventurous 3... Qf6?! would have failed to 4 fe5!± △ Nc3-d4-(Nf3), but even here, by linking his center pawns to fend off tactical tricks, White sets out to cast a shadow on his opponent's second move.

Convenient but pertinent for White now (after 3... Qe7 4 d3!) is 4... d5, since 5 Nc3[1] already leaves Black in search of an equalizing reply. Black's sensitive d5-square needs constant surveillance. In Raingruber–Melendez, *Modesto 1994*, Black overreached with 7... Ng4: (from Diagram 15-1) self-destructing on 4... Nc6 5 Nc3 Nf6 6 Nf3 Qc5 7 fe5 Ng4 8 d4 Qb6 9 Nd5 Bb4? 10 c3 Bc3 11 bc3 Qa5 12 Bd2 b5 13 Bb5 etc. (1–0 in 23).

Steadiest may be **4... d6**[2] (4... ef4 5 Bf4 Qb4 6 Nd2 Qb2 7 Bc7 Bb4 8 Nf3 only bothers Black), though **5 Nc3** (5 Bg2 Nc6 6 Ne2 Bg4= [13]) **Nf6 6 Bh3 Bh3** (6... Nc6 7 Bc8 Rc8 8 Nf3 ef4 9 Bf4 △ 0–0±) **7 Nh3 g6**[3] **8 0–0 Bg7 9**

f5 0–0 10 Bg5±

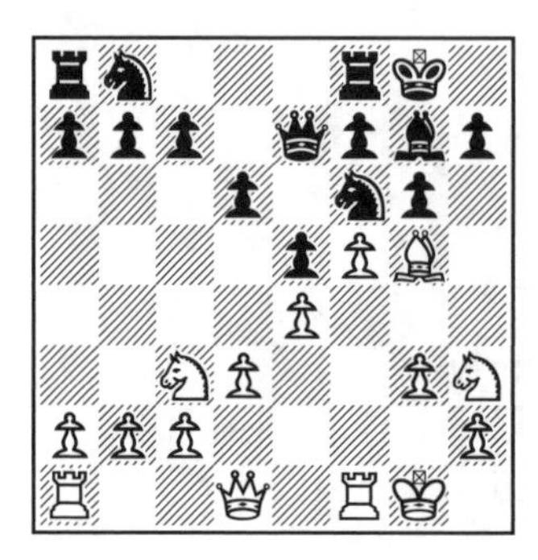

15-2

still challenges Black to justify the awkward location of his queen.

After 10... c6 (necessary) 11 Qd2 (g4!?) Nbd7 (11... Qc7 12 Bf6 Bf6 13 g4 gf5 14 g5 △ ef5) 12 g4 Qe8 13 Nf2, Black cannot easily coordinate his pieces. Answering with 13... d5 runs into 14 Bf6, which wins a pawn at the very least, so Black must presently remain passive in the center while anticipating the storming of his castled king. White, on the other hand, can organize his forces on the K-side with Bh6-Ne2-Ng3-h4-h5-Qg5 while keeping watch for the opportunity to exchange favorably on *f*6.

ILLUSTRATIVE GAME

Hebden—Vianin
Geneva 1987

1	e4	e5
2	f4	Qh4
3	g3	Qe7
4	Nc3!? (d3)	ef4
5	d4	fg3
6	Bf4!	d5
7	Nd5	Qe4
8	Qe2	Qe2
9	Ne2	Na6
10	Nc7	Nc7
11	Bc7	Nf6
12	Bg3	Ne4
13	Bf4	Bf5
14	Bg2	0–0–0
15	0–0	Bg6
16	Bh3	f5
17	Be5	Bd6
18	Bf5	Bf5
19	Rf5	Be5
20	Re5	Nd2
21	Kg2	Rhe8
22	Re8	Re8
23	Ng3	Nc4
24	b3	Nd6
25	c4	Re3
26	Rd1	g6
27	Rd2	h5
28	c5	h4
29	Nf1	Ne4
30	Ne3	Nd2
31	Nc4	Ne4
32	Nd6	Nd6
33	cd6	1–0

PROBLEMS

1. From Diagram 15-3, scan:

a) **5... d4?**
b) **5... de4.**
c) **5... ef4.**
d) **5... c6.**
e) **5... Nf6?**

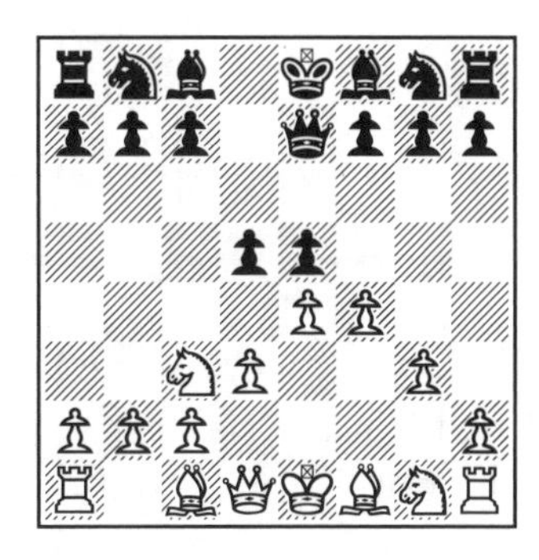

15-3

2. **4... f5** (see Diagram 15-4) just wastes more time. Why?

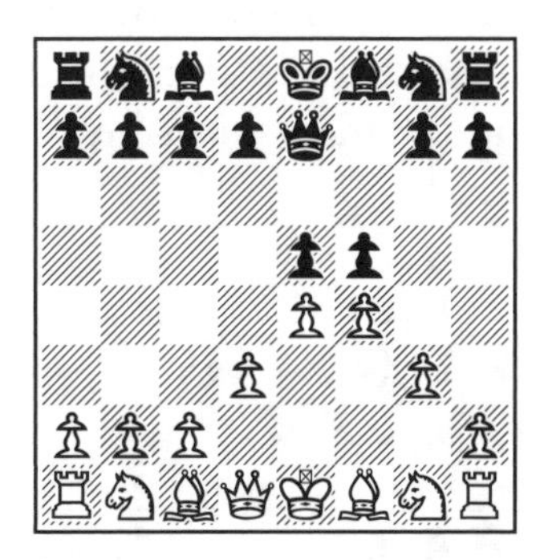

15-4

3. From Diagram 15-5, determine a course of action against:

a) **7... Nc6 8 0–0 0–0–0.**
b) **7... h6 8 Be3 Nbd7.**
c) **7... Qd7.**

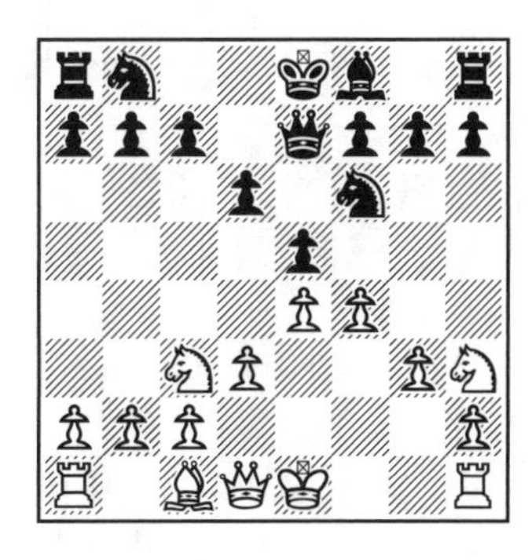

15-5

16: LESSER DECLINED VARIATIONS

Black's prospects in the Lesser Declined Variations for the most part do not inspire confidence. The most interesting lines of independent significance encompass 2... f5, the hot-off-the-press 2... Qf6, and 2... Nc6. The first of these is a reckless countergambit which has, understandably, rarely been seen.

1	**e4**	**e5**
2	**f4**	**f5**[1]
3	**ef5**	

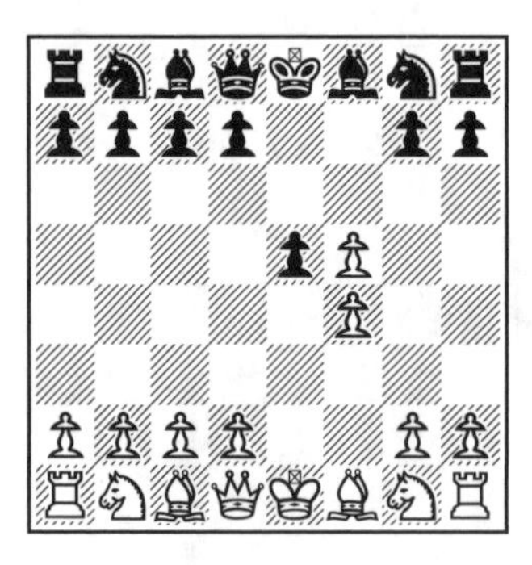

16-1

Continuing the symmetry with 3... ef4 simply invites 4 Qh5 Ke7 5 Qh4 Nf6 6 Qf4 d6 7 d4[2]±. An attempt to confuse the issue by **3... Qh4**[3] backfires too. There follows **4 g3 Qe7 5 fe5 Qe5** (5... Nc6 6 d4 d6 7 Qh5) **6 Be2!±.**

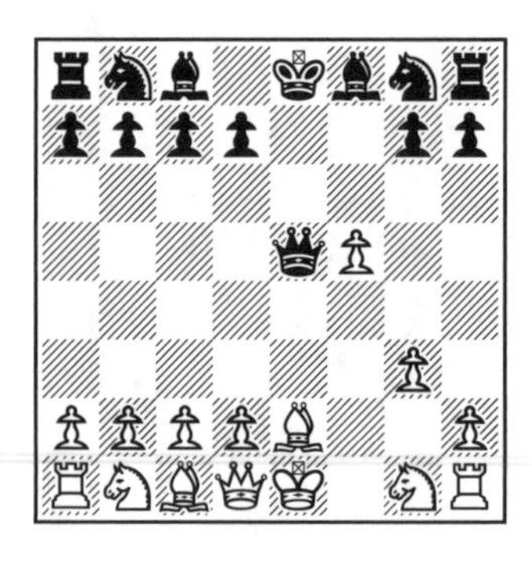

16-2

By kicking the Black queen around while pursuing his own development, White can gain more than enough time to redress the weakening of his light squares. Black, by contrast, may soon have to pay for his violations of opening principles. For example, after 6... Nf6 (not 6... Qf5 7 Nf3 Qh3? on account of 8 Ng5 △ Rf1/ 0–0+–) 7 Nf3 Qf5 8 0–0 d6 9 d4 Qd7 10 Nc3 Be7 11 Bc4 Nc6 (11... d5 12 Ne5) 12 Nd5±, how can

Black safeguard his king? In this line he will be fortunate to survive to an ending.

A word about the "routine" 2... Nc6 3 Nf3 is also in order. For one thing, 3... Bc5 transposes to lines in the discussion following Diagram 12A-1. For another, 3... d6 4 Bb5! inveighs against both 4... Bg4 5 0–0 a6 6 Bc6 bc6 7 d3⩲ [13] and 4... Nf6 5 Nc3 Bd7 6 d3 transposes to the line of Diagram 13-2.

On the other hand, (on 2... Nc6 3 Nf3) the countergambit 3... f5 was seen in the game Gallagher–Wohl, *Commonwealth Ch. 1992* which continued 4 ef5 e4 5 Ne5 Ne5 6 fe5 Qe7 7 Qh5 Kd8 8 d4 ed3 9 Bd3 Qe5 10 Kd1 Nf6 11 Qf3 Bc5 12 Nc3 d6 13 Bf4 Qd4 14 Kd2 Bf5. Though White won in 62 moves, improvements for both sides were likely.

However, a clearer path for White to advantage in the line directly above is: 3... f5 4 d3 d6 (4... fe4 5 de4± leaves White with mobile bishops and a free hand in the center, whereas 4... ef4 5 Bf4 Bb4 [5... d6 6 Qd2 Nf6 7 Nc3 △ 0–0–0] 6 c3 Ba5 7 e5± △ d4-Bc4-Na3-0–0–0 ensures that White will retain his advantage well into the middlegame) 5 Nc3 Nf6 6 Be2 Be7 7 0–0, but the initiative of the first move serves White well on 7... 0–0 8 Kh1 Kh8 9 fe5 de5 10 ef5 Bf5?! 11 Ne5!±.

And (following 2... Nc6 3 Nf3) as for the alternative 3... ef4, 4 d4 d5 (4... g5 5 h4 g4 6 Ne5 transposes to the discussion preceding Diagram 3A-4.) 5 ed5 Qd5 6 Qe2!± △ Nc3-Bf4-0–0–0-(Qb5) makes a very favorable impression on White's behalf.

Finally, there is the so-called Nordwalder Variation from 2... Qf6. To be anticipated next is 3 Nc3 Qf4 (3... ef4 4 Nf3 [Nd5!?] Ne7 5 d4 d6 6 Qd2 g5 7 h4 g4 8 e5 de5 9 Ne5 △ Qf4) 4 Nf3 Bb4 when 5 Bc4 (White it should be noted, can play for positional compensation on 5 g3 Qf6 6 Nd5 Qd6 7 c3 Ba5 8 d4 ed4 9 Qd4 f6 10 Bf4 Qc6 11 Bh3.) Bc3 6 0-0!? gets crazy. A game, A. Sanchez– Lugo, went 6... Ba5!? (6... Bb4 7 d4 Qe4 8 Bf7 △ Ng5/Ne5) 7 d4 Qe4 8 Bf7 Kd8 (8... Kf8) 9 Bg8 Rg8 10 Bg5 Ke8 11 Ne5 h6 12 Qh5 g6 13 Qh6 Qd4 14 Kh1 Qe5 15 Qh7 Qg7 16 c3 d6 17 Rae1 Kd7 18 Rf7 Kc6 19 Rg7 Rg7 20 Qg7 1–0.

PROBLEMS

1. Easier to meet is **2... c6.** After **3 Nf3 d5** (see Diagram 16-3), what move is best?

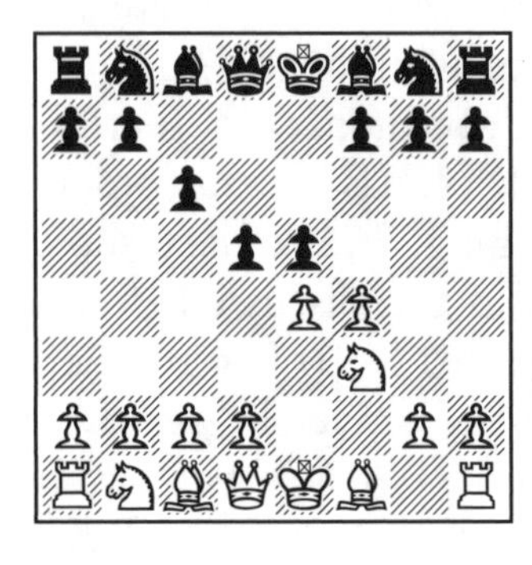

16-3

2. From Diagram 16-4, squelch:

a) **7... Kf7.**
b) **7... Qe8.**

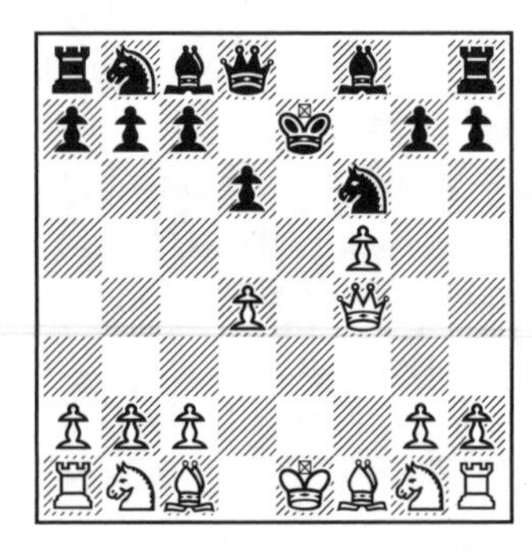

16-4

3. Also inadequate is **3... e4.** Following **4 Qh5 Ke7 5 d3 Nf6 6 Qh4 d5 7 de4 de4 8 g4** (see Diagram 16-5), reprove:

a) **8... Qd4.**
b) **8... g6.**

16-5

ANSWERS

ANSWERS TO PROBLEMS

3A King's Gambit—Kieseritzky Variation

1. a) **4... f6** is refuted by **5 Ng5!** (the thematic retort to ...f6 whenever Black does not have ...Kd7 at his disposal — compare Problem 4A#2) **fg5 6 Qh5 Ke7 7 Qg5 Nf6** (7... Ke8 8 Qe5 Qe7 9 Qh8 Qe4 10 Kd1) **8 e5 Kf7** (8... Ke8 9 ef6 Bd6 10 Be2 and White wins) **9 Qf4±.**
   b) **6 Rh4±** (Nh4!?) and Black's P/f4 is untenable.
   c) **7 g3** (Ng5) **Bg4 8 gf4 Bh4 9 Kd2±** [1], e.g., 9... Qf6 10 Kd3 c5 (10... d5 11 Nc3 or 10... Nc6 11 Be3) 11 c3 △ Be2/Qa4.

2. a) **12 Nd3±** △ Nf4/Bf4 since 12... Qd4? fails to 13 g3!
   b) **12 Rh6!+−** wins at least two pieces for a rook, e.g., 12... Bh6 13 Bf7 △ Bh6.

3. a) **9 Bf7 Kd8 10 Nd5! Qd6 11 Bf4+−** △ Ng6/Nc4-Bc7.
   b) **9 Bf4 d6 10 Bf7 Kd8 11 Bg5+−** △ Nd5/Ne4-0−0.
   c) **9 Nf7** (9 Bf7!?) **Bg7** (9... Ne4 10 0-0 Qh4 11 Nh8 g3 [11... Ng3 12 Re1 Be7 13 Bf4 Ne4 △ g3±] 12 Bf7 Kd8 13 Qh5±) **10 Nh8 Ne4 11 Nd5 Nc3** (11... Qd7 12 Nf7) **12 Ne7 Nd1 13 Nc8 Bh8 14 Kd1 Bd4 15 Re1 Kd8 16 Ne7 Bf2 17 Rf1** △ Nf5/Bf4+−.
   d) **9 Bf7!** (9 0−0!? while enticing but unclear is 9 Bf4 d6 10 Nf7 Rf8) **Kf8** (9... Kd8 10 Bb3 Rf8 11 Bf4 d6 12 0−0! gives White a good version of Problem 3A#3c) **10 Bb3 d6** (10... Nh5 11 Nd5 △ Nf4) **11 Nf7 Rg8** (11... Ne4 12 Ne4 Qe4 13 Qe2 Qe2 14 Ke2 Rg8 15 Ng5 h6 16 Nh7) **12 Bf4±**, e.g., 12... Be6 13 Be6 Qe6 14 Ng5 △ d5-Ne6, etc., or 12... Ne4 13 0−0 or 13 Kf1, which may be even better.

4. a) **12 Ne3 Bg6 13 h5+−.**
   b) **12 Nd5 Bg4** (12... Kd7 13 Nde3 Be4? 14 Nf2, etc., and if 12... Kd8, then 13 0−0 △ Bg5) **13 Bg4 Na6 14 0−0±** [9].

5. a) **10 Nf7 Qe4 11 Qe2 Qe2 12 Ke2 Nd4** (or 12... Bd4 13 c3 △ Nh8) **13 Kd2±**, e.g., 13... Ne6 14 Nh8 Bb2 15 Be6 de6 16 Rh7 Ba1 17 c3 (threatening Bg5) Nf6 18 Rc7 when due to White's initiative Black

cannot hold all of his pawns.

b) **12 Nd5 Qc5?** (12... Nf3 13 Qf3±) **13 Be5 f6 14 Qd4**+−.

3B King's Gambit—Kieseritzky Variation

1. a) **10 Nd5 f6?!** (10... d6 11 Nc7 transposes to Problem 3B#1b, while 10... f3 can be met by 11 Nc7) **11 Ng6**±.
   b) **10 Nd5 Qh4** (10... Qd8 11 Nf7 Rf7 12 Nf4, e.g., on 12... Rf8 White has 13 Nh5) **11 Nc7 Kd8 12 Na8 de5 13 de5 Bd7 14 Qd6** [8] ±. If 14... g3 (14... Nc6 15 e6 △ Bf4), then 15 Qb8 Ke7 16 Qd6 Kd8 17 Rf4! wins.
   c) **10 Bf4! Bf4 11 g3 Be3** (11... Be5? 12 Rf6 △ e5-Qd3) **12 Kg2 Qb6** (12... Qh6 13 Bf7 Kd8 14 Bh5!) **13 Bf7 Rf7 14 Rf7** [8] ± △ Re7/Qf1.
   d) **10 Nf7 Rf7 11 e5 Qh4 12 Bf7 Kf7 13 Bf4 Bf4** (13... Kg7 14 Ne4 d5 15 Nf6 Bf4 16 Rf4) **14 Rf4 Kg7 15 Ne4** [8] ±.

2. a) **9 g3 Bg5 10 Rh5! Rh5 11 Bf7 Kf8 12 Bh5 Bf4 13 Ng6 Kg7 14 Nf4 Nf6 15 Nc3 Qe7** (15... Qh8 16 e5!) **16 Nfd5 Nd5 17 Qg4 Kh8 18 Nd5**+− [9].
   b) **10 g3 Bg5 11 Qd2 Bf4 12 Nf4 h4 13 Nc3 h3 14 0–0–0**± [8].

3. a) **11 Nc3!** [5] ±, e.g., 11... Qe7 12 Qd6.
   b) **11 Bf4 Bf4** (11... c6 12 Bh6 Rh6 13 Ne3 Qe7 14 0–0) **12 Nf4 de5 13 Qd8 Kd8 14 0–0–0** △ Nd3±.

4. a) **14 Rh4 Ng6 15 Rg4!**+−.
   b) **14 Nc3 Nb6 15 Bb3 Rg7 16 Raf1** (e5!?) **Bg5 17 Qf2 Be3** (17... Qe7 18 e5) **18 Qe3 Qe7 19 e5 de5 20 Ne5**± transposes to Diagram 3B-3.
   c) **14 Nc3 c6 15 e5 Qf4 16 Nf4 de5 17 de5 Bg5 18 Rag1 Bf4 19 Bf4**± [1].
   d) **15 Raf1 Bf6** (15... Nh6 16 Rh4) **16 Nd5 Bh8 17 Qg4! hg4 18 Rh7 Nf3 19 Rf3 gf3 20 Rh8**+− [3] △ Bh6/Rg8!-Nf6.

5. a) **10 Rf4 Rh7 11 Qf1 Qe7 12 Rf6**± [11]. For example, if 12… d6, then 13 Bh6 when good for White are 13… Bh6 14 Bf7 △ Ng6 and 13… de5 14 Bg5 ed4?! (or 14… Qc7 15 de5 Qe5 16 Bf7) 15 Rf5 Qc7 16 Bf4 △ Re5/Bf7.
   b) **10 Rh5** (Qd2) **Bf4 11 gf4 d6 12 Ng4 Bg4 13 Qg4 Ng4 14 Rh8 Kd7 15 Rd8 Kd8** [3] ±.

6. a) **12 Nc3 c6** (12... Bg7 13 Nd5) **13 Bg5 Na6 14 Kd2 Bg7 15 Raf1 0–0 16 Qe3**+− [1].
   b) **12 0–0 Rh7** (12... Rg8 13 Bh6!) **13 Nc3**±. After **13... c6 14 e5** (Bg5) White has a strong initiative, e.g., 14... d5? 15 Bd5!+− [13].

3C King's Gambit—Kieseritzky Variation

1. a) **9 ed6 Qe4 10 Qe2**±.
   b) **9 Qg4**±, e.g., 9... Ne5 10 Qg7 or 9... f6 10 Qh5 Qf7 11 Qf7 △ Bc4-ef6-Bc7.

2. a) **10 Qc8** △ Qb7± leads to immediate trouble for Black.
   b) **10 Qf5!** just puts White's queen on a better square. Again, after **10... Bc3** (10... Qe7 11 Qc8 Qd8 12 Qb7 Bc3 13 bc3 Nbd7 14 Bd3± △ Bf4 and 10... Nbd7 11 Bf4 Qe7 12 Bd3 Nc5 13 0–0–0 Bc3 14 bc3 Nce4? (14... Qe6±) 15 Be4 Ne4 16 Rhe1 d5 17 Rd5 +–), **11 bc3 Nbd7 12 Rb1**± yields White the better chances, i.e., 12... Nb6 13 Bf4 Qe7 14 Bb5 △ 0–0, etc.
   c) **10 Bf4 Bc3** (10... Ne5 11 Qg3) **11 bc3 Nf6 12 Qf5 Qe7 13 Bd3**±. White's bishops compensate fully for the broken pawn formation.

3D King's Gambit—Kieseritzky Variation

1. a) **7 Bc4 Nh6 8 Bf4 f6 9 0–0!**± [5]. Note: On 9... fe5 White has 10 Be5 since 10... Qh4 11 g3 Qh3 is handled by 12 Rf2 △ Rh2/Bh8.
   b) **7 ed5** (gf3) **Qd5 8 Bc4 Qe4 9 Kf2 fg2 10 Re1 Qf5 11 Kg2** [3] ±. Note: After 7... Nf6 8 c4 White need not fear 8... f2 9 Kf2 g3 10 Ke1. Also clear-cut is 7... Be7 8 g3 Qd5 9 Bc4 Qe4 10 Kf2 △ Re1.
   c) **7 Ng4 de4 8 Bf4**± [13].

2. a) White's plan should incorporate Bc4-0–0. For example, **8 Bc4 Nd5 9 Bd5 Qd5 10 Ng4 Bg7** (10... Bg4 11 Qg4 Nc6 12 Nc3) **11 c3 Qf5 12 Be5**± △ 0–0-Ne3 is a plausible scenario.
   b) **8 Qd2 Be7** (an important new idea here is 8... f6 when 9 Nd3 de4 10 Nf2 Nf4 (10... f5±) 11 Qf4 Qd4 12 Nc3 Bd6 13 Qe4 Qe4 14 Nfe4 Be7?! [14... f5 15 Nd6 △ 0–0–0] 15 Nd5±) **9 ed5**± [8]. Note: After 9... Bh4 10 Kd1 Nf4 (10... Ng3? 11 Bg3 △ Qe3+–) 11 Qf4 Qf6 12 Qf6 Bf6 13 Bd3 White is better.

3. **9 Ne4 de4** (9... Be4 10 Qg4) **10 Bc4**± [8].

4. a) **12 Qe2 Rg8** (12... h5 13 Nf7! or 12... Ne5 13 Qe5 Rg8 [13... 0–0 14 Qh5 △ Bd3/Re6] 14 Qh5±) **13 Nf7! Bf7 14 Bc7+–** [1]. And if 11... Bd6 then 12 Bb5 looks good for White as 12... c6 13 Nf7 Kf7 14 Bd6 cb5 (14... Re8 15 Rhf1 Kg7±) 15 Rhf1 Nf6? 16 Be5 suggests.
   b) **13 Nf7! Bf7** (13... Kf7 14 0–0 Ke7 15 Rae1 Qg8 16 Bf5 Nf8 17 Be6 Ne6 18 Rf6!) **14 0–0 Ne5 15 Rae1 1–0,** Teschner—Dahl, Berlin 1946.

5. a) **13 Be5 Kd7 14 Bf6 Qf6 15 Rhf1 Qg7** (15… Qh4 15 g3!) **16 Re6+−** [9]. Note that 13 de5 allows 13... f5 blockading. In the main line, if 16... Ke6, then 17 Bf5 △ Qb4 after all replies except 17... Kf6 or 17... Kf7, when 18 Qe3! is immediately decisive.
   b) **13 Be5 Kd7** (13... Be5 14 Re5 or 13... Rf8 14 Qh6) **14 Bh8 Qh8 15 Qh6+−** [9].

3E King's Gambit—Kieseritzky Variation

1. a) **8 Qh5** △ Ne4 ±.
   b) **8 Qh5 Kd8 9 Qe2±.**
   c) **8 d4 fe4 9 Bf4 d5 10 g4±** [8]. Similar is 9... Be6 10 Nc3 d5 (not 10... Nd5? 11 Nd5 Bd5 12 Qh5+− △ Qb5-Qb7) 11 g4 △ g5, and White has excellent play.

2. White plays thematically with **8 d4 Bh6 9 Nc3 Qe7** (9... Nc6 10 Ne2) **10 Nd3!** (10 Rh2) **Bg4** (10… Bf5 11 Bf4 Bf4 12 Nf4 Ne4 13 Nd5) **11 Be2 Be2 12 Qe2 Nc6 13 Nf4** (e5!?) **Nd4 14 Qd3** (△ Nfd5) **Bf4** (14… Rg4 15 Qd4 Bf4 16 Bf4 Rf4 17 0–0–0) **15 Bf4 Ne6 16 0–0** (or Be3 △ 0–0–0) ⩲ [1]. Note that both 10... Nc6 11 Bf4 and 10... Ne4 11 Nd5 △ N5f4 are good for White.

3. **8 d4 Bh4 9 Bf4±.**

4. **12 Nd5 Bg5 13 g3±.** From Diagram 3E-10, the move 12 Bg4? is poor because of 12... Bg4 13 Qg4 Nd4, etc.

5. **15 Bf4 Qg6** (15... Qa5 16 Qf2) **16 d5** (16 Qf2? Ne4!) **Bd5** (either 16... Bb6 or 16... Bc5 can be met by 17 dc6 bc6 18 e5!+−) **17 Nd5 Nd5 18 ed5 Bc5 19 Rde1±.** Also, on 15... Qg4 or 15... Qg7 White has 16 Qf2! since his e-pawn is taboo. If 16... Ne4?! then 17 Rhe1 △ d5 works, as Black's queen is on a bad square.

6. After **12 Qf4±** White's development is notably superior, and Black may soon have to contend with Nb5, e.g., 12... Nc6?! 13 Nb5! Qb2 14 Rd1! may already be winning for White, while 12... Qe5 13 Qe5 △ Nd5 offers White a superb ending.

3F King's Gambit—Kieseritzky Variation

1. a) **8 Nc6 bc6 9 Nd2** △ c3±.
   b) **9 Be2!** leaves Black with nothing better than **9... Bg7 10 c3±**. On 9... Qb4?! White has 10 Nd2 Nd2 (not 10... Qd4?? 11 Ne4 △ Nf6+− or 10... Nd4 11 c3 Nc3 12 bc3 Qc3 13 Rc1 △ Be5+−) 11 Nf6 Kd8 12 Bc7! Kc7 13 Nd5+−.

2. a) **11 dc5 dc5 12 Be2±**, e.g., **12... 0−0 13 Bg4 Nf4 14 Nf4 f5 15 Qb3 Kh8 16 Be2 fe4 17 Nd5** △ 0−0−0.
   b) **11 Qe2** △ 0−0−0 or 0−0±, for instance, **11... c5? 12 dc5 dc5 13 ef5 Qe2 14 Be2 Nf4 15 Nf4 Bf5 16 0−0 0−0 17 Bc4 Kh8 18 Ne6 Be6 19 Be6** and White will win.
   c) **11 Be2±**, e.g., 11... Nf4 (11... c5? 12 dc5 dc5 13 Bg4 △ Qf3-0−0−0) 12 Nf4 f5? 13 Qb3! Kh8 14 Nd5 Qf7 15 Bc4 Be6 16 ef5 Qf5 17 0−0−0 with a big advantage for White.
   d) **11 Nf4 f5?! 12 Nd5 Qf7 13 Bc4 Be6 14 Nc7 Qc7 15 Be6 fe4 16 Qg4 e3 17 Nc4 Rf8 18 Ne3+−** when, e.g., 18... Bf6 19 Nd5 Qg7 20 Qg7 Bg7 21 Nc7 △ Na8 is a graveyard smash.

3. **9 Nc3 Nc6 10 Be3 d5 11 e5 Nh5 12 f4 Ng7 13 Qf3±** [8].

4. a) **12 Ne4 Be4** (12... Qe4 13 Bc7 or 12... de4 13 Nc5 b6 — not 13... 0−0−0? 14 Nb7! — 14 Qb5) **13 Nc5±**.
   b) On **11... f5** an effective plan may be h5!-0−0−0!-Qe3-Be2-Nf1-Ng3-Rdf1, zeroing in on Black's P/f5.
   c) **12 Ne4 de4 13 Nc5 Bh6 14 Qe3 Bf4 15 Qf4±** [8].
   d) **12 Ne4 de4 13 Nc5** (Ne5) **f5 14 0−0−0±,** e.g., 14... b6?! 15 Na6.

5. White is better because of his much greater control over the central squares and his lead in development. Play might proceed **14... Bg7** (14... Bb7? 15 Nf6) **15 0−0−0** when White can choose between Ng3 and d5-d6, depending on Black's reply.

6. a) **11 Ne4 Re8** (11... Be4 12 Qg4) **12 Kf2 Re4 13 Qd2±** △ g3-Bg2 gives White a good version of Diagram 3F-4.
   b) **11 Ne4** △ Ne5±. Also interesting is 11 h5.
   c) **11 Qb3 d5** (11... Kh8 12 h5 Nbd7 13 g3 △ Ne4, as 13... Ndf6? is refuted by 14 h6+−) **12 g3 Nd2** (12... c6 13 Ne4 fe4 14 Ne5 yields good play against Black's king and the P/g4) **13 Kd2 c6 14 Re1±**.

3G King's Gambit—Kieseritzky Variation

1. a) **11... f5** (11... d5? 12 Bc7) **12 0–0 Ndf6 13 Nd2 Bh6** (13... d5 14 Ne5 △ Ng6) **14 Rae1±** is terrific for White.
   b) **12 0–0 Bh6 13 Qe3 Bf4 14 Rf4 d5** (14... Nd5? 15 Qe4+–) **15 Nd2 Nd2 16 Qd2 Ne4 17 Be4 de4 18 Re1 f5 19 Ne5** (Nc5) **Rg8 20 Nc4** △ Ne3±.

2. a) **15 Rf8!+–** wins at once.
   b) **15 Nf4! Nf4** (15... Ng3 16 Qf2+–) **16 Rf4 d5 17 Nc3** (△ Ne4) **Bd6 18 Rf6 Qg8 19 Ne4** (thematic) **de4 20 Qe4 Be7** (20... Kd7 21 Raf1 Be7 22 Rf7) **21 Raf1+–** △ Rf7-Qe7 etc.
   c) **15 Qf2 Qd7** (15... Qe6? 16 Qg3 ed3 17 Re1+–, 15... Qg5 16 hg5 Nf1 17 Nf4 △ Qf1+–, and 15... Nf1? 16 Be7+–) **16 Qg3 ed3 17 Re1±**.

3H King's Gambit—Kieseritzky Variation

1. a) **12 Ne4 de4 13 Ne5±** [9].
   b) **12 Bg5 Ng5 13 Qe7 Ke7 14 hg5** △ Nf4± [13].

2. **15 Be3 Bf5** (15... Be6 16 b3 △ Nf4±) **16 Nf4±** [5]. After 16... Bg6 anticipated is 17 Bd3 Ne7 18 Rhf1 Bd3 (18... Rae8 19 g3 Bh6 20 Nh5! Be3 21 Re3 Bh5 22 Rfe1) 19 Nd3 Nd5 20 Rf5 Ne3 21 Ke3 Rae8 22 Kf2 Re1 23 Ne1± △ Nd3-Nf4-Rh5 (or Nh5).

3. a) **14 Nf2! Rhe8 15 Nde4 Be4 16 Qg4 f5 17 Qh3!±** △ Bb5-Rhe1. Also note that a timely b4 may win a piece.
   b) **14 Nf2!±,** continuing as in the first part of this problem.

4. **18 Re5! Qe5** (18... de5 19 Bh6 Rd5? 20 Bf5) **19 Bh6 Qd5 20 Bg7+–** △ Bf6-Bh7.

5. a) **18 Qf5** △ Qg4± wins back the pawn at once.
   b) **19 Qd2 Bg5 20 hg5 Qg7 21 Qf4 Rhg8** (21... Rdg8 22 Re7! △ Rf7 since 22... Qg5?? loses to 23 Re8!) **22 Rh5 Rd7** (to prevent Re7) **23 Qg4 Kd8** (23... h6?! 24 Re7± or 23... f6 24 Reh1 h6 25 Qe6! hg5? 26 Rh6 △ Rh7+–) **24 Reh1 f6** (24... Rh8 25 Qf5 Qg6 26 Qf6!) **25 Qf5±**.

4A King's Gambit—Fischer Variation

1. a) Returns the pawn too easily: with **5 ef5 Bf5 6 Bf4**± White gains a tempo, since Black's P/d6 belongs on *d5*.
   b) **6 h4! f6** (6... g4 7 Ng1! gives White a favorable version of Diagram 4A-3) **7 Qd3 Bg4** (7... Nc6 8 Bd2 Bd7 9 Nd5 Qd8 10 0–0–0 △ Re1) **8 Bd2 Nd7** (8... Nc6 9 d5! Ne5 10 Ne5 fe5 11 Qb5) **9 0–0–0 0–0–0 10 g3**±. Black's pieces are misplaced and he will soon lose his extra pawn.

2. a) After **7 Qd3 Nc6 8 a3**± Black has development problems. Note that 6 Ng5?! fg5 7 Qh5 Kd7 would have been a speculative alternative for White.
   b) **7 Qd3 Nd7** (7... Nc6 8 d5! △ Qb5) **8 Bd2**±.

3. a) **15 Bg5 0–0–0 16 Nf4 Qf7 17 Ne6 Rde8 18 Ng7**+–. Not conclusive, but highly suggestive of play in this particular line.
   b) **15 Nd4 0–0–0 16 Ne6**±.

4. **11 Nd5 Qd8 12 Rh4!** △ Nc7+–.

5. a) **15 Bg5!+–,** e.g., 15... Bf8 16 Nf6 mate! or 15... Qd7 16 Be7, etc.
   b) **15 ed5 a6 16 Ba4 b5 17 dc6 ba4 18 Re1**+– with a crushing attack, e.g., 18... 0–0 19 Rg1 △ Nh2, etc.

4B King's Gambit—Fischer Variation

1. a) **10 gf4 g3 11 Be3 Bg4 12 Qd2±** [5].
   b) **10 Bh6 Qf6 11 Qd2 Qf2 12 Kd1 g2 13 Bg2 Qg2 14 Rg1 Qf3 15 Qg5±** [5].
   c) **10 Bf4! Nf4** (10... Bf4 is similar) **11 gf4 f5** (11... c5 12 dc5 dc5 13 Qd5!) **12 Bg2 fe4 13 Be4 Bf4 14 Nf4 Rf4 15 Qd3 Qe7 16 0–0–0±** △ Nd5!/Rdf1.
   d) **10 Qd3 f5** (10... b6? 11 Qb5 △ Qh5+– or 10... c6 11 Nf4) **11 Nd5 Qf7 12 Nef4 Nf4 13 Bf4 Bf4 14 Nf4** △ Bg2-0–0±.

2. **12 Ne4 Qg7** (forced) **13 Nh5 Qg6** (both 13... Qg8?? 14 Nhf6 and 13... Qf8 14 Nhf6 Kd8 15 de5 also fail) **14 Nef6! Kf8** (14... Kd8 15 de5 △ Bd3!) **15 de5+–** leaves Black without an adequate defense against Qd8 mate. After **15... f2** (15... Nd7 16 Bd3! or 15... Bd7 16 Bd3 Nf5 17 Bf5 △ Qd6 mate!) **16 Kf2 Qf5 17 Bf4! Nd5 18 Bd3 Ne3 19 Bf5!** (19 Qd2) **Nd1 20 Rad1 Bf5** (20... Bf4 21 Rd8 △ Rh8-Re8 mate) **21 Rd8 Ke7 22 Rh8 Bf8 23 Bg5!** etc.

3. a) **15 Nh5** (threatening both Ng7 and Nef6-Qd8#) wins.
   b) **15 Nd6 Kf8 16 Nc8 Nd5 17 Nd5 Bc1 18 Qc1 de5 19 Qh6+–.**
   c) **15 Nh5! Qg6** (15... Qe5? 16 Bh6+–) **16 Nef6±,** e.g., 16... Nf6 (16... Kh8? 17 Bd3! Nf5 18 Bf5 △ Bh6+–) 17 Nf6 Kh8 (17... Kg7? 18 Bd3 △ h5+–) 18 Bd3 Bf5 19 Bh6 Qh6 20 Bf5 Nf5 21 Ng4 Qg6 22 Qf3 Rg8 23 Nf6 △ Rad1.
   d) **15 Nd6 Kf8** (15... Kd8?! 16 Bf4 △ Bc4-Nf7 when 16... Ne5? 17 Be5 △ Nf7 wins outright) **16 Bf4±**. Weak is 16... Ne5?! (16... Nd5? 17 Nc8 Rc8 18 c4 Nf4 19 Qd7+–) 17 Nc4! Nd7 18 Ne5 Nf6 19 Qd8 Ne8 20 Bc4 with decisive threats. Not even 16... Ng6 17 Nc8 Rc8 18 Qd7 bails Black out. Steadiest seems **16... Nc5,** although after **17 Bc4 Be6 18 Qd4! Bc4** (18... b6 19 b4) **19 Qc5!** Black must go in for **19... Be6 20 Nb7,** since 19... Ba6?? loses immediately to 20 Nf5.

4. a) **10 Bc4 c6 11 d5±.**
   b) **10 Bf4±,** e.g., 10... d5?! 11 Be5 Nf6 12 Bf6 △ Nd5.
   c) **10 Qe2!±** △ Ne4/Qb5.

5. a) **10 a3±.**
   b) **10 ef5±.**
   c) **10 ef5 Nh5 11 Nd5** △ Nef4±.
   d) **10 Ne4 d5** (10... Bf5? 11 Nd6) **11 Nc3±** △ Bd2-0–0–0, after which Black's position is loose.

6. a) **14 Nf6** △ Ng4+–.
   b) **14 Nd5!±.**
   c) **14 Kd2! Nc6** (14... Nbd7 15 h5 △ Re1) **15 h5!±,** e.g., 15... Qe7? 16

Nf6 Qf6 17 Qe4!+− △ Qg4/d5.

4C King's Gambit—Fischer Variation

1. No. **12 Bd2! f6** (else Bc3) **13 0–0–0±** is good for White, e.g., 13... h5 can be answered by 14 Re1. Note, however, that 12 Bd2 loses force after 11... Bg7, since the unusual resource 12... Kf8! leaves White with dubious compensation for his two-pawn deficit. One example is 13 Bc3 Qc7 14 Bg7 Kg7 15 0–0–0 Be6 and White's attack soon fizzles.

2. **19 e5!** keeps White on top, e.g., 19... de5 20 fe5 Qh4 21 Qg3 Qg3 22 Rg3±.

4D King's Gambit—Fischer Variation

1. **9 gf3** appears best. Here **9... gf3 10 Nf4 Ng3 11 Rh2 Bg4 12 Kf2 Nf1 13 Qf1** [5] ±.

2. a) **10 0–0–0±.** After 10... Bg7? or 10... Nc6?, 11 Qb5 △ Qf5/Qb7.
   b) **9... f5** restricts the mobility of the B/c8. White continues to control the dark squares on and around *f4*. **10 0–0–0±** with the plan h5-Qe3-Bc4(Bd3)-Ne2-Ng3 gives White quite good play. Note: Following 9... d5, White can proceed in similar fashion, although 10 Ne4 is also good — contrast Diagram 3F-2.

5A King's Gambit—Cunningham Variation

1. a) **8 g3! fg3 9 hg3 Bg3 10 Bg5+−**, e.g., 10... Ne7 11 Qd4 0–0 (11... Rg8 12 Rh7) 12 Rg1 (or even 12 Qg1).
   b) **8 Bf4±.**
   c) **8 g3±.** If 8... Qf6?!, then 9 Nd5 Qa6 10 Kf2+− wins a piece.
   d) **8 Bf4 Ba6 9 Kd2±.**

2. **9 Qd3! Bg4 10 e5 Qb6 11 g3!±** [1]. Note: After 11... fg3? (11... Bg5 12 gf4±) 12 hg3 (△ Qh7) Bf3 13 Kf3 Qc6 14 d5, White wins.

3. **7 e5!** For instance, 7... de5 (7... d5? 8 Nd5) 8 de5 Nc6 9 Bf4±.

4. **8 Qd3** (again thematic) **Qe7** (8... fe4?! 9 Ne4 d5 10 Nf2!) **9 Kd2 fe4 10 Ne4 Bf3** (10... Bf5? 11 Nd6!+−) **11 Qf3 Nc6 12 c3 0–0–0 13 g3±.**

5. a) **7 e5!±,** e.g., 7... g5 8 h4 g4 9 Ne1 △ Bf4.
   b) **7 h4** (Kf2) **g4 8 Ne1 Bh4 9 Bf4±** [9]. Note: 7... c6 (instead of 7... g4) 8 hg5 Bg5 9 g3! is great for White. This was evidenced in the game Bishop—Harris, *San Jose 1988*, which went 9... d6 10 gf4 Bh6 11 Bh3 Bh3 12 Rh3 Qf6 13 Qg1 Nd7 14 Qh2 0–0–0 15 Be3 Nf8 16 Rg1 Ne6 17 Rg8 Rdg8 18 Rh6 Rg2 19 Qg2 Qh6 20 Qg4 (or 20 f5) Kc7 21 f5 Qg7 22 Qh3 Nf8 23 Bh6 Qf6 24 Bg5 Qg7 25 e5 de5 26 Bh6 Qf6 27 de5 Qe7 28 Qg3 Nd7 29 e6 Kc8 30 Qg7 Re8 31 Bg5 Qf8 32 Qf8 Nf8 33 e7 Nd7 34 Ne4 Kc7 35 f6 b6 36 Bf4 Ne5 37 Be5 Kd7 38 Nd6 Ke6 39 Ne8 h5 40 Nc7, 1–0.

6. **7 ef5!** — thematic here when Black has not played ...d6, although e5 is also good. On **7... d6** (7... Qe7 8 Kf2 Bh4 9 g3!) **8 Qd3 Bh6** (not 8... Nh6?! 9 Qe4 Be7 10 f6! or 8... Qe7?? 9 Kf2 △ Bf4-Re1/Nd5) **9 Nd5 Ne7 10 Nf4 Nf5** (10... Bf5 11 Qb5) **11 g4! Bf4** (the threat was g5-Qb5, and 11... Nh4?? 12 Qb5 △ Qh5/g5+– drops a piece) **12 Bf4 Ne7 13 h3±** △ Kd2 (or 13 Qb5), White gets a clear initiative.

5B King's Gambit—Cunningham Variation

1. **9 h4!** (9 Bf4 also works) **Bf6** (9... Be7? 10 Qf5 Ke8 11 Qh5 Kd7 12 Be6!) **10 e5! de5 11 de5+–,** e.g., 11... Be5 12 Qf5, 11... Be7 12 e6 △ Qf3, etc., or 11... Qe7 12 Bf4! △ 0–0–0.

2. a) **10 Be6 fe6 11 e5!±** already forces Black to return the piece, since after 11... Nd5? (11... Ng8 12 Qf7 △ Qg7+–) 12 Nd5 ed5 the intermezzo 13 e6! leaves Black defenseless. Here, following 13... Rf8 14 Qh6 Rf1 (14... Bf6 15 Bg5) 15 Kf1 Qc8, the shot 16 Bg5! is immediately decisive. Examples include 16... c6 (16... Bg5 17 Qh5, etc.) 17 Qh5 Kd8 18 Be7 and 16... Nc6 17 Qh5 Kd8 18 Qf7. Black's best try to hold the extra piece stems from **11... de5 12 de5 Nd5,** but White still crashes through with **13 Qf7 Kd7 14 Nd5 ed5 15 Qf5 Ke8** (15... Kc6 16 Qe6) **16 Bg5! Nc6** (16... Rf8 17 Qf8!) **17 e6 Qd6** (17... Rf8 18 Qh7) **18 Qf7 Kd8 19 Qf8!**
   b) **10 e5 de5 11 de5! Qd4 12 Qd4 Nd4 13 ef6 Bc5** seems reasonable at first, but **14 Re1!±** keeps White in charge with an extra pawn to boot. For instance, on **14... Be6** (14... Kd8 or 14... Ne6 can be met by 15 Be3) **15 Be3 0–0–0** (15... Nc2 16 Bc5 Na1 17 Be6 Nc2 18 Re2+–) **16 Be6** Black has little to show for his pawn minus.

3. a) **12 Rf4! Qh6 13 Qf3 Qg7!** (13... Qh2 14 Kf1 Qh1 15 Ke2) **14 Nb5!±** △ Nc7-Rf8.
   b) **12 g3! Qh5 13 gf4 Qh4 14 Rf2 g3 15 Rg2 ef4 16 Nd5 Na6 17 Qf3 0–0–0 18 Qf4 Qh5 19 Bd2 c6 20 Nb4±.**

5C King's Gambit—Cunningham Variation

1. **6 Be2!** may threaten a doubled discovered attack on **h5.** Now play might well proceed 6... d6 7 Nd5! △ Nf4±. For additional ideas, see the discussion following Diagram 4A-2.

2. **9 Qe2 Qe7 10 Qe7 Ke7 11 Ng5 f6** (11... Be6 12 Be6! fe6 13 Nh3 △ 0–0-Bf4-Rae1±) **12 Nf7 Re8 13 0–0 Be6** (13... g5 14 Re1 Kf8 15 Re8 Ke8 16 Nd6 cd6 17 Ba3 Kd7 18 Re1 △ Re6) **14 Nd6 cd6** (14... Kd6 15 Bf4) **15 Re1! Kf7** (15... Kd7? 16 d5+–) **16 Re6 Re6 17 Bf4**±.

3. **14 Qc6**± (14 c4 Nc5!? is less clear), e.g., 14... Qf5 15 c4.

6 King's Gambit—Becker Variation

1. a) **7 Ng5 fg3 8 Bc4 g2** (8... Nh6 9 0–0) **9 Bf7 Kf8 10 Rg1**+– △ Qf3-Ne6/Ne4.
   b) **7 hg5 hg5** (7... h5 8 Bf4 △ Bg3) **8 Rh8 Bh8 9 Bg5 Bf6 10 Qd2 Bg5 11 Ng5 Nf6** (11... Nc6 12 c3 △ (Bc4)-Na3-0–0–0) **12 Qf4 Qe7 13 Nc3**±.
   c) **7 gf4 g4 8 Ng1**± [9].
   d) In this line, Qh5 is White's concept move following which White can look for (1) Bc4-Qf7; (2) Bg5 (after ...fg3 and hg5 hg5, Rh8 Bh8); or (3) Qf5 check (after ...gh5). Also, clearing the f- or g-file to prepare Rf1 or Rg1-(Rg6) is often important. Finally, b3 △ Ba3 may be a good reaction to ...Qe7. Thus **6... f5 7 Ne5** (ef5) **Be5** (7... Nf6 8 Ng6 Rg8 9 e5 △ Bc4) **8 de5 Qe7** (8... gh4? 9 Qh5 or 8... fg3 9 Qh5 △ ef5 or 8... fe4 9 Qh5 △ hg5 or 8... d6 9 hg5 △ Qh5-b3) **9 gf4 d6** (9... gf4 10 Qh5) **10 hg5 Nc6** (10... de5 11 Qh5 Kf8 — 11... Qf7 12 g6 — 12 Nc3 or even 12 b3 Be6 — 12... ef4 13 Nc3! — 13 Ba3 c5 14 ef5 △ g6/Bc4) **11 Bc4 Be6 12 Be6**± △ g6-g7-Rg1-Rg6.

2. **8 Bf4 fe4 9 Qg4 Bd4 10 Qg6 Kf8 11 c3 Bf6 12 Ng4**±.

3. **10 Ne3**±, e.g., 10... fe4 (10... Nf6 11 Nf5) 11 Qh5 Kf8 12 Bc4 △ Rf1-Nd5 or 10... Qe7 11 Qh5 Kd8 (11... Qf7 12 Nf5 Bf5 13 Qf7 △ ef5) 12 ef5 Nf6 13 Qf3 △ Na3-Bd2-0–0–0.

7 King's Gambit—Alapin Variation

1. a) **6 h4±** transposes to the line leading to Diagram 7-4, although 6 ed6 and 6 c4 are also interesting.
   b) **6 h4 h6 7 hg5 hg5 8 Rh8 Bh8 9 Nh4!±** [5].

2. a) **8 Qh5 Kd7** (else 9 Bg5) **9 Bb5! Ke6** (9... c6 10 e6! Ke6 11 Bd3! Ne7 12 0–0!+– or 9... Nc6 10 Qf7 Qe7 11 e6 Kd8 12 Bg5! Qg5 13 Qf8#) **10 Be8** (even better than 10 Bg5 Bb4 11 c3 Qf8) **Qe7 11 0–0 Qg7 12 Bg5 Be7** (else 13 Bf6) **13 Rf5** (quickest, although 13 Bf6 still wins) **Bg5 14 Rf7!+–.**
   b) After **8 Bg5 h5** (8... d5 9 Qh5 Kd7 10 Qf7 △ e6-Bf6) **9 Be2!±** White undermines Black's tenuous defense.
   c) **8 Qh5 Kd7 9 Nc3 c6 10 0–0–0±** △ ed6-Be5 or even Qf5. Here **10... Kc7?** is refuted by **11 Qf7.**
   d) **8 Nc3 c6** (8... d6 9 0–0–0 or Nd5) **9 0–0–0±** △ d5-Bc4.

3. **11 hg5 Qg5 12 Nd5 Na6 13 Ne2 c6 14 Ndf4 h5 15 d5!±** [1]. Note: 11... c6 can be met by 12 Qd2 △ 0–0–0±. White can assail targets on *f5* and *h7* while holding the riposte g6 in reserve.

8 King's Gambit—Schallopp Variation

1. a) **6 Qe2** (Also possible is 6 Bc4, but with White's queen knight already on **c3,** 6 Bb5 is not desirable — cf. Problem 9A#3c.) **Qe7 7 Qe7 Ke7 8 Bc4±** [13] — cf. Diagram 11A-4.
   b) **6 Bc4 0–0 7 0–0 c6** (7... Nbd7 8 d3! Nb6 9 Bf4 Nbd5 10 Nd5 Nd5 11 Bg5) **8 dc6 Nc6 9 d4 Bc3 10 bc3 Qc7±** [5].

2. a) **8 c4 Qe4** (8... Qe6 9 Kf2 c5 — 9... Qf6 10 c5 Be7 11 Qd2! g5 12 b4 △ Bb2 — 10 Bd3 Qh6 — 10... 0–0 11 Bh7! △ Ng5/d5 — 11 Re1 Kf8 12 Qe2 △ Qe8/b4) **9 Kf2 Bf5 10 c5 Be7 11 Bb5 c6 12 Bc4±,** and if 12... Be6, 13 Re1 Qg6 14 Be6 [9], etc.
   b) **8 Bf4 Nc6** (8... Qe4!? 9 Qe2 Bf3 10 gf3 Qe2 11 Be2 Bd6 12 Bb5 Nd7 13 Bd6 cd6 14 Kf2) **9 Bc7! Bf3** (or 9... Kd7 10 Bg3 Re8 11 Kf2 Kc8 12 c3 h5 13 Qb3 Qf5 14 Bb5! Re6 15 Rae1 as in Barle—Mariotti, *Portoroz 1975)* **10 Qf3 Qf3 11 gf3 Rc8 12 Bf4 Nd4 13 0–0–0! Bc5 14 Be5 Ne6 15 Bb5±** [5].
   c) **8 c4 Bb4 9 Kf2 Qd8 10 c5! c6 11 Bc4 Be6** (11... 0–0 12 h4! g4 13 Ne5±) **12 Be6 fe6 13 Qb3 Na6 14 Qe6 Qe7 15 Ng5+–** [13].

9A King's Gambit—Modern Variation

1. **5 Bb5** (Bc4) **c6 6 dc6 bc6 7 Bc4 Bh4 8 Kf1 Bf6 9 d4±** [1].

2. a) **7 0–0 Ne7 8 d4 0–0 9 Ne5±** [1].
   b) **7 d4 Bf3 8 Bf3 Qh4 9 Kf1 c6±** [1]. Here White can continue with **10 Ne2!** (g3) when possible are 10... Bd6 11 Qd2 g5 (11... Nf6 12 Nf4 △ g3) 12 g3 Qh3 13 Bg2 Qf5 14 gf4 and 10... g5 11 g3 Qh3 (11... fg3?? 12 hg3+–) 12 Bg2 Qf5 13 gf4 gf4 14 Bf4 Bh6 15 Qe1 Ne7 (15... Qc2? 16 Ng3 Kd8 17 Qe5+–) 16 Qf2, etc.

9B King's Gambit—Modern Variation

1. a) **8 Nc3 Bb4 9 0–0 Bc3 10 Qe2±** [8], e.g., 10... Be6 (10... Kf8 11 Bc6) 11 bc3 0–0 (11... Qc3 12 Bd2! △ Rfc1-Bc6!) 12 Qd3.
   b) **7... Bd6** (7... g5 8 Qe2) **8 0–0** (Qe2) **0–0 9 Nbd2!** (9 c3 Nd5!) **Bg4** (9... Nd5 10 Ne4 Bc7 11 c4, 9... Qb6?! 10 Nc4 Qb5 [10... Qc7 11 Nd6 Qd6 12 c3 h6 13 Bc6 bc6 14 Ne5 g5 15 Qf3 Ba6 16 Rf2] 11 Nd6 Qb6 12 Bf4 Qb2 [or 12... Bg4 13 Nc4 Qb4 14 Qd3 Bf3 15 Rf3 b5 16 Nd6 Qd4 17 Qd4 Nd4 18 Rf2 {19}] 13 d5 Qb6 14 Kh1 Ne7 15 c4 Ng6 16 Bg3 Rd8 17 Qd4! [19], and 9... Ne7!? 10 Nc4 Bc7 11 Nce5 Ned5 12 Bc4 △ Bb3-c4) **10 Nc4** (10 c3 Bc7 11 Nc4 Ne7 12 Ba4 b5 13 Bb5 Qd5 14 Na3 Qh5 15 Bd3 Ned5 16 Nc4 Rae8 =̄∞) **Bc7** (10... Bf3 11 Rf3 Bc5 12 Bc6! Qd4 13 Qd4 Bd4 14 Kh1 bc6 15 Bf4 [19]) **11 Bc6 bc6 12 Qd3 Qd5** (12... Bf3 13 Rf3 Nh5 [13... Nd5 14 Bd2] 14 Bd2 Qd5 15 Re1 Rad8 16 Bb4 [19]) **13 Nfe5⩲** [1].

2. a) **9 0–0 Bh6 10 d4 0–0 11 Ne5 Nd5 12 Nc3±,** e.g., 12... Ne3 (12... Nc3 13 bc3 g5 14 Bf3) 13 Be3 fe3 14 Bc4 Be6 15 Be6 Qe6 16 Ng4 Bg7 17 d5! cd5 18 Qd5.
   b) **8... Bg4 9 0–0 g6 10 Re1±.**

3. a) **10 Kd1 Bd6 11 Re1 Kf8 12 Re4±** wins a pawn in all lines.
   b) **10 Qd4 0–0 11 Bf4 Qe7 12 Kd2! Rd8 13 Bd3 c5 14 Bd6 Rd6 15 Rae1! Be6** (15... cd4 16 Re7 dc3 17 Kc3 Kf8 18 Rhe1 Rd8 19 Ng5) **16 Qe4,** 1–0, Krutskalns—Endre, *Corres. 1970.*

10 King's Gambit—Lesser Accepted Variations

1. **4 d4 g5** (4... Qf6 5 Nc3) **5 d5!** △ h4± gives White a very favorable version of the Kieseritzky Variation. Analyzed by Gallagher is 4... d5 when White can consider the line 5 ed5 Qd5 6 Be2 Bg4 7 c3 (Nc3!?) Bd6 8 0–0 0–0–0 9 b4 △ a4-a5-b5/Ne1-Bf4. White's queenside attack looks to be quicker than Black's projected Kingside attack..

2. In this line Black's N/g6 prevents ...g5 and offers White too free a hand in the center. As a result, Black cannot expect to hold his P/f4. Possible are:
   a) **6... 0–0 7 Nc3 Nc6** (7... c6 8 Ne2) **8 Nd5** △ Nf4±.
   b) **6... d6 7 Nc3 Be6 8 Qd3 Bc4 9 Qc4 Nc6 10 Nd5** △ Nf4±.

3. a) **8 Bc4**± places Black in immediate difficulties. The threat of 9 Neg5 cannot be prevented by 8... f6? because of 9 Qd3! Bf5 (what else?—9... Ne7? 10 Qb3!+–) 10 Nd6 Bd6 11 Qf5 Ne7 12 Qe6 or even 12 Qb5. As 8... Qe7 fails to 9 Kf2!, necessary seems 8... Be6; but 9 Be6 fe6 10 Qd3 still puts Black at a big disadvantage.
   b) **8 h5 Nh4 9 Bf4 Bg4 10 h6! 0–0 11 hg7 Re8 12 Kf2 Ng6** (±) **13 Bg3 f5 14 Qd2 f4** (14... fe4?? 15 Bc4 △ Qh6 is mate soon) **15 Bf4 Bf6 16 Bc4 Be6 17 Rae1** (17 Bc7!) **Nd7 18 Bc7 Qc7 19 Nf6 Nf6 20 Be6 Re6 21 Re6 Ng4 22 Kg1 Qd7 23 Rg6 hg6 24 Rh8, 1–0,** Kuznetsov—Bonch-Osmolovsky, *Moscow 1964*. Note: 10... Bf3 can be met by 11 gf3 when 11... gh6 (11... Qd4? 12 Qd4! Nf3 13 Kf2 Nd4 14 hg7 Rg8 15 Rh7+–) 12 d5!± guarantees White a lasting initiative. For instance, 12... Nd7 13 Qe2 0–0 (forced) 14 Bh6 Re8 15 0–0–0± △ Rh4-Qg2.

11A King's Gambit—Falkbeer Variation

1. **5 fe5 Qe5 6 Be2** leaves Black to choose from: (1) 6... Bg4 7 d4 Qe6 (7... Be2 8 Nge2 Qd6 9 Bf4± [15]) 8 Qd3 c6 9 Bf4 Nf6 10 0–0–0 Be2 11 Nge2 Bd6 12 d5 Nd5 13 Nd5 cd5 14 Qg3 Bf4 15 Nf4 Qh6 16 Rhe1 Kf8 17 Qa3, 1–0, Tolush—Alatortsev, *Moscow 1948;* and (2) 6... Bd6 7 Nf3 Qa5 (7... Qe7 8 0–0 Nf6 9 d4 0–0 10 Bg5 Qd8 11 Ne5 Be5 12 de5 Qd1 13 Rad1 Ng4 14 Nd5 Nc6 15 Nc7 Rb8 16 e6! f6 17 Bg4 fg5 18 Rf8 Kf8 19 Rf1 Kg8 20 Rf7 g6 21 Nd5, 1–0, Fraser—Farrow, *Corres. 1896(?))* 8 d4 Nf6 9 Bd2 Bb4 10 a3 Bc3 11 Bc3 Qb6 12 Bb4 Na6 13 c3 Nb4 14 ab4 0–0 15 Ra5 a6 16 0–0 Be6 17 Ne5 Rad8 18 Bd3 Nd5 19 Qh5 h6 20 Rf3 Nb4 21 cb4 Qd4 22 Kh1 Qb4 23 Ra1 Qb2 24 Raf1 c5 25 Nf7 Bf7 26 Rf7 Rf7 27 Qf7 Kh8 28 Qf8, 1–0, Hanstein—Jaenisch, *Berlin 1842*.

2. a) **8 d4 Qe7** (8... Bd6 9 0–0 Nf6 10 Re1) **9 Qe2 Qe2 10 Ke2 Bd6 11**

Ne4 Bc7 12 Ne5±, and if 12... Be5, then 13 de5 △ Nd6/Bf4.

b) **8 Qe2±**, e.g., 8... Bg4 (8... ef4 transposes to Problem 11A#2a) 9 Qe5 Bf3 10 gf3 △ Ne4 leaves White a pawn up.

3. a) **7 dc6 Nc6 8 Bf4±** [8]. Here if 8... Bf3 (8... Bb4 9 Bb5 or 8... Qe7 9 Qe2 △ 0–0–0), then 9 Qf3 Nd4 10 Qe3.

   b) **7 Nd5 Qd5 8 Bf4 Qe4** (8... Be7 9 Bd3 Bf5?! 10 c4 Qd7 11 0–0 Bd3 12 Qd3 0–0 13 Rad1 Na6 14 Ne5 Qd8 15 Qb3 [14]) **9 Qe2 Qe2** (9... Bf5 10 0–0–0) **10 Be2 Be7 11 0–0 Be6 12 c4 0–0 13 Ng5 Bg5 14 Bg5±** [8].

   c) **7 dc6 Nc6 8 Bf4±** [13].

   d) **7 Bf4 Bd6 8 Ne5!** [14] **0–0 9 Bd3 Nc6 10 0–0±** when 10... Nd4 11 Bh7 Kh7 12 Qd4 Kg8 13 Rad1 Be6 14 Bg5 Be7 15 Bf6 Bf6 16 Nd5 Bd5 17 Qd5 Qb6 18 Kh1 Qb2 19 Nd7 Rfe8 20 Nf6 gf6 21 Rb1 Qc2 22 Rb7 Qg6 23 h3 (23 Rb3 △ Rg3) △ Rf3-(Kh2)-Rg3 is to be anticipated.

4. **13 ef6 Bh5 14 fg7 Kg7 15 Bh6 Kg8** [9] +–. After 16 Qd5 Bg6 17 Bc4 [13], White has too many threats.

5. a) **12 Be2! g6 13 Bh5** △ Bf4±.

   b) **12 0–0 Nh5 13 Bf4 Nf4 14 Rf4±** is better for White due to 14... cd5 15 Nd5 △ Nc7 and 14... Re5 15 dc6 △ cb7/Rf7.

11B King's Gambit—Falkbeer Variation

1. a) **7 Be4 Qg4 8 Qg4 Bg4 9 Bb7+–** [19].

   b) **8 Qe2!±** [8].

2. a) **8 f5! Nf5 9 0–0 Ne3 10 Be3 Qe3 11 Kh1 Bd6 12 Nf4! 0–0 13 Qh5 g6 14 Ng6! hg6 15 Bg6! fg6 16 Qg6 Kh8 17 Nd5 Rf1 18 Rf1 Qe2 19 Qh6 Kg8 20 Nf6, 1–0,** Murey—Nikitin, *USSR 1970.*

   b) **8 0–0 Qb6 9 Kh1 Be7 10 Qe1±** [5].

3. a) **7 Bb5 c6 8 Qd5+–** [1].

   b) A reasonable follow-up to **6... c6** is simply **7 Qe2±**, i.e., 7... Be7 8 dc6 Nc6 9 Be3! △ 0–0–0 [13] does not leave Black enough compensation for his pawn minus.

4. **10 Rd1** (Qc4) **Qa2** (10... Qc6 11 Bf6 △ Qh5 or Qe4) **11 Bf6 gf6 12 Qe4 Qe6 13 Bd3 Nc6 14 Nf3 Bd7±**.

5. a) **10 Qe4 Ne4 11 Bg7 Rg8 12 Be5 Nc6 13 Bd3** (Nf3!?) **Ne5 14 Be4 Nc4 15 Bb7 Rb8 16 Bc6 Bd7** (16... Ke7 17 b3 Rb6 18 Bf3) **17 Bd7 Kd7 18 0–0–0±** [1].

b) **10 ed5 Bf1 11 Kf1 Nd5 12 Bg7 Rg8 13 Re1 Kd7 14 Rd1 Kc6 15 Bd4 Nf4 16 Nf3 Nd7 17 Be3** (g3) **Ne6** (17... Ng2? 18 Nd4 Kb6 19 Bf2+−) **18 Kf2**± [1].

c) **10 Qc4 Qe7 11 Bd3 Nc6 12 Nf3 0–0–0 13 0–0 Be6 14 Qa4 Qc5 15 Kh1 Ng4 16 Be1 f6 17 b4±.** Black gave up the ghost in the game Spielmann—Wadling, *Vasteras 1940*, after 17... Qh5? 18 Bg3 Kb8 19 b5 Ne7 20 f5 Bf7 21 Rab1 Nc8 22 Nd4 Rd6 23 Nc6 Ka8 24 b6! Rc6 25 Qc6! Nb6 26 Qc7 Rc8 27 Qd6 Ne3 28 Rb6 Nf1 29 Bf1 Be8 30 Rb7 Kb7 31 Qa6, 1–0.

11C King's Gambit—Falkbeer Variation

1. a) **7 Bd3 f5** (7... Bf5 8 Qe2 Qd5 9 Nbd2+−) **8 Qe2 Qd5 9 Nbd2!** [8] ±.

   b) **7 Be3! c6 8 Bc4 b5** (8... Qa5 9 c3 Nd7 10 dc6 was Horn—Thomas, *London 1938)* **9 Bb3 c5 10 d6! c4 11 Qd5** (+−) **Nd7 12 Qf5 Nd6 13 Qd5 Be7 14 0–0 0–0 15 Nc3 Nf6 16 Qd2 cb3 17 ab3 b4 18 Nd5 Nf5 19 Ne7 Qe7 20 Rfe1 Rfd8 21 Bd4 Nd4 22 Nd4 Qc5 23 Rad1 Rd5 24 h3 Rad8 25 c3 h6 26 Qd3 Qd6 27 Qf3 Nh5 28 Re4 Nf6 29 Re3 Nh5 30 Rdf1 Nf6 31 Rfe1 Qc5 32 Kh2 Rc8 33 R1e2 Kf8 34 Re5 Rcd8 35 Nf5 Qb6 36 Qg3 Nh5 37 Qh4 Re5 38 fe5 Rd1 39 Re3 Qg6 40 Qb4, 1–0,** Alekhine—Tarrasch, *St. Petersburg 1914*.

   c) **7 Nbd2** (Bd3) **Nd2 8 Bd2 Qd5** (8... cd5 9 Bc3) **9 Bd3**± [13].

   d) **7 c3 Qe7** (7... Bc5 8 Qa4 △ Qe4+−) **8 Qa4 Nc6 9 Be2 Nc5 10 Qc2 g6 11 dc6 Bf5 12 cb7 Rd8 13 Qd2 Rd2 14 b8=Q Rd8 15 Qb5 c6 16 Qc6 Bd7 17 Qd5 Ba4 18 Qe5 Rd1 19 Bd1 Nd3 20 Kf1 Ne5 21 Ba4 Kf8 22 fe5 Qb7 23 Bh6 Ke7 24 Bg5 Kf8 25 cb4 Qa6 26 Kf2 Qa4 27 Bf6, 1–0,** Spielmann—Von Bardeleben, *Prague 1908*.

   e) **7 Bc4 0–0 8 Nbd2** [14] ±.

2. a) **9 Bc5 Nc5 10 Nc3**± [9].

   b) **9 Bc5 Qc5 10 Nc3 0–0 11 Ne4 fe4 12 Qc4 Qc4 13 Bc4 Kh8 14 Ne5**± [13].

   c) **9 Qe3 Qd5 10 Nc3**± [8].

   d) **9 Bc5 Nc5 10 Qe3**± [8], i.e., 10... Qd5 11 Nc3 Qe6 (11... Qd6 12 Rd1) 12 Nd4 Qf7 13 0–0–0 △ g4, etc.

3. a) **9 Nfd2! f5 10 Nc3 Qd4 11 Nce4 fe4 12 c3 Qe3** (12... Qb6 13 Nc4) **13 Qh5 Kf8 14 Bc4 Qf4 15 Qd5**+− [9].

   b) **9 Nfd2! Bh4 10 Ne4 fe4 11 Qe4 Kf7 12 Bd2 Bf6 13 Nc3 g6 14 Bd3**+− [1].

4. a) **13 0–0–0 0–0–0** (for 13... Be4 14 Ng5 see Illustrative Game I in Chap. 11C) **14 Rd4! Ng6 15 g4**+− [9].

   b) **12... Nd5** (12... Bc2 13 Rc1 Nd3 14 Bd3 Bd3 15 Rc7 Nd7 16 Kd2

Be4 17 Re1 f5 18 Ng5 [15]) **13 0–0–0 c6 14 Ng5 Nd7** (14... f6 15 Re1 Kd7 16 Nf7 Rg8 [16... Re8?? 17 Re8 △ Nd6] 17 c4 △ Re7+– is crushing.) **15 Bc4 Be6 16 Rhe1**± [9].

c) **13 0–0–0 Bd5 14 Bb5 Bc6 15 Rhe1 Ne6 16 Bc4 Bf3 17 gf3 Nc6 18 f4**± [15].

5. a) **15 Ng5 Kd5? 16 Re4! Be8 17 Rd4 Kc6 18 Be2 Nd7 19 Bf3 Kb6 20 Rb1 Ka5 21 Rb7 h6 22 Rc7 Rb8 23 Nf7 Bf7 24 Rcd7, 1–0,** Bronstein—Vaisman, *Sandomierz 1976*. Note: 15... Be8 16 Bc4±, i.e., 16... b5? 17 Bb5 Bb5 18 Nf7+–.

b) With **14... Kf8** Black deactivates his king and shuts in his R/h8. Following **15 Re4**± △ Bc4-Rhe1 White will complete the centralization of his pieces and prepare to invade on the seventh rank. Note that 15... b5?! does not really thwart White's plan, since 16 Nd4 a6 17 Bd3 Nd7 18 Rhe1 Nc5 19 Re7 Nd3 20 Kd3 Rc8 21 Nc6 leads to a won game for White.

6. a) **15 c4**± (Bd3), i.e., 15... b5 16 Kb2! (16 cb5 h6!) Bc4 17 Bc4 bc4 18 Rhe1 Kf6 19 Rd4± [13].

b) **15 Ne6 fe6** (15... Ke6 16 Bc4 Kf6 17 g4 g6 18 g5 Kg7 19 Rhe1) **16 Bc4**± [1]. If 16... Rf8?, then 17 Rhe1 Rf6 18 f5! Na6 19 Be6 Nc5 20 Bg8 Kf8 21 Bh7 Rd6 22 Rd4 Rad8 23 Bg6! Nd7 24 g4 (△ g5), 1–0, Krnic—Cortlever, *Wijk aan Zee 1972*. Better is 16... Nd7, but 17 Be6! [13] still keeps White on top.

c) **15 c4** (or Re1 △ Nh7) **Be6 16 Rd8 Kd8 17 Ne6 fe6 18 Bd3 h6 19 Re1! Kd7 20 Re3** △ Rg3+– [1].

d) **15 Bc4!** △ Rhe1±.

12A King's Gambit—Classical Declined Variation

1. a) **5 Qh5** (Bc4) **Qe7 6 Bc4! g6 7 Qe2 Nh6 8 Nc3 Nd7 9 Nd5 Qd6 10 Qe4 0–0 11 b4! c6 12 bc5 Nc5 13 Nf7! Nf7** (13... Ne4 14 Nd6 Nd6 15 Ne7) **14 Ne7 Kg7 15 Bb2 Kh6 16 Qe3 Na4 17 f5 g5 18 Qh3#,** Zelevinsky—Ravinsky, *USSR 1961*.

b) **5 ed5!**±, i.e., 5... Nd5 (5... Qd5 6 Qf3!) 6 d4 △ Bc4-0–0 leaves White a sound pawn ahead. Note that prior to Diagram 12A-6, White could also have essayed 4 Nc3, the critical scenario being 4... d4 5 Na4 Bd6 6 fe5 Be5 7 Ne5 Qh4 8 g3 Qe4 9 Qe2 Qh1 when, instead of 10 Ng6?! as in Erzukkowski—Lipski, *Warsaw 1974*, White should have played 10 Nf3! with advantage in all lines. One example is 10... Ne7 11 Kf2 Bg4 12 Bg2 Qh2!? 13 Qe7! Ke7 14 Nh2 Bc8 15 Nc5 c6 16 b3, etc.

2. **5 d4 Bd4 6 Qd4 Qh4 7 Qf2** (!) **Qf2 8 Kf2**± [5]. Note that 5... Nf6? 6 fe5 Ne4 7 Qd3!+– only worsens matters.

3. a) **7 d4 Bd6 8 Nf3 Ne4 9 Bd3 Bf5** (9... Nf6 10 0–0 or 9... Re8 10 0–0 h6 11 Nbd2 Nf6 12 Nc4 Nc6= [19]) **10 0–0** (±) **Bg6 11 Qc2 Re8 12 Nbd2 Nd2 13 Bd2 Nd7 14 Bg5 Nf6 15 Rae1 Re1 16 Re1 c5 17 Bg6 hg6 18 Qf2 Qa5 19 Qh4 Nh7 20 Be7 Be7 21 Qe7 cd4 22 Qb7 Rf8 23 Nd4 Qa2 24 Nc6 a6 25 Qb4 Ra8 26 c4 g5 27 Ne7 Kh8 28 c5 Nf6 29 c6 Nd5 30 Qb7 Re8 31 c7 Ne7 32 Re7 Qb1 33 Kf2 Qc2 34 Kg3 Qd3 35 Kf2 Qc2, ½–½**, Flis—Szymcak, *Polish Ch. 1983*.

   b) **7 d4 Bd6** (7... Ne4 8 Qf3 f5 9 Bf4 Bb6 10 Bd3 0–0 11 0–0 c5 12 Bc4 Kh8 13 Ng6, 1–0, Cripe—Ham, *1987*) **8 Nf3 Ne4 9 Be2 0–0 10 0–0 c5 11 Nbd2** (11 Bd3) **Nd2** (11... cd4 12 Ne4 △ Bd3±) **12 Bd2 Nc6** [5] (12... cd4 13 cd4±) **13 Bd3!** (13 Bg5) ∞ with sharp play, e.g., 13... cd4 (13... Bg4 14 Qc2 △ Bh7/Rae1-d5 is possible) 14 Bh7!? Kh7 15 Ng5 Kg6 16 h4 △ h5.

4. a) **5 Na4** (or 5 h3)± [1]. Note: 5... Bb6 6 Nb6 ab6 7 h3! (avoiding 7 Bc4 Nc6 8 0–0 Nf6 9 d3 Na5=) Be6 8 d4 is good for White. Another possibility is 5... ef4 6 d4 Bf3 7 gf3 Qh4 8 Ke2 Bb6 9 Nb6 ab6 10 Qd2 g5 11 Kd1$\overline{\overline{\infty}}$ [19].

   b) **5 fe5** (d4!?) **de5 6 Ne5 Qd4** (6... Nf6 7 Qe2) **7 Nd3**±, e.g., 7... Ba7 8 Nd5! Qe4 9 Qe2 Qe2 10 Be2 Kd8 11 Ne5 Be6 12 Nf4 [13].

5. **6 Na4!**± takes the initiative, e.g., 6... a6 7 Nc5 dc5 (7... ab5 8 Nd7) 8 Bc6 Bc6 9 d3 ef4 10 Bf4 △ 0–0-Ne5, etc. Note that 6... Bb6 7 Nb6 ab6 8 d3 Nge7 (8... Qe7?! 9 0–0 Nf6 10 Kh1 h6 11 Qe1 0–0–0 12 a4 ef4 13 Bf4 Nb8 14 Nd4 c6 15 Qc3 Ne8 16 a5 ba5 17 Ra5 Nc7 18 Bc4 b5? 19 Bb5! cb5 20 Ra7 1–0, Hebden–Lane, *London 1987* or 8... ef4 9 Bf4 Qf6 10 Qc1 Nge7 11 0–0± [1]) 9 0–0 0–0 10 f5 f6 11 Bc4 Kh8 12 a3 Be8 13 Ba2! Bf7 (13... d5 14 ed5 Nd5 15 Nh4 △ Qg4, etc.) 14 c4! [13] offers White a strong kingside attacking orientation.

12B King's Gambit—Classical Declined Variation

1. a) **10 Qe2**± [9] allows White to open the e-file to his benefit!, e.g., 10... Nc3 (10... Ng5?? 11 Qh5+–) 11 Qe6 Kd8 12 dc3 (△ Bg5 check) leaves White a pawn up with a strong attack to boot.

   b) **10 Qe2 Nc6 11 b3**± [9].

2. **9 Ne2 Nbd7** (both 9... Qb6 and 9... 0–0 lose a pawn to 10 fe5) **10 Ng3 0–0 11 Rf1 Qb6 12 Qe2**± △ fe5(f5)-Bg5-0–0–0(Kd2)-Nf5 is a typical sequel. As White's kingside attack continues to build, the fate of Black's queenside diversion will depend on Ba6-Rae8-d5, etc.

12C King's Gambit—Classical Declined Variation

1. a) **10 g3 Bf2 11 Ke2 Qh5 12 h3!±** [1]. Note: After 12... Ne3 13 g4 White is in the driver's seat.
   b) **10 Qf3±,** i.e., 10... fe6 11 Rf1 Qh4 12 Rf2 Bf2 13 Qf2 Qh2 14 Nb5 Qh1 (14... Rf8 15 Nc7) 15 Ke2 Qh5 16 Qf3 Qf3 17 gf3, and if 17... Kd7 (△ ...c6), then 18 Nd4, etc.
   c) **10 Kf1 Qh4 11 ef7 Kf8 12 Qf3** △ Bf4±.

2. a) **8 Qh5 g6 9 Bf7±**, i.e., 9... Ke7? (9... Kf8 10 Qh6 Ke7 11 Nd5 Kd7 12 Be6 Ke8 13 Qg7) 10 Nd5 Kd7 11 Be6 Ke8 12 Qh6+−. Best may be 9... Kd7, though 10 Be6 Ke8 11 Qh6 Nd4 12 Qg7 △ Nd5 still gives White some advantage in a double-edged position.
   b) **8 f5±**, i.e., 8... Ne3 (8... Nf2 9 Qh5 or 8... Bf2 9 Kf1 Be3 10 Bf7 Kf8 11 Qg4) 9 Bf7 Kf8 10 Be3 Be3 11 Ne6 Be6 12 fe6 Qf6 13 Qe2 Nd4 14 Nd5± [13].
   c) **8 f5 Bf2 9 Kf1 Ne3 10 Be3 Be3 11 h4 Bg5** (11... g6? 12 Nf7 Rf7 13 Qf3+−) **12 hg5 Qg5 13 Rh5±** [6].

3. a) **8 f5 Bd7 9 Bg5 Nd4 10 Bd7! Qd7 11 Bf6 gf6 12 Nd4 Bd4 13 Nd5±** [9]. Note that 13... Qd8 14 Qg4 Kh8 15 Qh4 Kg7 16 Rf1 c6 fails to 17 Rf3 △ Rg3, etc.
   b) **8 Na4 Nd4** (8... Bb6?! 9 Nb6 ab6 10 Bc6 △ fe5-Ne5 or 8... ef4 9 Nc5 dc5 10 Bf4) **9 Bd7! Nd7 10 Nc5 Nf3 11 Qf3 Nc5 12 Qg3!±** [13].

12D King's Gambit—Classical Declined Variation

1. a) **10 fe5 Nd7 11 Bf4 Qe7 12 c3⩲.**
   b) **10 Bb3 c4 11 dc4±**, e.g., 11... Ne4 (11... ef4 12 Qd8 △ Bf4-Bc7) 12 Qd8 Rad8 13 Ne5 or 11... Qd1 12 Rd1 Ne4 13 Re1!, etc.

2. a) **10 Bf7! Kf7 11 Ne5+−.**
   b) **10 Be3** [5] **Qe7** (or 10... b6?! 11 Bd5 Qd7 — 11... Qd6? 12 Bf7! — 12 Qd2, etc.) **11 Qd2** (0−0!?) **Bf3 12 gf3 Ne5 13 Qf2±**. Note that 10... 0−0 (not 10... Ne5? 11 Ne5 Bd1 12 Bf7 Ke7 13 Bc5 Kf6 14 0−0 Ke5 15 Rf5 mate, Alekhine—Tenner, *Cologne 1907)* 11 0−0 Ne5 (11... Nd4 12 c3 b5 13 Bd5 c6 14 Bd4!) 12 Bc5 (Ne5!?) Bf3 13 gf3 Qg5 14 Kh1 Nc4 15 Bf8 Ne3 16 Rg1 Qf4 17 Bg7 Ng7 18 Qe2± is even better for White.
   c) **10 0−0 Nd4** (10... Na5 11 Bb3) **11 Qd2 Nf3 12 gf3 Bh3 13 Rf2 Nh5 14 Be3±** △ f4-Kh1-Rg1.

3. **10 ed5 Nd5 11 h3±**. For instance, 11... Bf3 (11... Be6 12 fe5) 12 Qf3 Nf4 13 0−0 0−0 (13... g5 14 g3 Rg8 15 gf4 gf4 16 Kh2 Rg3? 17 Qh5 △ Bf4!-Rae1) 14 Bf4 ef4 15 Qf4 △ d4± offers White strong central

control plus a good bishop.

4. a) **10 fe5! Nc2** (10... Nh5 11 Qf2 Nb3 12 Nc5 Na1 13 Nb7 and 10... de5 11 Nc5 Nc2 12 Kd1 Na1 13 Bg5 Kh8 — 13... Qd6 14 Bf6 △ Nd7 — 14 Qe5) **11 Kd1 Na1 12 ef6 Qf6 13 e5!**±, i.e., 13... Qf2 14 Nc5. Black cannot save his N/a1.
   b) **10 Kd1 Na1 11 Qg7 Rf8** (11... Kd7? 12 Nc5 △ fe5+−) **12 Nc5 dc5 13 fe5 Ne4** (13... Qd7 14 Qf6+−; 13... Nh5 14 Qg4+−; 13... Nd7 14 Bg5) **14 Rf1 Qe7** (14... Qd7 15 Bf7 Qf7 16 Rf7 Rf7 17 Qg8 Rf8— 17... Ke7 18 Qa8—18 Qe6 Kd8 19 de4+−) **15 Bh6**± [1]. Note: 15... 0−0−0? (15... Rd8 16 Qg4) 16 Qg4 (△ Qe4) Kb8 (16... Qd7? 17 Qd7) 17 Bf8 Qe5 18 Bg7 Qe7 (18... f6 19 Kc1 △ Qe4/Bf6) 19 Kc1!+− [1].

5. a) **12 Nb3** (or Nb7) **Nc2 13 Kd1 Na1 14 Na1 Rg8 15 Qh6 Rg2 16 Qf4**±.
   b) After **11... dc5** White must play accurately, e.g., 12 0−0? b5 13 Bb3 c4! 14 dc4 Rg8 15 Qh6 f3, and if 16 Bg5, then 16... Ne2 △ ...fg2-Rg6-h6 allows Black to whip up an attack. Simply **12 Bf4!,** however, avoids all that; whereupon, **12... Qe7** (12... b5? 13 Bb5 Nb5 14 Bg5 Rg8 15 Qf6 Rg5 16 Qc6 Kf8 17 Qb5 Rb8 18 Qc4 Rb2 19 Rf1! and 12... Nc2? 13 Kd1 Na1 14 Bg5 c6 15 Bf6 Qd6 16 e5! △ Rhe1) can be met by **13 Bg5**+−.
   c) **12 Kd1 Na1 13 Nb7! Qe7 14 Bb5 Nd7 15 Bf4 Rb8 16 Bc6**+− △ Kd2-Ra1/Bh6/Bg5. Black is considerably tied down and his N/a1 is lost. E.g., 16... f5 17 Qe7 Ke7 18 ef5 Rf5 19 Re1 Ne5 20 Be5 Re5 21 Re5 de5 22 Kc1 Rf8 23 Bf3 △ Kb1-Ka1.

6. a) **10 Ng5**±. A natural sequel is 10... Ne6 11 Be6 Be6 (11... fe6 12 fe5 Ne5 13 d4 △ 0−0-Nf7) 12 f5 Bd7 (12... h6 13 fe6 △ ef7) 13 Qh5 Qe7 (13... g6 14 Qh6) 14 0−0. Black is bottled up and cannot easily castle, as 14... g6 15 Qh6 0−0−0? 16 f6 Qf8 17 Qg7 demonstrates.
   b) **10 Be6 Ne6** (10... fe6 11 fe5 Ne5 12 0−0±) **11 0−0** (f5!?) ± is a little better for White.
   c) **10 Qf3 0−0** (10... Nd4 11 Qf2 0−0 12 0−0 Qe7 13 a4± △ b4-c3 followed by kingside expansion) **11 0−0 Na5 12 Bb3 Nab3 13 ab3 Qe7 14 Be3**± △ f5-g4, etc.

13 King's Gambit—Solid Variation

1. **4 Nc3 Nf6** (4... Nc6 5 Bb5 △ Bc6-fe5 is uncomfortable for Black, and 4... ef4 5 d4 g5 6 h4 f6 7 Qd3 transposes to Problem 4A#2b) **5 h3 Bf3** (5... Be6 6 d4!, i.e., 6... Nh5 7 fe5) **6 Qf3**±. One follow-up is 6... ef4 7 d4 g5?! 8 h4! g4 9 Qf4 Nc6 (9... Be7 10 Bc4 △ e5) 10 Be3 Be7 11 0–0–0 Rg8 12 Bc4. Here 12... Na5? 13 Bf7! Kf7 14 e5 Nc4 15 ef6 Bf6 16 Nd5 △ Nf6 etc., only makes matters worse.

2. **7 Bc6 Bc6 8 fe5 de5 9 Ne5**+– [1].

3. **10 Be2**± avoids ...b5-b4-Ne4 and threatens d5-Nd4/e5.

4. a) **5 d3 fe4** (5... d5 6 ed5 △ Qe2) **6 de4 Bg4** (6... Ne4? 7 Qd5+– or 6... Nbd7 7 Ng5±) **7 fe5 Bf3** (7... de5 8 Qd8 Kd8 9 Ne5+–) **8 Qf3 de5 9 Be3** △ 0–0±.
   b) **4... Nc6 5 d3 Nf6** (5... Na5? 6 Bg8! Rg8 7 fe5 fe4—or 7... de5 8 Ne5 △ Qh5—8 de4 △ Qd5) **6 Nc3** △ 0–0±, i.e., 6... Na5? 7 fe5 △ Ne5, etc.

5. **10 g3! fg3** (10... Ng3 11 Rf4) **11 Bf7 Kd8 12 Qh5 gh2 13 Kh1**+–.

14 King's Gambit—2... Nf6 Variation

1. **7 c4!**± is strong, as 7... dc4 (for 7... Bb4 see Illustrative Game II in Chap. 14) 8 d5 Nc5 9 Bc4 and 7... Nc6 8 cd5 (Nc3) Qd5 9 Nc3 Bb4 10 Kf2 (a3) Bc3 11 bc3 quickly show. Perhaps 7... c6 is more logical, though 8 Nc3 (cd5) Be7 9 Be3 0–0 10 Qd2 b6 11 Bd3 Na6 12 cd5 cd5 13 Rd1 f5 14 ef6 Rf6 15 0–0 Nac7 16 Ne5± [13] presents White with a lasting central space advantage. In this line, Black will not have an easy time safeguarding his king.

2. a) **9 Nbd2**±, i.e., 9... cd4 10 0–0 Bf5 11 Nb3 △ cd5 or 9... Nd2 10 Bd2 Qb6 (10... Qa6 11 Qe2) 11 cd5 △ 0–0.
   b) **9 Nc3 Nc3** (9... cd4 10 Nd5 Qa5 11 Bd2!) **10 bc3 Bd3 11 Qd3 cd4** (11... Be7 12 cd5 Qd5 13 c4 △ d5) **12 cd4 Bb4 13 Kf2** △ Rb1±.
   c) **9 0–0**±. One possible sequel is 9... Bf5 (transposing to Ivanovic—Osterman, *Belgrade 1979*, is 9... Be7 10 cd5 Qd5 11 Qc2 Nc5 12 Bc4 d3 13 Qc3 Qd8 14 Ng5!) 10 Bg5 Be7 (10... Ng5 11 Ng5 Qg5 12 Bf5 Qe3—12... dc4 13 Qd4—13 Kh1 dc4 14 Qa4 △ Qc4) 11 Be7 Ke7 (11... Qe7 12 cd5) 12 Nh4, etc.

3. **10 Qc2 c6 11 Nc3 Nc3 12 Bh7 Kh8 13 bc3**± [9]. Note: Black must agree to 13... dc4 14 Be4±, as after 13... g6? 14 Bg6 fg6 15 Qg6 his king becomes too exposed. A representative line is 15... Bf5 (15... Qd7 16

Bg5 is similar) 16 Qh6 Bh7 (16... Kg8 17 Ng5 Bg5 18 Bg5 Qd7 19 g4!) 17 Bg5, whereupon 17... Rg8 18 Bf6 (h4!?) Bf6 19 ef6 Rg6 20 Qh5 Nd7 21 Ne5! should win for White. For instance, 21... Ne5 (21... Rf6? 22 Nf7 Rf7 23 Rf7 Nf8 24 Qe5 is mate in 3!) 22 de5 Qd7 (22... Qf8 23 e6) 23 Rae1 Qe6 24 Rf4 △ Rh4, etc.

15 King's Gambit—Keene Variation

1\. a) **5... d4?** loses a pawn to **6 Nd5** (△ fe5) since **6... Qd6 7 fe5** △ Bf4 is even worse.

b) **6 de4 ef4** (6... Nf6 7 fe5 Qe5 8 Nf3 Qa5 9 Bd2 [13] when 9... Bb4? 10 a3 Be7 11 Nd5 is terrific for White) **7 Bf4±** hands White a dangerous lead in development for the small price of an isolani. Examples include 7... Nf6 8 Qe2 Bg4 9 Nf3 Bf3 (9... c6 10 0–0–0 Qe6 11 Qd3! △ Qd8/Ng5) 10 Qf3 c6 11 e5 △ Bc4 and 7... c6 8 Qd2 Nf6 9 0–0–0.

c) **6 Nd5 Qd8 7 Bf4 Na6 8 Nf3 c6 9 Nc3 Bb4 10 Bg2 Qa5 11 Bd2 Bg4 12 0–0 Qb6 13 Kh1 Nf6 14 a3 Be7 15 b4 0–0 16 Qe1±.** White is a healthy pawn up.

d) **6 fe5 de4 7 Ne4 Qe5 8 Nf3 Qd5 9 Qe2 Be7 10 Nfg5 f5?! 11 Nc3! Qh1 12 Bf4 Bd7 13 0–0–0 Nf6 14 Bd6 0–0 15 Qe7 Na6 16 d4 Qh2 17 Bc4 Kh8 18 Nf7 Rf7 19 Bf7 c5 20 Be5 Nb4 21 Rd2 Qh1 22 Nd1 Ne4 23 Bg7 Kg7 24 Be8, 1–0,** Krantz—Dehmelt, *Postal 1986.*

e) **6 fe5 Qe5 7 d4 Qe7 8 e5 Bg4 9 Be2 Be2 10 Qe2** △ Nd5±. White is probably winning here.

2\. **5 Nc3±** is a clear refutation. Neither 5... fe4? 6 de4 nor 5... ef4? 6 Nd5 △ Bf4 looks tenable for Black. Best may be **5... Nf6,** though **6 fe5 Qe5 7 Bf4 Qe7 8 Qd2 fe4 9 0–0–0!** does not bode well for the second player. For instance, possible is 9... d5 10 de4 Ne4 11 Ne4 de4 12 Bg5!, etc.

3\. a) Black hopes to improve his chances by omitting ...h6. However, **9 Nd5 Nd5 10 ed5** crosses him up as White's P/d5 prevents Black from obtaining counterplay with ...d5. Best may be **10... Nb4** (10... Nd4?! 11 c4 Nf5 12 fe5 Qe5 13 Qf3 Ne7? 14 Ng5+– results in a family fork) when **11 c4 e4 12 de4±.**

b) **9 0–0 Nb6 10 a4 Qd7** was reached by a different move order in Christiansen—Gibbons, *Los Angeles 1980*, when **11 Nf2 Qc6** could have led to **12 Ng4!** △ fe5 with advantage to White.

c) **8 Nf2 Nc6** [16] **9 Nd5!?±,** e.g., 9... Nd5 10 ed5 Nb4 11 c4 ef4 12 Bf4 Qe7 13 Kf1 0–0–0 14 a3 Na6 15 Qg4 Qd7 16 b4 Qg4 17 Ng4 h5 18 Nf2 Be7 19 Be3 Bf6 20 Rb1 Kb8 21 Ne4 △ Nf6-Bd4-Bg7/Kg2-Rhf1. White appears to have his way in the center, although both sides ultimately plan to generate pawnstorms on opposite wings.

16 King's Gambit—Lesser Declined Variations

1. **4 Ne5**± [8]. Both 4... de4 5 Bc4 Nh6 6 Nc3 Qd4 7 Qe2 Bf5 (7... f6 8 Nf3 or 7... f5 8 d3) 8 d3! and 4... Qe7?! 5 ed5! f6 6 d6 Qe6 7 Bc4 are very awkward for Black.

2. a) **8 Nc3 Qe8** (8... Nc6 9 Be3 △ Bc4/0–0–0) **9 Be2**± prepares Be3-(Bc4)-0–0–0. Insufficient is 9... Nh5? 10 Qf3!, although 9... Nc6 10 Be3 behooves Black to meet Bc4 without losing his P/c7, as 10... Bf5?? 11 Bc4 is immediately decisive.
   b) **8 Nc3! Kd8 9 Be2 Nc6** (9... Nh5?! 10 Qh4 Nf6 11 g4) **10 Bd2** (Be3) **Be7 11 0–0–0 Qd7 12 g4**± △ Nf3-Rhe1.

3. a) **9 Nc3**+– does not alleviate Black's discomfort. White's intended Nge2 will have to be dealt with. For instance, after 9... Kf7 10 Nge2 Qb4 11 a3 Qe7 12 Nd4 △ Bc4-g5, how does Black organize a meaningful defense?
   b) One good line is **9 g5 Nh5 10 f6 Kf7 11 Be3 h6** (11... Be6 12 Be2) **12 Bc4**+–. Either 12... Be6 13 Be6 Ke6 14 f5! or 12... Ke8 13 Nc3 △ f7-Rd1(0–0–0)-(Bc5) quickly shackle Black with insuperable difficulties.

THEORY REFERENCES

[1] *ECO C* Beograd, Yugoslavia 1981 by Chess Informant.
[2] Evans, Larry *CL&R* Oct 1977 p. 558.
[3] Freeborough, E. and Ranken, C.E. *Chess Openings, Ancient and Modern* 1974 by Hippocrene Books, Inc. NY.
[4] Gligoric, Svetozar *CL&R* Oct 1977 p. 543.
[5] Hay, Trevor *King's Gambit* 1973 by Chess Digest, TX.
[6] Horowitz, I.A. *Chess Openings: Theory and Practice* 1964 by Simon & Schuster, NY.
[7] Kastner, Jeff *CL&R* Jul 1978 p. 373, Jul 1980 p. 46.
[8] Keres, Paul *Theory of the King's Gambit*.
[9] Korchnoi, Viktor and Zak, Vladimir *The King's Gambit* 1975 by Chess Digest, TX.
[10] MCO-*11* 1972 Walter Korn by Pitman Publishing Co., NY.
[11] Pachman, Ludek *The King's Gambit Accepted* edited by Schroeder, J.R. in Classic Chess Openings #4.
[12] Thimann, R.G. *King's Gambit* 1974 by The Chess Player Ltd., Carlton, England.
[13] Estrin, Y. and Glazkov, I. *Play the King's Gambit* 1982 by Pergamon Press, Great Britain. This includes Vol. I (the King's Gambit Accepted) and Vol. II (the King's Gambit Declined).
[14] Bangiev, Alexander *Developments in the King's Gambit 1980-88* 1988 by Quadrant Marketing Ltd., London.
[15] Leach, Colin, *Falkbeer Counter-Gambit* 1988 by Caissa Books Publishing Ltd., London.
[16] Silman, Jeremy *Theory and Analysis #464* 1987 p. 1.
[17] Soltis, Andrew *Winning with the King's Gambit, Vols. 1 and 2* 1992 by Chess Digest, TX.
[18] Schiller, Eric *Who's Afraid of the King's Gambit* 1989 by Chess Enterprises, Coraopolis, PA.
[19] Gallagher, Joe *Winning with the King's Gambit* 1993 by Henry Holt and Company.
[20] Narciso, Marc *King's Gambit Norwalder Variation* in *The New Myers Openings Bulletin #4*.
[21] Burkett, Kevin *Chess Life* Jan 1994 p. 14.

Other Sources Checked:

Dahlgrun, H. Harro *Königsgambit* 1974 by Kurt Rattmann, FRG.
Fine, Reuben *Basic Chess Endings* 1974 by David McKay, Inc., NY.
Fine, Reuben *Ideas Behind the Chess Openings* 1972 by David McKay, Inc., NY.
Fine, Reuben *Practical Chess Openings* 1948 by David McKay, Inc., NY.
Fischer, Bobby *My 60 Memorable Games* 1969 by Simon and Schuster, NY.
Gallagher, Joe *Trends in the King's Gambit Vol. 2*

Hoene, Jr., Howard F. *Winning Chess Gambits* 1982 by Aardvark Printing, WA.
Kmoch, Hans *Pawn Power in Chess* 1959 by David McKay, Inc., NY.
Marovic, D. Susic, I. *King Pawn Openings* 1972 by David McKay, Inc., NY.
Myers, Hugh *The King's Gambit Jungle* in *The New Myers Openings Bulletin #1* and #3.
Patek, V. *100 Partija Kraljevog Gambita* 1974 by Sahovska Naklada, YUG.
Sergeant, Philip *Morphy's Games of Chess* 1957 by Dover Publications, Inc., NY.

INDEX OF COMPLETE GAMES

INDEX OF MAIN REFERENCE LINES AND EARLY DIVERGENCES

All main reference lines lead to main body diagrams. All moves listed without White responses are early divergences presented as problems or notes.

ACCEPTED VARIATIONS (1 e4 e5 2 f4 ef4)

(3) Kieseritzky Variation

(10) Lesser Accepted Variations

DECLINED VARIATIONS (1 e4 e5 2 f4)

(11) Falkbeer Variation

(12) Classical Declined Variation

(16) Lesser Declined Variations

COLOPHON

Typeset in Adobe's Goudy Oldstyle with Thinkers' Press C.R. Horowitz, 12/14.
Data Entry, Copy Editing, Diagrams: Bob Long and many others
Cover: Greg Sterling & Bob Long
Layout: Bob Long
Proofreading: Robert Raingruber & Bob Long

Thinkers' Press is known worldwide for its quality chess literature. We provide quick delivery and postpaid shipping of all of our products. You can be assured of top-notch materials; what we sell through this catalog is guaranteed or your money back. Please order by catalog number.

THE OPENING

Alekhine's Defense Four Pawns Attack: *GM Larry Christiansen, Manuel Joseph, Bob Raingruber, flexi*

Ultimately, this attack is probably the one Black fears most. Designed like our King's Gambit book, it arms White with a very powerful weapon for his 1. e4 arsenal. Published in 1989. OP57882. **$12.95**

Bronstein-Ljubojevic: Four Pawns Attack: *Tom Tucker & Bob Long, flexi*

A 20-page supplement to the above book on a highly-tactical line not contained in the ADFPA book. Controversial and exciting. OP57889. **$4.00**

Benoni Defence Taimanov Variation 8 Bb5 (A67): *Maurizio Tirabassi, flexi*

While Black seems to keep coming up with ways of diverting White's latest innovations, in this line he has been running into a brick wall. Black's congestion and development problems last throughout the game. Published in 1993. OP77529. **$12.50.**

Bird Variation in the Ruy Lopez *Rotariu and Cimmino, flexi*

128 pages. ICCF GM Rotariu explores the correspondence weapon 1. e4 e5 2. Nf3 Nc6 3. Bb5 Nd4 by giving hundreds of annotated and unannotated games such as Rohde-Christiansen 1985 (won by Black). 17 main lines plus complete games indices. © 1992. **$14.00**

Blackmar-Diemer gambit keybook: *Rev. Tim Sawyer, flexi*

Master Sawyer's compilation of 743 (mostly) annotated games, arranged in 7 chapters (Avoided, Declined, Bogoljubow, Euwe, Ziegler, Gunderam, and Teichmann), presents a great number of scintillating games where Black is often crushed under the weight of a mighty piece onslaught by White.

While this opening is exciting, controversial, and dangerous, it will also add many points to your rating. Chapter one is loaded with ways of beating Black when "he" avoids your opening. The whole book is chock full of brilliant tactical counterstrokes. OP57887. **$21.95**

Caro-Kann Defence Advance Variation (B12): *Tirabassi, flexi*

More than the Seirawan ECO book. 3... c5, 3... Bf5, 3... Na6 are covered. Includes the hot 3... Bf5 4. Nc3 e6 5. g4 line. Many games and analyses. 128 pages. OP77558. **$14.00**

Caro-Kann Defence Knight Variation 4... ♘f6 (B15-B16): *S. Curtacci, flexi*

Popular with Karpov, Seirawan. and many others. Our Italian IM offers this system as a secret weapon because the lines are not as numerous nor complex as many others are. Figurine algebraic notation with 100s of decisive annotated and unannotated games. Indices, 96 pages. *ECO* style. OP72982. **$12.50**

Cambridge Springs Variation in the Queen's Gambit (D52-QO15.2): *S1E, flexi*

Ten major chapters including the Anti-Cambridge Springs. This rough and tumble chess variation begins: 1. d4 d5 2. c4 e6 3. Nc3 Nf6 4. Bg5 Nbd7 5. e3 c6 6. Nf3 Qa5. 282 games and analysis. © 1994. OP92788. **$12.50**

Dutch Defence Leningrad Variation 7... Nc6 (A89): *Luccioni, flexi*

If you are playing to win a critical game, many of the best players turn to the Dutch Defense. The Leningrad is such a solid line that you must know a lot of things. OP87982. **$14.00**

English Opening (A21): *Maurizio Tirabassi, flexi*

96 pages. Covers the "new" 1. c4 e5 2. Nc3 Bb4!? 200 games plus extensive analysis as well as original analysis of this hot system to combat the English. © 1994. OP77557. **$12.50**

English Opening Lukin's Variation (A21): *S1E, flexi*

This very enterprising line goes: 1. c4 e5 2. Nc3 d6 3. Nf3 f5 4. d4 e4. A combination Old Indian/Dutch/English. White has had no end of grief looking for a good 5th move. © 1994. OP95525. **$16.50.** If you want the book + ChessBase disk (PC) combo then it's SW95527 for **$28.95.**

French Defence Winawer Variation C15-C19: *Myers, flexi*

46 complete games + extensive bibliography covering 27 chapters. An amazing book and excellent introduction for beginner and advanced player. © 1994, OP87987. **$17.50.**

The Göring Gambit: *Cimmino, flexi*

128 pages on C44. 210 games plus lots of analysis on one of the most difficult and yet fascinating gambits in the history of chess (1. e4 e5 2. Nf3 Nc6 3. d4 ed 4. c3). © 1993. OP77552. **$14.00**

Grünfeld Indian Exchange Variation 7 Nf3 c5 8 Be3 (D85): *S1E, flexi*

More English instruction than the usual S1E book. With the introduction of 7... c5 White's advantage in the past has become "unclear." 247 games or fragments. © 1994. OP95299. **$16.50.** Or get the book + ChessBase disk (PC) combo. It's SW95522. **$29.95**

Italian Game C53-C54: *S1E, flexi*

288 complete or partial games are referenced. To many this is known as the Giuoco Piano. Lots of old and new games are given. Includes the Möller and d3 lines. Of the "main lines" are older games! There are number of 1993 references. Also includes the Evans Gambit. © 1994, OP95528. **$16.50.** Or get the book + ChessBase disk (PC) combo. It's SW95529. **$28.95**

The King's Gambit As White 3: *Bob Raingruber and Lou Maser, flexi*

Rewrites to the Berlin and Fischer systems plus new additions to various declined methods in this "heavily expanded" edition. More problems and almost three times as many games as before. OP58295. **$22.95**

Keres Defence: *G. Falchetta, flexi*

A system in vogue in order to solve the problem of the QB: 1. d4 d5 2. c4 Bf5.

White's objectives are on the Q-side but Black can also get active play there as well as a solid game. Figurine algebraic notation, hundreds of annotated games, clearly diagrammed, and many decisive contests. Indices, 128 pages. © 1992. OP72988. **$14.00**

Semi-Slav Defence Botvinnik Variation (D44): *Konikowski and Thesing, flexi*

244 pages. Botvinnik's variations in any opening are usually important and this one is particularly true. 1. d4 d5 2. c4 c6 3. Nf3 Nf6 4. Nc3 e6 5. Bg5 dc4. © 1993. OP77572. **$15.50**

Ruy Lopez (Vol. 1) Exchange Variation: *Falchetta, flexi*

Lots of analysis in 175 pages as well as 132 well-annotated games. More to come. OP87985. **$15.50**

Sicilian Defence Najdorf Variation 7... ♕c7 (B96): *S. Curtacci, flexi*

91 pages. A hot line of interest with thousands of copies sold in Germany alone. Other moves have been 7... Be7, 7... Qb6, and 7... b5. Current practitioners are Kasparov, Chandler, Tukmakov, Gelfand and many others. Black's play has resulted in great tactical and positional tension.

The author suggests you fasten your seat belt. If, however, you have a faint heart, this book is not for you, he says! New winning chances for Black. OP72985. **$12.50**

Sicilian Defence Najdorf Variation (B98-B99): *Curtacci, flexi*

292 pages. 21 lines, a huge and easy to read index of variations. Over 300 complete games plus lots of analyses on 1. e4 c5 2. Nf3 d6 3. d4 cd4 4. Nd4 Nf6 5. Nc3 a6 6. Bg5 e6 7. f4 Be7. White presses and Black tries to complicate. © 1993. OP77559. **$18.50**

The LDL Sicilian: *Alex Dunne, flexi*

An eight-chapter dissertation of the Lasker-Dunne-Line. Featuring a "new" winning method against the Sicilian Defense using a fianchetto system.

This suggestion by the great Lasker is 30 pages in length and designed to fit inside a standard business envelope. OP58298. **$5.00**

Schaak: *collected by Jaap van der Kooij (Dutch), flexi*

These regularly updated pamphlets each contain an average of 100 correspondence games (mostly master level) on a particular opening. Presented in easy-to-read Dutch algebraic and unannotated.

The collection is too large to list here, but you may contact Thinkers' Press for a complete listing by name of opening, *ECO* number, and move order. At this writing 200 pamphlets exist.

Prices are **$4.00** each; **$3.50** each for 10 or more copies; **$3.00** each for 25 or more copies. Or, you can buy 100 or more for **$2.00** each.

TREATISES

The Genesis of Power Chess: *Leslie Ault, flexi*

Dr. Ault's contention is that a thorough grounding in strategy and tactics is necessary for strong, consistent, and effective play. Examples from master play and Ault's own master praxis will convince you of his step-by-step approach. The emphasis often revolves around getting a winning endgame or great pawn play—typical master achievement. One of our most important works. 352 pages, 700+ diagrams. © 1993. TR72872. **$25.95**

Practical Chess Analysis: *Mark Buckley, 3rd printing, flexi*

A brilliant exposé of how masters

analyze. The methods and aims are illustrated through many fine examples. If you really want to follow a long thread of analysis, in your head, the author shows you how it can be done, really!

The goal is to systematize the way you think so can carry these logical chains of reasoning, in your mind, to their conclusion including long chunks of analysis, not covered here-to-fore.

Buckley is a Senior Master from California. To be reprinted in 1995 for the 3rd time! TR58527.

Win At Chess: *Ron Curry, flexi*

This expert has been teaching improvement to amateurs and average players for years with his own special brand of philosophy, techniques, and openings. The success and comments of his students offer proof of the worthiness of his methods. This is to be our entrant in the intermediate level instructional chess market. Nearly 300 pages. Summer 1995. TR77992.

How to Become a Candidate Master: *Alex Dunne, 3rd printing, flexi*

Most of us non-masters want to make the "expert" rating, and this book contains 50 annotated games whose sole purpose is to get you to win more often and tone up that killer instinct.

A wide variety of opening, middlegame, and endgame play is displayed to get you used to winning in *any* phase of the game. There is also a "think and grow rich" tone presented throughout by the author. TR58288. **$18.95**

Answer Guide to How to Become a Candidate Master: *Alex Dunne, 2nd printing, flexi*

This book came about due to the tremendous popularity of the preceding book. Besides the brief biographical background of the author, there are answers to the questions posed in the book, ratings of the combatants, and corrections to the first edition of HTBACM. Published in 1986. TR57885 **$4.95**

Thinkers' Chess: *Gerzadowicz, flexi*

The best tips from 26 different game sources. The author annotates all skill levels from 1400-2400—compiled from the most interesting games supplied by readers of *The Chess Gazette.* Deep instructional ideas and just plain fun with words, the players, and chess. © 1995. TR87277. **$17.95**

Strategical Themes: *Unger, flexi*

Four principle applications, little known or used by the average player, are illustrated with (60) games and discussion (analysis): the pawn roller, centralization, the bad bishop, and the double fianchetto. One master told me this is the best exposition of the bad bishop he has seen. TR59828. **$13.95**

Chess Master . . . At Any Age: *Rolf Wetzell, flexi*

Rolf Wetzell was 50 years old when he attained a master's rating after years of fruitless pursuit at the 1800 level.

Using all kinds of psychological insights, analysis, discussions with friends, etc., he finally made it. He shows you how and what he found necessary to do when one isn't blessed with instant natural talent. The charts, aphorisms, philosophies, dietary and other considerations abound. This is a HOW TO book that really worked. Includes 16 dissected games using his methods. One of our hottest books in years. 300 pages. TR77997. **$23.95**

GAMES COLLECTION

CJS Purdy's Fine Art of Chess Annotation and Other Thoughts: *compiled by Ralph J. Tykodi, flexi*

100 superbly annotated games by the man Fischer referred to as one of the best annotators of chess games.

For years Purdy, an Australian, edited *Chess World* magazine and a large majority of his readership was in the USA. In 1953 he won the world's First Correspondence Championship.

Included with the master-grandmaster level games are many aphorisms/maxims from his writings to help you improve your chess ("Purdyisms") and avoid those nerve-wracking blunders. See ad at back for more details. GC58279. **$16.95**

New York 1991: *S1E, flexi*

100 selected games from this powerful event. GC95289. **$11.00.** As an introduction to the superb S1Editrice line from Italy, we will offer this book to you at **$4.00** with the purchase of ANY other S1E book from this catalog.

BIOGRAPHICAL

The Journal of a Chess Master: *Stephan Gerzadowicz, flexi*

An amazing collection of annotated games mostly from correspondence events played against many of the best players around and annotated in a belles-lettres style that William Shakespeare would have loved.

Several times finalist in national correspondence events, "Gerz" elucidates on the Pirc/King's Indian/Modern systems, and others, from years of experience on either side of the board! Rave notices and reviews (so much so that a second volume is in preparation). BI58292. **$19.95**

Henrique Mecking Latin Chess Genius: *Stephen Gordon, flexi*

One of the brashest, brightest players, of the 70s and the first player of great significance from South America.

Master Gordon annotates 24 of Mecking's best games and provides another 320 in the most complete collection ever of this Brazilian fireball. Also includes his recent return to chess.172 pages. BI72989. **$17.95**

Persona Non Grata: *GM Viktor Korchnoi & Lenny Cavallaro, flexi*

Korchnoi's defection from the USSR and his battle for the World Chess Championship, at Baguio City in the Philippines, is the theme.

This book contains many items missing from his Anti-Chess" such as photos, seven annotated games (3 by Kortchnoi, the other 4 by Alburt and Shamkovich), an afterword, letters, and other appended items (ten in all).

Kortchnoi's notes are a motherlode of information on such topics as pushing passed pawns.

Published in 1981 during his match with Karpov. BI58522. **$8.95.** We also have a very small supply of hardcovers (BI58525) at **$22.50** each.

Grandmaster Fearless: *edited by Long, flexi*

This pamphlet came on the heels (1982) of "Persona Non Grata" and will be included FREE with any paid order for that book.

Kortchnoi's results in the USSR championships included title wins 4 times! An article, written by Bronstein, praises Kortchnoi's play.

There are 13 games and 6 are annotated. Also included are Kortchnoi's scores against all world champions he has played (Karpov was the only player with a better percentage at that time). BI58287. **$3.00**

Viktors Pupols, American Master: *Larry Parr, flexi*

A book about a player who is just as interesting in person as he is in the book. His knowledge of chess, illustrative positions, and chess humor makes Pupols a fascinating and humorous study.

All types of openings, opponents and a 100 tournament first-places!

Tired of boring chess or boring chess masters?, grab this book and reminisce about driving to far away tournaments, dealing with obnoxious people, and discovering new chess theory. Pupols' Latvian Gambit flattened Fischer numerous times when Bobby was just a youngster. Foreword by GM Yasser Seirawan. BI59852. **$6.50**

Confessions of a Chess Grandmaster: *GM Andrew Soltis, 2nd. ed, flexi*

Do only born geniuses have a chance to become a GM? This and lots of other questions are discussed in this huge autobiography.

Soltis' gift as a writer and chess player. is evidence in this autobiography. Virtually all new, original information whether it is about Fischer, Zuckerman, or the Russian GMs.

Soltis discusses his penchant for "bizarre" systems in "normal" openings and gives lots of details, especially in his Sicilian lines. He also discusses why he decides to drop certain variations just as they become popular. BI58282. An expanded edition will be printed in 1996.

ENDGAME

What Every GM Knows About the Endgame...: *GM Andrew Soltis, flexi*

This will be the best endgame book ever written for instructional purposes. One column has a diagram and analysis, the "adjacent" column has a discussion of "techniques" with GM Noah Tall and his student Pat. These techniques include the mismatch, zugzwang, Lucena, Philidor, elbowing, triangulation, the opposition and much more. Most of the examples are from current Grandmaster play! Mistakes and improvements by the world's best with instructional value less hundreds of hours of memorizing! Available Fall 1995. EG87279.

REFERENCE

The Complete Guide to Correspondence Chess: *Alex Dunne, flexi*

Everything about correspondence chess is here: players, rules, organizations, history, games, advice, rosters of winners, computers and cheating.

Dunne has been the "Check Is In The Mail" columnist for *Chess Life* for the past ten years. Nothing else like this in print. Now with every purchase get a 16-page supplemental update of addresses, prizes, events and lots of other information. RE58285. **$16.95.**

Russian for Chessplayers: *Hanon W. Russell, flexi*

A revised and expanded edition of his earlier book—this is completely re-typeset. The vocabulary is twice the previous size and now a pronunciation guide to the names of Soviet players has been included. How to handle nouns, verbs, and translate on the fly using HWR basics. RE58529. **$12.95.**

Lasker & His Contemporaries

In 1978 we began publishing translations, theories, photos, new articles, and some incredible game annotations cover Lasker and the other giants of chess from the Golden Age. An oasis in a Sahara of chess literature. All are 8.5" x 11" format and, unfortunately, several are in short supply.

Issue One: Capablanca—Lasker negotiations, Lasker's Profundity, the Earliest Recorded Lasker Game, Annotated Games, and the Ten Best Controversy. 36 pp. Some rust on staples. EN59855. **$15.00**

Issue Two: The Great Steinitz Hoax, Karl Schlechter, 1903 Lasker—Chigorin, Lasker the Mathematician, and the 1910 Lectures in South America. 40 pp. EN59857. **$15.00**

Issue Three: Lasker vs. the Devil, New York 1893, Frank Marshall, Chess and Strategy, Lasker's Forgotten Games, and "old" Lasker in the USSR. 48 pp. EN598958 **$15.00**

Issue Four: Doomsday Encounter, Khrulev on Lasker, Marshall and Lasker, Cambridge Springs, 1894 Match, Lasker's Visit to Spain, Chess Nerves, and the Annotated Lasker. 56 pp. EN59859 **$15.00**

The Lasker Poster: A beautiful, full size, two-color rendering of the artwork designed by Bob O'Hare for *Lasker & His Contemporaries*. Orange-brown and black. Few left. Price includes shipping. **$15.95.**

CHESS HAMMERS

Originally published as "Chess Analysis Reports." Use these just like a jackhammer to your opponent's game.

This is winning chess, ideas that you won't find in the regular opening books. And, if you look close enough, you will find lines that probably refute current thinking—no kidding!

There are 38 of these and you can get them all at special prices, see at the end. These typeset idea-starters run from 3 to 5 pages. Contributions by Masters Tom Tucker, Allan Savage, Tim Sawyer, and your editor, Bob Long.

1. Colle System: A New Idea for White. 1 d4 d5 2 Nf3 Nf6 3 e3 c5 **4 ???**

2. Richter-Veresov: A New Idea for White. 1 d4 d5 2 Nc3 Nf6 3 Bg5 Nbd7 4 Nf3 g6 **5 ???**

3. Nimzo-Indian Defense: A Gambit System for Black. 1 d4 Nf6 2 c4 e6 3 Nc3 Bb4 4 Qc2 0-0 5 a3 Bc3 6 Qc3 **???**

4. Old Catalan: A New Idea for Black. 1 d4 d5 2 Nf3 Nf6 3 g3 **???**

5. Catalan: A Surprise Weapon for Black. 1 d4 Nf6 2 c4 e6 3 g3 **???**

6. Colle System: A New Idea for Black. 1 d4 d5 2 Nf3 Nf6 3 e3 c5 4 c3 **???**

7. French Advance: An Interesting Idea for White. 1 e4 e6 2 d4 d5 3 e5 c5 4 c3 Nc6 5 Nf3 Qb6 6 Be2 cd 7 cd Nh6 8 Nc3 Nf5 **9 ???** **?** Includes 6 games.

8. Symmetrical English: A Gambit for White. 1 c4 c5 **2 ???**

9. French Defense Burn Variation: A Gambit Idea for White. 1 e4 e6 2 d4 d5 3 Nc3 Nf6 4 Bg5 de **5 ???**

10. Sicilian Defense Moscow Variation: An Unusual Resource for Black. 1 e4 c5 2 Nf3 d6 3 Bb5 Nc6 4 d4 cd 5 Qd4 **Qa5** 6 Nc3 Qb5 7 Nb5 **???**

11. Ruy Lopez Classical Defense: A Gambit Idea for White. 1 e4 e5 2 Nf3 Nc6 3 Bb5 Bc5 **4 ???**

12. Caro-Kann, Panov-Botvinnik Attack:

A Blow to the Gunderam Attack. 1 e4 c6 2 d4 d5 3 ed cd 4 c4 Nf6 5 c5 e5 6 Nc3 ed 7 Qd4 **???**

13. Réti System: An Unusual Idea for White. 1 Nf3 d5 2 c4 d4 **3 ???**

14. Caro-Kann Advance Variation: A New Resource for Black. 1 e4 c6 2 d4 d5 3 e5 **???**

15. Center-Counter Defense, "Modern" Variation: A New Resource for Black. 1 e4 d5 2 ed Nf6 3 c4 **???**

16. French Tarrasch, Guimard Variation: An Underestimated Resource for Black. 1 e4 e6 2 d4 d5 3 Nd2 Nc6 4 Ngf3 Nf6 5 e5 Nd7 6 Nb3 Be7 7 Bb5 **???**

17. The English Defense: Black Fights Back! 1 d4 e6 2 c4 b6 3 a3 **???**

18. Réti vs. Dutch: An Old Gambit Springs to Life. 1 Nf3 f5 2 e4 fe **3 ???**

19. QGA: A "Beginner's Move" for Black. 1 d4 d5 2 c4 dc 3 Nf3 Nf6 4 e3 **???**

20. Center-Counter with Colors Reversed: A Surprise for White. 1 e4 e5 2 d4 ed 3 Qd4 Nc6 **4 ???**

21. The Old Indian Defense: Pseudo-Saemisch System for White. 1 d4 Nf6 2 c4 d6 3 Nc3 e5 4 d5 Nbd7 **5 ???**

22. Trompowski's Attack: Black's Critical Answer. 1 d4 Nf6 2 Bg5 Ne4 3 Bf4 c5 4 f3 Qa5 5 c3 Nf6 6 d5 **???**

23. The Larsen-Nimzovich 1 b3: White's Punishment. 1 b3 e5 2 Bb2 Nc6 3 c4 **???**

24. The Bishop's Opening: An Unusual Defense for Black. 1 e4 e5 2 Bc4 **???**

25. Caro-Kann Defense: A New Idea for Black. 1 e4 c6 2 d4 d5 3 Nd2 de 4 Ne4 **???**

26. QGD: Anti-Alatortsev. 1 d4 d5 2 c4 e6 3 Nc3 Be7 4 cd de **5 ???**

27. English Opening, Mikenas System: Improvements in the 8... h6 Line for Black. 1 c4 Nf6 2 Nc3 e6 3 e4 d5 4 e5 d4 5 ef dc 6 bc Qf6 7 d4 c5 8 Nf3 **???**

28. French Defense, Alekhine-Chatard Variation: The Recommended Defense Crumbles. 1 e4 e6 2 d4 d5 3 Nc3 Nf6 4 Bg5 Be7 5 e5 Nfd7 6 h4 a6 **7 ???**

29. Refuting the King Pawn Nimzovich Defense. 1 e4 Nc6 2 d4 d5 3 Nc3 de 4 d5 Ne5 5 Bf4 Ng6 6 Bg3 f5 **7 ???**

30. The Center Counter Wing Gambit: The End of Tunbridge Wells 1912. 1 e4 d5 2 ed Qd5 3 Nc3 Qa5 **4 ???**

31. Lisitsin Gambit 1 Nf3 f5 2 e4 fe 3 Ng5 **???**

32. Krejcik Gambit 1 d4 f5 **2 ???**

33. Alekhine's Defense 1 e4 Nf6 **2 ???**

34. Budapest Defense, Quiet Line 1 d4 Nf6 2 c4 e5 3 de Ng4 4 Nf3 Bc5 5 e3 Nc6 6 Be2 Ngxe5 7 Nxe5 Nxe5 8 Nc3 0-0 9 0-0 Re8 **10 ???**

35. Schlechter Gambit, Another ECO Unmentionable 1 f4 e5 2 fe **???**

36. Scholar's Mate Attack, What They Didn't Teach You in School 1 e4 e5 **2 ???**

37. Hillbilly Attack, Caro-Kann Comes to Dogpatch 1 e4 c6 **2 ???**

38. King's Gambit, ECO Fails Again! 1 e4 e5 2 f4 ef 3 Nf3 **???**

Each "Chess Hammer" is **$3.00.** Buy all 38 for just **$57.00.** More titles are expected.

CHESS PREVIEWS

Want to see some fresh, innovative, eye-opening, jam-packed information about chess openings? You know, stuff that will drive your opponents nuts?

The original idea was to provide a free gift for each monthly purchase of a certain amount to all of our good and regular customers. They were 14-16 pages in length and put together by Master Tom Tucker. There were semi-annuals that added new material from the previous 5 issues. In fact, the semi-annual is a good composite and would give you a good picture of what it is all about. Try a few of these, you will be pleasantly surprised at how GOOD this material is!

1. The French Defense: Tarrasch 3... a6. 1 e4 e6 2 d4 d5 3 Nd2.

2. The King's Indian Defense: Smyslov's Variation 5 Bg5. 1 d4 Nf6 2 c4 g6 3 Nc3 Bg7 4 Nf3 d6.

3. The English Opening: Neo-Keres 3... c6. 1 c4 e5 2 g3 Nf6 3 Bg2.

4. The Closed Two Knghts' Defense 4 d3. 1 e4 e5 2 Nf3 Nc6 3 Bc4 Nf6.

5. Torre Attack 3... h6 Variation. 1 d4 Nf6 2 Nf3 e6 3 Bg5.

6. Semi-Annual Update. Previous 5 openings updated + 10 games.

7. Modern Benoni 7 Bf4 Variation. 1 d4 Nf6 2 c4 c5 3 d5 e6 4 Nc3 ed 5 cd d6 6 Nf3 g6.

8. Slav Defense Exchange Variation 6... Bf5. Killer stuff.

9. Pirc Defense Classical System 5 Be2. 1 e4 d6 2 d4 Nf6 3 Nc3 g6 4 Nf3 Bg7.

10. Dutch Defense Modern Stonewall 6... Bd6. 1 d4 f5 2 c4 Nf6 3 g3 e6 4 Bg2 d5 5 Nf3 c6 6 0-0.

11. LDL Sicilian. The Emergence of a Main Line. 1 e4 c5 2 g3 Nc6 3 Bg2 g6 4 Qf3.

12. Semi-Annual Update. An update of issues 7-11. 11 complete games.

Priced at **$4.00** each. Buy a complete set of all 12 for just **$36.00.** Get an accompanying binder, postpaid, for just **$3.95.** Chess Hammers and Previews are available only through Thinkers' Press.

I really believe in Thinkers' Press literature and not just because I am the publisher!

At one point in my publishing career I owned over 2,000 different chess titles + thousands of magazines. I kept noticing one thing over and over—most of the books looked bad whether there was anything good in them or not.

Do you recall how discouraging it was to pick up a book (to learn something), only to be put off because it is poorly organized, or there is no index when there should be, or the type is hard to read, or the material is a mishmash rehash of stuff you've seen before?

Well, now that we have desktop publishing, we are in for the treat of the same old stuff only on a broader scale—everyone's doing it!

My years of experience in typography and publishing doesn't make me a genius, just someone who cares about the final product and who tries to make each succeeding effort better than the one previous to it.

The price of our books is based on our costs and effort—not whether we think it will be a best seller or a chance to fleece the public.

We love all the comments we get about our books. We love it so much that it drives us on towards our next project—and we have lots of them coming up—for example, **Chess Centurions** by Alex Pyshkin on the Soviet and Russian championships from 1891-1991. A colossal work.

GM Soltis' book on the endgame, **What Every GM Knows About the Endgame...** will be the best book on the endgame ever published—I've seen them all! You'll actually learn how to play the endgame—for real!

We expect to publish a 10-volume CJS Purdy set—the likes of which you have never seen. Don't overlook our first volume.

There were a few high-quality chess publishers such as G. Bell & Sons, and Simon & Schuster, and so we hope that one of these days we will surpass them.

With your efforts, we will.

Thanks to everyone who purchases Thinkers' Press products.

Bob Long

S1Editrice

Three annual yearbooks for correspondence chess players. Similar to the *Chess Informants,* these same size books have 350-400 games per issue and are annotated by the best postal chess masters around. Thinkers' Press has become the exclusive North American distributor for all S1E books. Their line of opening books are featured in earlier pages of this catalog and denoted by their figurine algebraic notation, though usually there is an introduction in English.

Chess Correspondence Yearbooks:

OP72852	CCYB#2	$24.95
OP72855	CCYB#3	$24.95
OP72857	CCYB#4	$24.95
OP78227	CCYB#5	$24.95
OP72858	CCYB#6	$24.95
OP72859	*CCYB#7	$21.95
OP77528	*CCYB#8	$22.95
OP79757	*CCYB#9	$23.95
OP87897	CCYB#10	$22.00
OP89779	CCYB#11	$22.00
OP92958	CCYB#12	$22.00

* Includes *Chess Theory* booklet.

What Is CHESSCO?

Chessco is the retail arm of Thinkers' Press, Inc. We publish a monster-sized 128-page chess catalog with a plethora of supplements. This catalog is jam-packed with pictures and information on the following:

Books
Openings
Middle and Endgame
How to Books on: Combinations, Strategy and Tactics
Instruction
Reference
Entertainment
Game Collections
Matches & Tournaments
and . . .

Chess Equipment
Boards & Sets (nice ones!)
Clocks
Scorekeeping pads, etc.

Software + CDs
ChessBase & Smart Chess
Bookup
Deja vu
Chess Fonts

Used Book Lists

Special Sales Sheets

How can you get all this NEAT stuff? Easy Edgar. Send us **$2.00** and we'll send you such a pile of stuff you'll need the energy from two boxes of Wheaties®!

CHESSCO
P.O. Box 8
Davenport IA 52805
1-319-323-7117